Terye's Grandchildren

Tevye's Grandchildren

REDISCOVERING A JEWISH IDENTITY

Eleanor Mallet

THE PILGRIM PRESS CLEVELAND

DEDICATION *To David*

The Pilgrim Press, 700 Prospect Avenue, Cleveland, Ohio 44115-1100
thepilgrimpress.com
Copyright © 2004 Eleanor Mallet

Excerpt from "Names, Names in Other Days and in Our Time" from
OPEN CLOSED OPEN, copyright ©2000 by Yehuda Amichai, English
translation copyright © 2000 by Chana Bloch and Chana Kronfeld, reprinted
by permission of Harcourt, Inc.

Excerpts from "The Small Station Called Treblinka," copyright © by Halina
Birnbaum and Acum Ltd., are reprinted by permission of Acum Ltd.

Printed in the United States of America on acid-free paper

09   08   07   06   05   04   5   4   3   2   1

Library of Congress Cataloging-in-Publication Data

Mallet, Eleanor, 1943–
    Tevye's grandchildren : rediscovering a Jewish identity / Eleanor Mallet.
      p.   cm.
    Includes bibliographical references (p.).
    ISBN 0-8298-1620-8 (cloth : alk. paper)
    1. Eleanor Mallet, 1943–   2. Jews—United States—Biography.
3. Jews—History—20th century.   4. Jews—Identity.   5. Israel—Social life
and customs.   6. Germany—Ethnic relations.   I. Title.

E184.37.M35A3   2004
973'.04924'0092—dc22
[B]   2004048871

CONTENTS

PREFACE

Tevye was buffeted by history. He was the father in Sholem Aleichem's turn of the century story *Tevye the Dairyman*, later made into the hit musical *Fiddler on the Roof.*

His traditional *shtetl* world of Orthodox Jewish life in Russia was breaking apart. Each of his daughters took a different path—one turned down the matchmaker and married for love; another married a revolutionary; another a non-Jew; yet another a capitalist who went to America. Tevye himself planned to set off for Palestine but was diverted by a pogrom in his village.

In a historical sense, I am Tevye's offspring, a great-grandchild, to be exact. My parents would be grandchildren, my children, great-great-grandchildren. Each of these fractures that spewed from Tevye's family foreshadowed what were to become the new streams of Jewish life (and death)—immigration to America, assimilation, socialism and revolution, Zionism, the Holocaust. Each became part of the spectrum of Jewish life that was passed on and transformed by new generations.

What happened to us in this great fracturing of Jewish life? It has been a dizzying century. This book is a journey into fractious history, both my own and that of the Jewish people. I began this study in order to understand and connect to what made up the rich, complex, and contradictory heritage I had come into and passed on to my children. I am a middle-aged woman, yet at the time I began, my Jewishness was inert: I had yet to wrestle with it and bring it to life.

Mine was a generation of Jewish invisibility. Yet Jewishness at some level had a passionate center for me. What drove me to begin writing this book were two contradictory feelings: A dissonance I felt about my Jewishness and my passionate attachment to it.

In one sense my exploration has been an effort to buttress the scaffolding—the Jewish scaffolding—to generations on either side. My parents had both died; my children had left home. My search was to find out how Judaism has flowed through my family over three generations: my parents,' my own, and my children's. Each of us has sought a Jewish wholeness. But each generation also found it necessary to break free of the understanding—and limitations—of the previous one.

One of the ways Judaism is passed along is through story. What we take from the Jewish narrative—from Torah to the particular one we learn in family—shapes us into whom we become. These stories help form our deepest feelings about being safe or not, belonging or not, being loved or not.

The Jewish story is also filtered through history. The story of my post–World War II generation was overwhelmed by the tragedy of the Holocaust. I was profoundly ignorant of the wider Jewish past as it was lived at different times and in different cultures. I was also a product of twentieth century assimilation—schooled well in the wider narrative of western, that is, Christian, civilization and, concomitantly, in burying my own heritage deep inside.

So I lived with a sense of disconnection from and silence about a troubling past. As I got further into my investigation, what I found inside were shards, fractures, and wounds. It was, in a sense, a contaminated Judaism, better equipped to defend itself than to nurture, more capable of fostering the mentality of the outsider than a sense of belonging. The Judaism I was imprinted with was obsessed with Jewish suffering and survival, and, ironically, even suspicious of religion.

This journey has been an effort to heal the effects of intolerance and shame that were laced through my personal heritage. I sought to understand how my particular history had developed. I wanted fluency in and literacy about Jewish life across the span of history. I wanted to loosen the grip assimilation had on me as well as the grip of the Holocaust, allowing it to begin to slip into its place in history. But mostly I wanted to give myself the time and space to grow a deeper sense of Jewishness within. I wanted to feel the embrace of a Judaism that could nurture—a Judaism from which I could draw a sense of belonging and feel a sense of wholeness. And I wanted to take my legitimate place in the continuum of Jewish identities.

This book is anchored in the premise that, to live in a multicultural world, we must understand and come to grips with our own ethnic, racial, and religious pasts, especially those that contain difficult histories. The question of how to be comfortable in one's heritage and be part of the mainstream is the American, if not the world's, challenge. My book is the story of one individual grappling with that question.

Many Jews, as well as those of other backgrounds, are searching for ways to be less conflicted about their heritage. This is my attempt to understand the deep disquiet that lies beneath our outward success.

The journey I took turned out to have three trajectories. One was as a journalist, my profession for the previous eighteen years. I went to museums of Jewish history and the Holocaust; movies ranging from those about hip Israelis to the Nazi Klaus Barbie; lectures on midrash and Israeli art. I traveled and interviewed people who were searching, as I was, for a stronger footing for Jewish identity.

Second, I became a researcher. I delved into the vast literature of Jewish history. I read about Maimonides and Spinoza, Theodor Herzl and Abraham Isaac Kook, the Spanish Inquisition and Sephardic Jews, novels by Israeli writers Aharon Appelfeld and Amoz Oz, Holocaust memoirs from Bolivia and Shanghai. I wanted to locate myself in this Jewish universe. I was in search of a usable past.[1] I wanted to tease apart family memory from history, to know where I had come from, not my genealogical past, but my cultural and psychological heritage. I wanted to unpack how I came to be what I am, my particular strand.

Third and perhaps most important, I wanted to live the experience, not just observe from the outside or read about it in books. I wanted, as I had not done before, to live in Jewish time and space. So I lived in Israel for two months so I too could feel what Shabbat is like in the Jewish state; I studied Hebrew here and in Israel, to get the words of this ancient, living tongue to come out of my mouth. I wanted to write about the experience, not as journalism or as a scholarly treatise, but as my personal story.

What I have tried to do is connect up the spare outline of my past with its fleshy history. The result is a series of pieces, many beginning in different places with different lenses on Jewishness. Taken together, they form the mosaic that is my stream of Jewish history.

Most of all I wanted to understand what it was like to be my brand of Jew. I came of age in the '60s, imbued with beliefs in expanding rights and progress, honed by hard-driving assimilation, Holocaust tales playing in the background, and with this new love object in the foreground: Israel. I wanted to get my Jewishness out into the air, piece it together and integrate it into the rest of me. I wanted to widen the space for Judaism and Jewish culture in my life, for Yiddish and Hebrew, for ritual, and for understanding Jewish history over its long arc and in its many places. I saw in my children that Jewishness did not have to be sealed off. I wanted to get rid of my own silence.

NOTES

1. A term used by several authors: David G. Roskies in *The Jewish Search for a Usable Past,* Ismar Schorsch in *Text and Context: The Turn to History in Modern Judaism,* Josef Haim Yerushalmi in *Zakhor: Jewish History and Jewish Memory.*

Part One

B E G I N N I N G S

1

THE BEGINNING

We are born in the middle of somebody else's story and die before we finish our own. We make up stories to place our present between past and future. . . . Our stories fix our identities.

—Yaron Ezrahi, *Rubber Bullets*

One day I was sitting in the kitchen watching my two grown sons laugh and joke with each other. It was a pleasure to see the fun they were having; yet I was on the outside. I could only understand a word here and there of what they were saying—as they were speaking in Hebrew.

Suddenly, I was reminded of sitting in the kitchen of my childhood. There, too, I listened, on the outside, to warm banter in a foreign tongue. Only then it was my parents and they were speaking Yiddish. Again, I could only catch the meaning of a few words. Still I was fascinated. Those Yiddish words seemed threads, pathways back to the old, nearly extinguished world of eastern European Jews, just as the Hebrew banter of my sons was a glimpse, a pathway into new and mysterious Israel, a world that has grown up in my lifetime.

Both kitchen scenes, my mother's suffused with Yiddish, my own with Hebrew, were compelling to me. In both, the private kitchen space was filled with the intimate, vulnerable sounds of Jewish languages. Both evoked for me some elemental core of Jewishness, that power of survival that reaches deep into the Jewish past and around the globe. Yet I had only the vaguest idea of the outlines of Jewish history.

At that same moment in the kitchen, I caught this view of myself in the middle, inalterably American. I was poised between these two generations, the speaker of English-only, that formal, powerful, and most of all safe language. My parents were, my children are, bilingual. Each had, or have, access to a Jewish language, culture, and sense of identity that I didn't.

Both of my sons, taking different paths, had reached young adulthood as forthright Jews. They grew up in a far richer, more comfortable time to be Jewish than I. Jewishness for them is alive and expansive, not simply defensive, as it had been for me. It is a history, a culture, a people, a cycle of rituals to draw sustenance from and be embraced by. I was astonished, proud of their knowledge and sense of belonging, and left behind.

So, too, I caught a glimpse of how constrained and circumspect my Jewishness was. Growing up in the 1950s, what I had felt most strongly was that I was held in place by two powerful forces. One was the imperative to assimilate. Being accepted as a Jew, you might say, was the sacred Jewish mission of that day. As a child of second generation immigrants, that meant ironically quieting, even shedding, Judaism in order to fit in. The other driving influence was the information that was being disclosed about the Holocaust. Those events that would not recede into history floated menacingly into our secure lives, creating a perpetual fear that existed just below the surface. Can it happen again? Can it happen here? What made it happen? And, of course, why us?

To protect myself, I hid my Jewishness in a tangle of memory, history, fear, and pride. And growing up in the shadow of the Holocaust, I developed an excessive, perhaps obsessive, concern with the workings of government and politics, with antisemitism and discrimination of any kind.

Outwardly I was like most Americans, free to make my way. Judaism was, after all, heralded as one of the three great religions of the land. The phrase "Judeo-Christian tradition" evoked an easy fraternity. But was I, as a Jew, really on the same solid ground as Christians? Or did this smooth outward fellowship gloss over the cataclysmic history? I had known inside that we were different, no matter how much we kept it under wraps. It was the great and indelible dissonance of our otherwise comfortable lives. I'd feel my suppressed difference surface, and even a feeling of physical threat, when I would hear Louis Farrakhan or members of the Christian Coalition talk about Jews, or of a bomb exploding on a Tel Aviv bus, or even the high, whiney, and to me vulnerable sounds of klezmer music.

A litany of harsh words and deeds filled much of the previous decade. It came from many quarters: the finger-pointing morality of the culture wars, the rise of terrorism, militant Islam and militias, and political figures such as Pat Buchanan. I reacted to these with a diffuse sense of vulnerability, poignantly aware that I had been marked by history. I seemed lacking in the capacity to assess the actual danger of these forces. They all seemed of a single tone and calibrated at the highest level. Each tirade felt like it echoed the conspiracy against Jews in our European past.

The negative feeling toward Jews has deep roots. "Europe was and is a Christian civilization," said Leonard Glick, professor of Anthropology and Jewish History at Hampshire College. And Jews did not fit in. "Christianity is not just a religion, it is a total view of how the world is constituted. And it is dominated by one book, the New Testament. In the Gospel of John, Jews are not just another people but *the* other people. Jews were the antagonists in the Gospels."[1]

And Christianity, say Christians, triumphed. Jews are equated with darkness. "Jews are stationary and useless antiquity," wrote St. Augustine.[2]

Such a negative mindset toward Jews has ebbed and flowed through the centuries. But even in good times, feelings against Jews remained in strains of eastern and western European culture.

There has also been a particular Jewish finger pointing in the last decade: American Jews were going to disappear—and this time it would be our fault. The myriad of facts and figures that came out of the 1990 Jewish population study was somehow distilled down to a single one—52 percent, the purported rate that Jews were intermarrying. Never mind that some argued the study was flawed and the number was lower, likely 40 percent.[3]

The singular message was this: How could it be, after two thousand years of living as a persecuted minority mainly in the fold of Christianity, that American Jews, with their astonishing success in this most successful of countries, will fail to deliver three-thousand-year-old Judaism to the next generation? This uncomfortable question tapped into the deep resonance that survival has in Jewish history.

In one sense, the huge issue made of 52 percent was another wrinkle in the strident culture wars. The American family was in trouble, it was said, and women were blamed for divorce and child problems. The scolding culture's Jewish wing added the condemnation of assimilation. It is in the family, and fundamentally from mothers, that Judaism is passed on. It is women who were marrying late and failing to produce a higher birth rate.

In the torrent of words that followed the study, a chorus derided American Jewish identity: "The kind of Jewish we have tried to share is so pallid and so meaningless, it has nothing to say to young people," said Daniel Gordis, of the University of Judaism in Los Angeles to a Jewish leadership group.[4] He argued that without a reinvigoration of tradition, what is passed on to many is not powerful enough to keep Judaism alive.

"It (Judaism) has lost its religious core," said Rabbi Arthur Hertzberg. "No wonder the draws of American culture are more powerful."[5]

Others charged that American Jewishness was too focused on the Holocaust and Israel and neither was adequate; the Holocaust only offered victimhood and Israel a kind of surrogacy. The lack of religiosity of many American Jews, these critics argued, meant there was too little substance to bind the next generation.

Now assimilation was the enemy, not Hitler. Jewishness would vanish through the astonishingly successful way that I, and many of my generation had led our lives. What an indictment.

It was a shocking idea indeed to consider that assimilation, that fast train my parents, and even their parents, boarded, which was to bring all things great and good, had all of a sudden become a dirty word. I could not help wondering whether the powerful promise of assimilation that was to heal Jewish wounds and make Jews whole had a flaw in it and would be our downfall.

Yet another seemingly countervailing force emerged in our culture at the same time: multiculturalism, an expanded definition of what it means to be an American. One reason for this redefinition was the influx of immigrants—Hispanics and Asians—who did not blend and melt as was expected, actually demanded, of previous immigrant groups. But it was African Americans who led way in finding their separate and distinct voice as a minority within the larger culture. Sociologist Nathan Glazer argues that a major force behind the development of multiculturalism was ironically, the failure of white society to accept African Americans in their schools and neighborhoods.[6]

Multiculturalism is pervasive now. Some Jews look at the concept coming out of American culture as a way to strengthen Jewish identity. Historian David Biale argues that, throughout history, Jews have been multilingual and multicultural. They did not live in isolation but interacted with the surrounding culture while maintaining their own.[7] It is only in modern times that Jews were swept up in relinquishing their own differences in order to belong. This model from the past may be useful today.

My son Max came to understand the powerful sense of identity that is gained from fully exploring Jewishness. It was not until he started taking history classes in college that he began to dig in and galvanize as a student. It was then that he made rigorous intellectual learning a central part of who he was. Interestingly, those first classes were in Jewish history.

Suddenly, he understood the personal importance of history. It gave him, as he explained it, a way to connect to the Jewish past, situate himself in it, and understand where he had come from, as an essential part of who he was. That experience was so powerful, it led him to study Hebrew in college and then in Israel. He went on to study French and Serbian and is now a doctoral student in European history.

What a change in thinking. My generation was always measuring itself against this stringent imperative of "too Jewish." Names were changed, noses shortened, hair straightened in order to blend in. Was there now room to stretch out and give Jewish identity larger space in which to breathe? I too wanted to slip in under this umbrella and explore my own complex difference. Why not loosen the bonds enough to allow distinct pools of culture to flourish?

My sons embracing Jewish heritage, the culture wars, multiculturalism —all came at me like bullets flying overhead. What was my Jewish identity and that of those like me in the post–World War II generation who came of age in the high tide of assimilation? What was it like to be my kind of Jew, the generation not only faced with assimilating the Holocaust and its backdrop of European persecutions, but now emerging from stringent assimilation?

In order to join this safe, secular, mainstream America, I had gone through a series of doors, leaving Jewishness behind. The watchword of my generation was invisibility. We were not only white, we were opaque.

Here I was at midlife; I hadn't lived as a Jew in the conventional or fulsome ways. I was a product of, and had made my contribution to, this century of Jewish assimilation. I had raised my children to be Jewish but it was in a makeshift way that depended more on osmosis than a deep imprint of religiosity or a binding institutional loyalty.

I was an outsider to traditional Jewish life. I didn't belong to a temple. I contributed to the Jewish federation but, other than a son who loved Jewish camp, I had little connection to its communal activities. I was raised Reform, but as an adult I was rather unaffiliated, along with close to a third of American Jews.[8]

From the start, my parents positioned me to look outward. I was poised to enter, experience, learn about, and live in worlds other than my own. I believe they felt—and I did too—that no matter how much I drank up mainstream America, Jewishness was fixed within in a place so deep and so inalterable that nothing would dislodge it, not the Holocaust and certainly not the seductions of modern life.

My education and career as a journalist have been secular. I learned far more about western civilization—the Greeks, the spread of Christendom, and the birth of democracy—than I did about the history of the Jews.

Not much remained with me of my Reform Temple education. If pressed, I could recall the mythic figures of Abraham and Moses and ex- otic places like Babylonia and Mesopotamia, but it was at about a sixth grade level. I knew far more about Columbus' voyage from Spain to the New World in 1492 than I did about the expulsion of the Jews from the same country in the same year. I knew nothing of the Sephardic Jews who made their way from Spain and Portugal to Turkey, Holland, Bulgaria, and even the New World.

For years, I felt this was as it should be. Wasn't it better, more American, to be focused on the future? I could hear my father saying, weren't we in America to leave behind, forget, what it was like to be a Jew in Europe? Part of the freedom of America was to let this dark Jewish history fade into the past. I was emboldened even more in this thinking by the culture of my own generation, which, with our 1960s antiwar protests and array of civil rights movements, acted as though history had begun anew.

But I was to find that even when history is kicked aside, it eventually works its way back into the present.

NOTES

1. Leonard Glick, *Ashkenazic Jews in European History*, tape 1, lecture, summer program in Yiddish Culture, National Yiddish Book Center, Amherst, Mass., 1995.

2. Ibid.

3. J. J. Goldberg, "Interfaith Marriage: The Real Story," *The New York Times*, Aug. 4, 1997, op-ed page.

4. Daniel Gordis, "Personal and Family Religiosity as a Gateway to Continuity," lecture at the Wexner Heritage Foundation New Member Institute, Oak Park, Ill., June 30, 1993.

5. Arthur Hertzberg, lecture at Case Western Reserve University, Cleveland, Ohio, February 25, 1999.

6. Nathan Glazer, *We Are All Multiculturalists Now* (Cambridge, Mass.: Harvard University Press, 1998), 95.

7. David Biale, Michael Galinsky, and Susannah Heschel, eds., *Insider/ Outsider: American Jews and Multiculturalism* (Berkeley: University of California Press, 1998), 8.

8. J. J. Goldberg, *Jewish Power: Inside the Jewish American Establishment* (Reading, Mass.: Addison Wesley, 1996), 59.

FATHER

When my father turned fifty, he became a race horse driver. The way he saw it was that he had grown up poor and a Jew. Other kids had the chance to participate in sports. But he didn't, he had to work. And what place was there for a Jew on a ball field, or the racetrack?

Sure, he spent Friday nights in front of the television in his big chair watching the fights. And I remember striding with him into the cavernous baseball park, my small hand in his large palm. But becoming a race horse driver, putting on the silks and getting in the sulky behind the horse, was different. It was the uncloaking of a long held desire—to enter that foreign world of a sportsman.

The horse world in the 1960s—the owners, trainers, drivers, grooms —was virtually all Gentile, as I recall it. He ventured deep into it. He would come back from early morning workouts, his clothes sweaty and with dirt caked on his boots and face. He loved the taste and feel of competition and danger. It was, as he saw it, the luscious freedom of America that, as a Jew, you could decide to be a race horse driver. And become one.

It was part of the freedom of America that allowed you to step away from being what you were born into. America held out that very near heretical freedom not to be yourself. You could lose yourself, the self you were born into, and go after the one you longed to be. Unless you chose to, you didn't have to live and breathe every minute of every day as a Jew. You could be a race horse driver.

Even before my father became a driver, he had something of the Wild West about him. He started his own business at the age of twenty-four and built it into a successful company employing more than a hundred people. He was an entrepreneur, an inventor of new products, a capitalist.

He had *seichel* (good sense). He would point to his bald head and urge my sisters, brother, and me to develop our own common sense, good judgment. He was the son of poor Jews from the Russian Pale. Like many of his generation, he came from a line of people who were held down for generations and then, so it seemed, burst forth in this new climate. Let loose to drink up the opportunities of this freeing culture, he left that insular world and exploded with dynamism and creativity.

America has a duality about it that made it a particularly good place for Jews. Sure, the culture demands conformity—the organization man, the man in the gray flannel suit. At the same time it reserves a special place for the nonconformist, the innovator, the person with the new idea. Such persons move about freely, including across class lines. They are granted a certain exemption from conventionality.

My father was one of those people. He didn't conform to what people expected. He was a Jew to the core—above all, imprinted by the brutal history—yet he had little to do with the tight-knit Jewish community we lived in. No temple men's club, no country club, no *macher* (big shot) in the Jewish federation. And he wasn't interested in any of the talk about such matters either.

He didn't want to be defined, crimped, or compromised by any group or institution, religious or social. His only standard was to be yourself. Live life according to the conviction of your ideals, stand up for what you believe in and shape your life as you see it. Be a race horse driver.

But the old world had its pull on him. My father would take us to his parents' on Sundays for brunch. There his entire clan from the old country would gather. Bubbie had a wide face, her short hair pulled straight back. In her shapeless dress covered by a bib apron, she shuttled back and forth bringing food from the large pots on the stove to the yellow Formica table. She never sat. I don't know what the grownups talked or argued about. It was Yiddish only around the kitchen table. There we were enveloped by Jewish life.

We children ate our soup and whatever else Bubbie brought us, then we slithered away between the adults. We wanted to avoid getting our cheeks pinched and play make-believe games. We rolled ourselves silly on the fat ottomans in the living room.

The memory of my father's family is vivid to me, even though his parents died within a year of each other when I was around six or seven. I remember standing with my father in the front hall of his father's Russian *shul* (synagogue) getting jostled among the chattering bearded men, their heads covered with *yarmulkes* (skullcaps). When my grandparents died, that world I had peered into faded from view.

Years later my husband David and I renovated an old house on the same street as that shul in Pittsburgh where I grew up. I felt a certain comfort moving onto that quiet street that my grandfather had been connected to. Yet I would not have dared approach the synagogue. It was a world no longer accessible to me. It belonged to black hatted men and their wives whose heads were covered in wigs or hats, pushing their baby strollers on the neighborhood streets. I would nod or smile; yet they wouldn't make eye contact with me, even though I too shared the street, I too was a Jew. They were encased in the thickened membrane of ultra-Orthodoxy and my Jewishness had constricted. So we led parallel existences, alien to each other.

Among all the uncles and aunts, cousins and second cousins, my father was the one the extended family relied on. He made the big bucks and he was generous. "Closed door" meetings went on in our living room. Relatives I never met called on Uncle Lou for money or advice about money. He put a nephew through college. For years, he supported a brother-in-law and his family. After my father died, I came across letters from his cousin who had spent her adult life in a mental hospital. In each letter, she thanked him for the money he had sent. The tribal imperative to help was still operative. Deserving or not, whether he wanted to or not, it was what you did for family.

Even though the world my father grew up in faded away, he regularly would be seized by a desire to connect to the Jewish culture of his past. My parents took us to New York to see Yiddish theater and walk among the pushcarts on the Lower East Side. While the High Holiday services at the Reform Temple seemed to do little for him religiously, he felt an intensity about it at a tribal level. It was a time to "rub shoulders with Jews," he would say. And he would drop in for chicken soup and a corned beef sandwich at the deli in the Lower Hill District, the neighborhood where he grew up.

Although my father outwardly assimilated into American culture, he also carried the shame of class, of foreignness, of being different. He had his dark side. He had a sense of being an outsider that remained fully intact even with all of his success. Part of this was rooted in being the child of immigrants. His parents never quite learned English. His mother would get him to take her to the movies and then in a not-very-low whisper, insist he translate for her. People around them would shush him. He never recovered from the public embarrassment, the mortification of doing his mother's bidding.

His parents' world remained small. In this great and free country, they stayed nearly within the ghetto boundaries laid down for them in the Pale and transplanted here; the Russian shul, the kosher butcher shop, Yiddish.

Sure, for them there was *the* world, the world you made a living in. It was a line you crossed, like passing through a checkpoint into a foreign land. As for the place of Jews in that world . . . well, that was another matter. Antisemitism to them, my father once explained, was as fixed as the sun, moon, and stars.

Those demarcations were etched permanently in my father too. Whatever else being Jewish was to him, it was a set of internal boundaries and restrictions. However far he went in life, however freely he moved or successful he was, he maintained a sense of difference, mostly of vulnerability.

Antisemitism was alive on the streets of the teeming immigrant neighborhood where he grew up. It seared a generation of American-born Jewish children. In elementary school a group of boys held him down on the ground, called him a Christ-killer and forced him to kiss a picture of Jesus.

A part of him lived in a holocaust—at least a pogrom. He had this primal fear that we could be set upon at any time. Or that in some future, inevitable turn of events, we could, would, be plucked from our lives.

I remember him poking his finger at the newspaper, that historic day in 1965 when the Papal encyclical Nostra Aetate was issued, declaring the Jews not responsible for Christ's death. He felt personally absolved, vindicated, from the injustices of his childhood and for Jews through history. But it was bittersweet coming at that late date.

Deep down was this wound: He was a Jew, he was the outcast Other. He made his way, but no helping hands were held out to him. He lived an existential aloneness, assuaged only by the enveloping warmth of Yiddish, powerful, closed, family bonds, and my mother.

Were he alive today, he would not be dislodged an iota from his conviction that antisemitism is a recurring disease. Today, I can hear him, he would be warning of the day when world capitalism reels downward, when fortunes are lost and people everywhere are in bread lines again. The Jews will be blamed for it, he would say, pointing his finger at me, maybe this time, Alan Greenspan. Or the Israeli struggle with the Arab world would be the spark for a new Jewish catastrophe. We would be routed out once again and set upon for fabled international conspiracies.

But if you turned that fear in him over, it contained something else—the hard shine of survival. It was as if he was also saying, "Yet, I, we, after all these centuries, are still here."

THE HOLOCAUST

In the year I was born, 1943, the furnaces at Auschwitz were going full force. Between 1942 and 1944, one million Jews were gassed and burned there.[1]

As a kid, it seemed I always knew about the six million. But it was from a well-meaning Sunday school teacher that I learned that Germans made Jews into soap and lampshades. The six million was so big as to be an abstraction. But soap and lampshades? I was morbidly fascinated.

I don't know what impelled her to share this information with a bunch of rowdy kids. It was the early fifties. Perhaps full revelations about what we now call the Holocaust were just becoming known. Perhaps she had only recently heard herself and had to ease her burden. I don't know. The sheer dead weight of these images obliterated all else she was to teach me of Jewish history, ritual, or belief. Those few words uttered by this ill-advised teacher surely influenced me more than the booming orations of the erudite rabbi.

I remember exactly how I heard it. I was sitting near the classroom door. She was wearing a fifties style suit, standing off to the side of her desk by the window. She told us what they had done to us. I wished I didn't know. But from that moment on I would always know.

Repelled as I was by these soap and lampshade stories, I tried to imagine how exactly they did it. Was the skin stretched to make a lampshade? To my literal mind, it did not make sense. Did some German father sit in the evening in his comfortable chair trying to read the newspaper, his kids chasing around him, as my sisters and I did with our father, only the lamp at the side of the chair was made of a Jew? I would come back to it again and again. It was completely absorbing. How could it be? Jews, like us, made into lampshades? As for the soap, I couldn't even fathom it.

These horror stories fixed something potent in me about what it meant to be a Jew. We, "this people apart," were different. I was confused about whether it was by our design or that of others. But one thing I came to understand, a colossal betrayal had occurred. It placed us outside the human family, making us grotesque. Some wholeness of being had been punctured, some rupture made in fundamental trust. And it did not heal or mature.

Ever since then, I have been drawn to the Holocaust, reading about it obsessively in histories, memoirs, and novels. And no matter what I read, these tales would always leave me with the same feeling. Yes, these things did happen. And I still could not grasp and comprehend them.

I have since read that making Jews into lampshades and soap may not have actually happened. But equivalent and worse atrocities did—taking the gold from the teeth of gas chamber victims and melting it down into gold bars that were cycled through Swiss banks to fuel the German war machine. Catholic priests in parishes across Germany turned baptism records over to the Nazis. That is how they figured out who the Jews were in a town: They had no baptism records.[2]

I did not experience the blunt trauma of the Holocaust directly nor the difficult heritage that has been passed on to children of survivors. I am simply a member of the community that was once victims. Still, the Holocaust's wake was engulfing. It has made itself felt in every aspect of being a Jew.

At twenty, I went on a college trip to the Soviet Union, Poland, and Czechoslovakia. I stood in front of the crematoria at Auschwitz, saw the dirty, striped prison uniforms on the floor in the barracks and the pictures of gaunt people with shaved heads. You could not tell the men from the women. I knew that this was part of who I was and where I had come from. My family had gotten in a different queue, one that came to the

United States before the crematoria lines were formed, but these broken pieces were part of my Jewishness. It was 1964. Israel was sixteen years old. The Eichmann trial had been held three years earlier. The Holocaust had just begun to be acknowledged.

Nowadays, the Holocaust seems a current news event. There are stories about the planned Jewish memorial in Berlin, the Pope's statements on Jews and Swiss bank accounts. There are new books on Pius XII, the pope during the Holocaust, and on the involvement of IBM with Germany during the war. Daniel Jonah Goldhagen's book *Hitler's Willing Executioners* made the bestseller list in the United States and Germany and Stephen Spielberg's *Schindler's List* grossed $317 million at the box office worldwide.

But in the years following the war, a certain silence, maybe numbness, prevailed. Survivors were busy rebuilding their lives. Then in 1961, the Israeli intelligence service Mossad brought Adolph Eichmann to Jerusalem for trial. The televised trial laid out the full scope of what happened in the Final Solution. Individual survivors knew what they had lived through, but in footage of the trial, their faces were filled with astonishment, as if to say, "This is what happened to us? How do we comprehend it?" In the same year Raul Hilberg's monumental book *The Destruction of the European Jews* was published. It laid out in minute detail the German bureaucratic machinery for destruction, including the role of Jewish councils. In some ways, we are still grappling today with trying to comprehend these atrocities.

Hannah Arendt in her controversial coverage of the trial was sharply critical of Ben Gurion's insistence on holding the trial. She saw Eichmann's crime, genocide, not as just the latest in the long history of Jewish suffering, but as a crime against humanity. She thought the trial belonged in an international tribunal. "In the eyes of the Jews, thinking exclusively in terms of their own history, the catastrophe that had befallen them under Hitler, in which a third of the people perished, appeared, not as the most recent of crimes, the unprecedented crime of genocide, but on the contrary, as the oldest crime they knew and remembered."[3]

She raised complicated questions that are still debated today about the universality of the Holocaust or its particular Jewish tragedy: about the Jewish people—its separateness from other peoples and nations or its place among them.

Whatever the lessons of the Holocaust may be, in the past half century, this monstrosity has made its way into the story of the Jewish people, of Israel, and into Judaism itself. In one sense, the Holocaust occupies sacred space. Collective memory is permeated with loss. Many are transfixed by voices such as that of Elie Wiesel, a kind of "rabbi" of the Holocaust, who keeps us there. Despite the charge that this focus on the Holocaust keeps Jews in victimhood, it has felt like something of an act of heresy to move on.

The Holocaust has become part of Jewish ritual. For as long as I can remember, we stood for the six million in temple. There is a Holocaust Remembrance Day, Yom HaShoah, in the spring. In Israel, Yom HaShoah is held a week before the celebration of Independence Day, giving ritual meaning to the trajectory of destruction to the birth of the state. In Israel where the religious and the secular meld together, there is another lesson to learn, the grave danger for Jews if they do not have their own state. Ralph Grunewald, director of external affairs at the U.S. Holocaust Museum, believes that in time commemorating the Holocaust will become an even more definitive part of Judaism.

There is a strain in Jewish thinking that wants to keep the Holocaust holy, keep it for the "people apart." It is an existential wound that will not be healed in a single generation. Perhaps Polish Catholic journalist Jerzy Turowicz captured this feeling in June 1986 during the controversy over the Christian crosses at Auschwitz. "Auschwitz represents for the Jews their total abandonment, the symbol of their absolute solitude in the face of death, the symbol of the passivity of the other nations in the face of their destruction."[4]

Some are reluctant to acknowledge that the sufferings of others in the war were also of unimaginable magnitude or the resonance the Holocaust has with other acts of genocide.

In Jerusalem's old city, maps along the wall of the Armenian quarter show pictures of starving children, piles of dead bodies, maps showing the routes of deportation, refugee caravans, "The Victims of the First Genocide in the 20th century," it reads, "Remember and Demand. 1.5 million killed by the Turkish government in 1915: Another million driven from their homes. The Turkish denial has continued for 83 years."

And new genocides abound. In the mid-1970s Cambodia's Khmer Rouge killed one million out of a total population of seven million. In 1994 in Rwanda genocide squads of Hutus killed 800,000 Tutsis with machetes in one hundred days.

Grunewald feels that the existence of the Holocaust Museum opens up the opportunity for others, from Cambodia, Rwanda, or Bosnia, to talk about what happened to their own people. And university programs have sprung up to study genocide.

The Holocaust surely has given resonance to other catastrophes in Jewish history and to a pervasive sense of Jewish vulnerability. I have often wondered the extent to which the Holocaust has poisoned Judaism, made a belief in God troubling if not impossible. Or looked at another way, perhaps people who are fervently religious have more of a protective membrane against absorbing the full magnitude of what happened in the Holocaust.

How the Holocaust will settle into Jewish memory—what will be drawn from it—may not be sorted out for many years. Will it be the lesson of withdrawal and bitterness, that we dwell alone, or one of healing and trust and that we share with others certain common catastrophes, if only through empathy? Likely, each generation will find a different way of telling these events in history.

I knew at twenty that being Jewish was about the fundamentals of existence, about survival. Ironically, it was not survival in a spiritual or theological sense, but right on the ground, politically and psychologically. The higher planes of faith, ritual, or the debates over the fine points of Jewish law never carried much heat for me. I was willing to concede, yes, I was stunted, stuck there, at the Holocaust, just as critics have charged. For a long time, there wasn't much else for me to Jewish history. Surely there was nothing else to German history.

Cruel as it seems to me now, I wanted my sons to know what it meant to be Jewish in this way too. I felt they had to if they were to know what it meant to me to be a Jew. On our first trip to Israel when they were eleven and thirteen, we saw the Western Wall and the orange groves at a kibbutz. But I also made sure to nudge them in front of the Holocaust exhibits at Yad Vashem. But they grew up in a vastly different time. And they would find far more expansive meanings in Judaism.

NOTES

1. Raul Hilberg, *The Destruction of the European Jews,* student edition (New York: Holmes and Meier, 1985), 239.

2. Guenter Lewy, *The Catholic Church and Nazi Germany* (New York: McGraw Hill, 1964), 282.

3. Hannah Arendt, *Eichmann in Jerusalem: A Report on the Banality of Evil* (New York: Viking Press, 1963), 245.

4. Bernard Wasserstein, *Vanishing Diaspora: The Jews in Europe since 1945* (Cambridge, Mass.: Harvard University Press, 1996), 154.

HISTORY AND MEMORY

There is a fable that still in the 20th century individual families
in Sofia (Bulgaria) kept keys to homes in Toledo Spain which their
ancestors had locked up and abandoned centuries earlier.

—Vicki Tamir, *Out of the Fire: Sephardim and the Holocaust*

"What is remembered?" intoned
Steven Zipperstein, a professor of Jewish culture and history at Stanford
University at a packed lecture that I was attending.[1]

Zipperstein's question was an evocative one to be sure: What has been
preserved fermented in memory, by later generations? The room was filled
with people older than me, many second generation immigrants. We were
in rapt attention, eager to understand the immigrant experience.

Zipperstein quickly answered his own question: "The darkness, the
pogroms, the government-sponsored discrimination, the terrible crossing
at sea, the hunger for kosher food, the vagaries of the new world."

Yes, the few facts passed on to me painted a dark picture indeed. My grandmother's father, Elyee, came first to earn money. After a year he sent money back from this country for tickets for his wife and family. They made their way, mostly by foot, from their village in Poland to sail from the port in Hamburg, Germany. But the night before they were to leave, their money was stolen as they slept. So they returned to Poland, by foot. After another year, he sent money again. The sight of a man being killed fighting for a piece of meat on the crossing remained imprinted in my grandmother's mind. When she arrived in Pittsburgh she was ten years old and went to work in a stogie factory.

But just as I was fleshing out Zipperstein's statement with my grandmother's story, he added: "It is a flattened sketch. It is the essence of what Jews assumed to be true." And he, a historian who deals in fact and the larger context, insisted: "There is a disjuncture between history and memory.

"They did not tell us about the towns and rivers. There is a lack of knowledge of birthplace. So many children were told nothing of the past. It is a vivid example of historical amnesia. That world was drained of color and texture."

Yes, what was passed on to me was the heroism, the hardship, the idealism, a black and white picture of bad there/good here, that was needed to make the emigration work. I recalled the time when I was in college and had an early impulse to uncover this past, I had proposed the idea of going to the Soviet Union for the summer. My father said to me in astonishment, "Why would you ever go back there?" To him, that was a darkness one did not return to.

But did that mean that our precious stories, the eastern Europe we have clung to in our imaginations, must be dislodged, discounted?

Zipperstein directed our attention to two maps: One was titled, "The Jewish Pale of Settlement in Western Russia," the other "Sites of Pogroms 1881." "Jews were limited to living in fifteen provinces, twenty-five including Poland. Moscow and St. Petersburg were outside the Pale.

"But no one in Russia had freedom of residence except the nobility and even they had to apply to move," Zipperstein said. "Few liked Jews. But there was a great variability in government policy. Russia did not know what to do with its Jews. The tsars had much bigger problems than the Jews! Rarely were the rules established with the Jews in mind."

A shocking statement, to be sure. I heard mumbled resistance in the group. Don't we hold in our collective memory a sense that Jews were special objects of antipathy for the tsars with their pogroms and the dreaded twenty-five-year army conscription? There wasn't tailor-made discrimination for Jews?

Zipperstein hacked away. "There was no monolithic policy in Imperial Russia for the Jews. In fact, there was no policy on anything!"

This was becoming a jolting encounter between decades of family lore layered into memory with the disciplined work of a historical account of Jewish life as it intersected with mainstream Russian history.

Between the 1880s and World War I, Jews of the Pale were on the move. Of the 5.2 million Jews in the Pale of Settlement (11.5 percent of the population), two million moved from the north to the Ukraine in the south. The Ukraine had the rich area of the grain business where Jews were middlemen, often providing transportation. Another two million, the poorest, emigrated to the United States. Jews were 9 percent of the total emigration to the United States from 1880 to 1924.

"Yes," Zipperstein said, "conscription into the Russian army contributed to the radicalization of the Jews in the 1870s. There were more Yiddish folk songs about conscription than love and marriage." But in 1874, the twenty-five-year conscription was lowered to three to four years.

Then he dropped the biggest blow of all: "The immigration was for social and economic reasons, not ideological or political. It was not for socialism or Zionism. Only forty-five thousand went to Palestine."

The pogroms (1881–84) "took on the role of metaphor—the last straw. Yet many of those who moved were from areas where there had been no pogroms."

A shudder of disbelief made its way through the group. People were shifting in their chairs, murmuring loudly in disagreement to the strangers sitting next to them. I too wanted to argue. You mean Russia wasn't a dark place politically? Surely a pogrom in one place must have set off fear hundreds of miles away and for years to come. And after the pogroms, weren't Jews further constrained and confined by new administrative measures?[2]

Was he saying that Jews were like most immigrants, they came for self-interest, not so much for political reasons?

Zipperstein was teasing apart memory from history, two very different records of the past. He was challenging and adding complexity to our fundamental premise that our existence in America is based in political oppression. He was shredding a narrative that had defined us in America for years.

Russia was also a place of increasing economic strangulation for Jews. At the turn of the century Russia was becoming more urban. The shtetl (small Jewish town of eastern Europe) was in decline. Jewish population had increased dramatically, more than tenfold in less than a hundred years. Jews were not permitted to establish businesses outside of the Pale, making for a growing impoverishment. The expansion of the railroad and the emancipation of the serfs in 1861, which created a flood of cheap labor, threatened Jewish economic life.[3]

Most who came to the United States were artisans. It was easier for them to move; they didn't need to know the language to work, as the shopkeepers did. Most were in the clothing trades. Word traveled that there were jobs in the garment businesses of German Jews who were already here.

"The Jews who came were at the bottom of the social and economic ladder. They were *prost* (unlearned)," he said. Now that was a word from my past that was associated with shame. It was the way my mother described my father's parents. Prost was something to obliterate, to get away from.

"Do you have statistics on blacksmiths in Latvia?" a woman asked, poignantly. "This is my grandfather," holding up a picture. I could hear in her voice a yearning to connect to the remnant of her family's past, to fill in that great void. Zipperstein's cold water bath in history that demanded context, causation, and a multiplicity of forces to move events was not having an impact on her cherished memories. She wanted to hear what she wanted to hear! The myths were not to be dislodged! I too found myself holding on tight to family legends, even as I had a sense of the stories shifting. I saw more clearly what previous generations did, had to do, to make their lives work, how important these conflated stories of ourselves were to survival. I wondered—if the emigration made for a flattening of memory, the Holocaust must have frozen it.

I only half listened to what Zipperstein was saying about blacksmiths, as I was focused on the maps he had given us. First I found Kiev, home to my father's parents. Then I located Riga, birthplace of my mother's father. Then I spied Suwalki, a province in Poland. Suwalki was where my mother's mother was born, a place as fabled to me as Brigadoon. Suddenly, I was chilled. I had never seen the word Suwalki on a map. So it was real, a place of air, trees, and children laughing. I thought of how, when that generation emigrated, a door closed on the old country, never to be opened again.

And I thought of how many maps of Russia I had seen as a student at Oberlin College. There I had this passionate interest in studying all things Russian—history, language, the revolution, Soviet government. I had studied maps of Russia at the time of Peter the Great, during the civil war, after the Soviet consolidation of power. I had taken three years of the language, even made a halting stab at reading Pushkin, Tolstoy, and Dostoevsky in Russian. But it turned out to be a misdirected search. All that effort and I did not get the education there that I had sought. I never found out about my roots, my Russia, my eastern Europe. I don't recall hearing the words Pale or pogrom or Jew, for that matter, in all that study. But then too, I was perhaps unable to bring to the surface what I wanted to know, as infatuated as I was with every word of that definitively authoritative education I was getting.

Jew, Pale, and pogrom remained words lodged in memory connected to stories, however flattened and distorted. And I didn't learn about these in my Jewish education either. It dwelt on even more disconnected places like the Fertile Crescent and the land of Canaan. Finally, here it was—a map of the Russian Pale, the sites of pogroms in 1881, Suwalki.

Sitting there, I felt so clearly the duality in which I lived. Russia was but one example. There was the Russia of my grandparents, a few nostalgic and perhaps inaccurate facts encapsulated in a great deal of emotional heat. On the other side were the tsars and revolution, a compelling story but with a far more distant connection to me.

I could see that my inability to bring those two worlds together contributed to the silence in me about being a Jew. Without that integration I wasn't able to carry my Jewishness forward into the outside world, propelled by any real sense of the past. So, too, without that intellectual understanding, the compelling quality of family myth is without nuance and complexity.

Part of America's magic is how, with such flourish, it erases the ghetto lines of the old country. But I saw clearly in that room with Zipperstein that some powerful remnant of ghetto—a beloved and frozen snapshot of eastern Europe—still existed in my imagination. Looking at those maps, I felt the two worlds finally coming together.

NOTES

1. "Eastern Europe and the Jewish American Imagination," conference at the national Yiddish Book Center, Amherst, Mass., March 1998.

2. David Vital, *A People Apart: The Jews in Europe 1789–1939* (New York: Oxford University Press, 1999), 294.

3. Salo W. Baron, *The Russian Jew under Tsars and Soviets* (New York: Macmillan, 1976), see chapters "Population and Migration" and "Economic Life."

MOTHER

Perhaps my parents were typical second generation; they had little evident baggage from the old country, and even that was tucked away as they propelled themselves forward. Perhaps that forgetting, that pushing aside was a necessary part of making it in this demanding, seductive new culture.

If my father lived the dark side of being a Jew, my mother's view was bright indeed, springing from Jewish concepts of justice, rights, and community. She believed in taking matters into her own hands and reaching out to the less fortunate. She was a child of the Enlightenment as it had pooled into Jewish life in Europe. Such powerful belief in progress and reason came to her through a father who adored her. I was imbued with these ideals from an early age.

Few stories survived the crossing. But much meaning was sucked out of one that did. My mother's father, Robert Margolis, emigrated here as a young man in the first decade of the century from Riga, Latvia. He came after being questioned by police for his socialist activity. On the way to the police station, the story went, he tore up the piece of paper that had the names of his fellow activists and swallowed it bit by bit.

My mother carried something of his high-minded, revolutionary spirit. I was imprinted with her impassioned imperative—what are you doing *today* to make the world a better place? This stringent moral requirement was her way of creating Jewish time and space for us. It was a Judaism of social activism, in every thought and action, in your bones.

Robert Margolis repaired watches. He and my grandmother spent their days in a small jewelry and watch repair store—Margolis Jewelers—on Eighth Avenue in Homestead, Pennsylvania, that famed steel mill town. It seemed he was as happy with capitalism as with socialism. By the 1940s, his passion had a new strain: Zionism. Whenever my mother thought of her father, her eyes would fill with tears that he died in his late forties, a few months before the state of Israel was declared. My grandmother belonged to Pioneer Women, an organization that raised money for Israel. She was always buying bonds for the Jewish state—I had the sense it might go under without her.

In the Jewish tradition of naming children for family members who have died, my mother named me Eleanor to honor her mother's father Elyee. But she also had another person in mind—Eleanor Roosevelt. Elyee had to do with where my mother came from; Eleanor Roosevelt had to do with who she was.

My mother's relationship with the Roosevelts was quite personal. My parents came of age in the Depression, which nearly shattered their dream of economic success. For my mother, FDR pulled us out of the Depression and set the American dream back on track. Roosevelt was a near-messiah. It was he who turned American might on the Nazis and won the war. Roosevelt was her hero, despite his reputed antisemitism and how little he did to rescue Jews during the Holocaust. These things did not dampen her feeling. Perhaps she felt it was the most you could expect from an American leader in relation to Jews in those dark times. Roosevelt's actions in the Depression and the war wedded my mother to the notion of the state as the ultimate protector.

Eleanor Roosevelt was a different kind of protector. Here was this woman who never quite fit into her own high-born beginnings and had the capacity to speak to all of America's vulnerable and downtrodden. She certainly spoke to my mother as a woman and, interestingly, as a Jew. Eleanor made my mother feel valued and visible, that her own voice could be heard. Under Eleanor's protective wing, my mother felt her Jewish values validated in the American political environment.

She believed in the power of people working together to better their lives. She was a social worker, working with the first Mothers Assistance Fund. Later she was a National Council of Jewish Women volunteer helping with the resettlement of Holocaust survivors. She had no truck for piety and little for ritual. She waited for no Messiah; in fact, she scoffed at the idea. The way she talked, if her family had stayed in Europe, she might have been among the Jews in the Warsaw ghetto uprising. Such thinking stemmed in part from her pragmatic female nature, but also from *her* aloneness, something that settled into Jewish air after the Holocaust. There would be no rescues.

I wonder now how much this sense of Jewishness laced its way into her mothering. After all, it is at the breast that one learns fundamental survival skills. I was always expected, it seemed, to stand on my own two feet. There were no rescues, and I, breathing the same air, expected none.

I never knew how far my mother's father went in school but he was "educated." More importantly, he believed in education. My mother was the first in her family to graduate from college. The reverence her parents had for her was perhaps akin to a Catholic family of that time having a son become a priest.

Education was the entry to America's great meritocracy. In fact, growing up, I thought education was a fundamental tenet of Judaism, which of course it is. But we were turned in a different direction. It was not a yeshiva —she sought but the best secular learning.

So my mother sent me to boarding school in Vermont, Putney School. She had decided that the local public high school, where many Jewish kids went and where she and my father had graduated, no longer suited. I don't know if the idea of this school was connected to some vestigial memory passed on to her of shtetl life in Europe or from some socialist utopian ideal forged the generation before in the desperate politics of the Russian Pale. But she had this belief in the inherent goodness of the utopian community.

And so she found Putney School, an experiment in communal life where the students worked on the farm in addition to going to classes and finding enrichment in the arts.

But on the ground in my everyday teenage life, another order prevailed. The other students were, for the most part, straight-haired, self-controlled Christian girls and boys. And, oh, the power I relinquished to

them, especially the girls. We may have sung as one, moving pieces like
The Messiah, but their Messiah was not the same as mine. I would never
talk or look like them. They were from the best families who had con-
nections to the best colleges. My father took eight years to get a degree
from Catholic Duquesne University in Pittsburgh because he had to work
and go to school at night. Their fathers were tall, thin, with shocks of
thick hair. What a contrast to mine—a bald, barrel-chested businessman.
I felt shame betraying him with my longing to be transformed and re-
planted in this other life even though it seemed their network did not
have a place for me.

It was not that being a Jew at this school mattered. Everyone was too
progressive to make an issue of differences. In fact, it was never spoken of.
At the same time, my Jewishness was no longer cultivated, as I stopped attending religious school. So I allowed this whole aspect of my past to retreat deep inside.

When my father married my mother, a bridge opened up for him to
leave the closed world of his family, although he always maintained his
sense of responsibility to them. He might not have gone to college, had it
not been for his father-in-law. My grandfather believed it was important
and paid the tuition.

My mother maintained a tie to the old world. Our library was filled
with books of Yiddish literature that had been her father's. These Yiddish
tomes remained a mystery to me. I couldn't read a word.

For my mother the heat of Judaism came from Yiddish language and
culture. The distinction between a Litvak and a Galitzianer still mattered
to her. She was nurtured by the richness of these remnants. A passion for
making society better was passed on to me. It shaped my work in children's
programs, the way I approached journalism, and how I raised my children.
And I felt a warmth and connection to the Jewish culture left behind,
however vague I was on its content.

My mother had many outlets for her Judaism. She was a Zionist, a socialist, and a passionate believer in rights and justice. She was of a generation of Jews with an "over-full" history.[1] Coming through the American
filter, these metamorphosed into American liberalism and Zionism and
even later grappling with the lessons of the Holocaust. For her, Judaism
was never as simple, as single dimensional, as going to temple.

My parents had such different and complicated perspectives: One so
dark and fearful, the other so optimistic and demanding. Together they
gave us this powerful message: Go out into this very large world. Make it

a better place. Be all you can be. Make whatever suits you your own. After all, at fifty, my father became the race horse driver.

In addition to the Yiddish books I could not read that were on the shelves of our home library, there were these mysterious academic journals. They were from some place called the YIVO Institute. My mother had a subscription and was a longtime member. The YIVO started in Vilna. From my mother I had a glorious sense of this fabled "old country" city as a center of Jewish life. Perhaps her father, who was from Riga, not far away, described it to her.

I had no idea what YIVO was and what exactly made Vilna special. Now I wanted to know what had fascinated my mother. What had she held onto from Vilna and YIVO and what kind of Jewishness had she drawn from it?

YIVO, I was to discover, was founded in 1925 and it stood for the Yiddish Scientific Institute. It was an academic institution, which studied Jews and Judaism with academic methods. Its driving force was Max Weinreich. Born in Latvia and educated in Germany, Weinreich was concerned with how Jewish life would continue in a modern secular world. He sought to synthesize Jewish tradition with the modernity encountered by Jews in the early part of the twentieth century.

It made sense that YIVO was in Vilna. Vilna, which was subsumed into the Russian Pale at the end of the eighteenth century, was long a center of Jewish life for its region—the Baltics, Belarus, Poland, and Russia. If ever there was a place early in the twentieth century where a Jewish culture—under the pressures of modernity—was surviving, it was Vilna. "As a Yiddish secular culture, Vilna was it," said Samuel Kassow, professor of history at Trinity College. "Other places—Kiev, New York—assimilation was well underway. Yiddish was in retreat. Warsaw, with 350,000 Jewish kids, could not support a Jewish high school."[2]

In western Europe—from the time that French Jews were first granted citizenship in 1791 following the French Revolution—assimilation barreled forward. But further east, in Vilna, things were different. Napoleon once referred to Vilna as the Jerusalem of Lithuania.[3] It held many of the crosscurrents of Jewish life. Vilna "brought together tradition and modernity in the name of Jewish national consciousness," said Kassow.

Its famed courtyard had nearly one hundred synagogues. It had the legacy of the Vilna Gaon—Elijah ben Solomon Zalmen—an important religious figure who supported the Jewish Enlightenment and stood against the spread of Hasidism.

Jews were 40 percent of Vilna's population; the city had six daily Yiddish newspapers. It was an incubator of key Jewish movements. The Jewish Bund, or labor guild, got started there in 1897, hoping for an alliance with a broader base of Polish workers. Zionism was strong. And it had the YIVO.

The sixty thousand Jews of Vilna were murdered in the Holocaust, part of the "virtual disappearance of Ashkenazic Jewish civilization from the European continent."[4] It does not exist now, even in name. Today, the city is Vilnius, Lithuania.

Kassow says everyone from Vilna came away with something. Poland and Lithuania have their independent states and the Jews have Israel. But the uniqueness that was Vilna is no more.

YIVO, however, managed to reopen in New York City, where it still serves as the archive for researchers on the life of eastern European Jews. I visited the modest YIVO offices when they were still on Fifty-seventh Street. Researchers bustled about and the phone rang constantly. Staff fielded questions on everything from information about small towns in eastern Europe, to how to say something in Yiddish. YIVO moved in 1999 to join the new Center for Jewish History.

In September 1938, as Jews were trying to flee Europe, a twenty-three-year-old American and recent graduate of Hunter College went in the other direction to Vilna to study Yiddish and Jewish history at the YIVO. It was Lucy Dawidowicz, who in 1975 wrote *The War Against the Jews.* But her memoir, *From That Place and Time,* makes her one of the last witnesses of Jewish life in Vilna on the eve of the Holocaust.

What she saw was Jewish life deteriorating. Vilna, which was part of Poland before the war, was the home of some Jews who were well-off, but most, caught in the vise of Polish antisemitism, were plummeting into poverty. In 1939, Yiddish schools lost their stipend and the boycott of Jewish stores was strangling Jewish shopkeepers. Dawidowicz herself became involved in a row when she tried to enter a Jewish stationery shop under boycott. Fear of war was in the air.

Dawidowicz fled less than a week before the Germans invaded Poland in September 1939. That year, Lithuania briefly controlled Vilna. The next year, it came under the Soviet Union before the Nazis marched in.

Almost everyone Dawidowicz knew at YIVO was murdered. Max Weinreich made it to the United States. The YIVO, renamed the Institute for Jewish Research, opened in New York with its library rescued from Europe, although a huge archive of Jewish life, hidden during the war, remains in Lithuania. About 4,000 Jews, mostly elderly, live in Lithuania today.

Even though I could read none of my mother's mysterious books on our library shelves, their silent and powerful presence had managed to carry secrets about our way of being Jewish to me. The code of the kind of Jews I had come from was becoming more legible.

What I found was that long before my generation, Jews had wrestled with the question of how Jewish life would embrace modernity and survive. Others too had looked to history as a source of identity. I was hungry to read works of history in order to understand my Jewish past.

NOTES

1. Arnold M. Eisen, *The Chosen People in America: A Study in Jewish Religious Ideology* (Bloomington: Indiana University Press, 1983), 6.

2. Samuel Kassow, "Vilna: Jerusalem of Lithuania," tapes from the 1996 winter seminar on Yiddish Culture, The National Yiddish Book Center, Amherst, Mass.

3. Ibid.

4. Lucy S. Dawidowicz, *From That Place and Time: A Memoir 1938–1947* (New York: W.W. Norton, 1989), xiv.

6

ASSIMILATION

For all of my mother's democratic aspirations, she had her social status aspirations too. That meant entry into the stiff Jewish establishment: the prestigious Reform Temple of the German Jews. Like many Jews of eastern European origin at that time, she wished us bathed in the cold water of Reform Judaism, rinsed of our warm, chaotic, and humble origins in order to emerge again into the higher class of the orderly German Jew. It was the reason, at least in part, that she held us back from my father's family. They were *prost*—simple or lowly in her eyes: She had her ambitions.

My siblings and I went to religious school, some years on Saturday, the Sabbath, and some on Sunday, the American way. We sat very still in dress-up clothes listening to the scholarly rabbi, the magnificent organ, and the choir. There was no Bar or Bat Mitzvah at that time. We learned no Hebrew. Too Jewish. We were American. Reform Judaism was Jewish, of course, but it was also an instrument of assimilation.

It was Judaism tamed, corralled. It was as if we were getting poured into a mold, a Protestant mold. Nothing much of it stuck with me. Perhaps because it was not of us, but what they—especially my mother—wished us to be.

Such were the ways this different religion of this strange and suspect people became understandable to established Christian America, and they to us. No men with untamed beards in black suits rocking back and forth, praying out loud, each at his own pace. No, all that went out with Yiddish and the old country. Our way was modulated, the rough undesirable edges taken off.

We were learning the ways, the self-control of those in charge, so that we too might arrive, undetected, at the corridors of power and gain, finally, that prize of belonging. And so we did.

It was the conforming '50s. Will Herberg's landmark book, *Protestant, Catholic, Jew,* appeared at this time, making Judaism, practiced by only 2 percent of the population, one of America's three great religions. Judaism too had arrived.

It was a time of friendly ecumenism. I visited an Episcopal Church occasionally with a friend and she came to Rodef Shalom with me. My parents were skeptical but hers felt it was what right-thinking, open-minded people were proud to have their children do. In much the same vein, Chanukah got beefed up to achieve some parity with Christmas, to be its Jewish vessel.

The holidays, in the home, left to women, had a warmth quite different from temple. My mother would bring out her "good" dishes and put the white linen cloth on the dining room table. My Aunt Izzie brought her gefilte fish, tsimmis, and chicken soup. Here a more potent Judaism, its food, was passed on.

Yet it was many years until I was able to take up this holiday making with enthusiasm. I lacked a comfort with femaleness and domesticity. I was also ill at ease with ritual, with the display, obedience, and deference that it entailed. I felt inauthentic, as if I was fitting myself into something that wasn't me. Then, too, my generation had a prickly relationship with authority of all kinds. Consequently, I took little part in the simple holiday rituals that seem to bring people such pleasure and sense of belonging.

If I held back from bonding with many of Judaism's rituals, I also sensed that my parents' Jewishness was elsewhere. It was not formed in text, in faith, in the big ideas, or even in ritual. What was it? It was the powerful grip of the Jewish family, its ethical moral dimension, its commandments to improve the world in some way, as events were argued, filtered, and shaped, around the kitchen table. It was not *the* answers, but a lifelong search for answers that centered on the authority of the individual in his or her search that came from within, not imposed from outside. It included the universals of justice, tolerance, and freedom, which were also the particulars of making the world just and safe for Jews.

My father also had social status aspirations. He was acquisitive and nouveau. He made money and showed it. He wanted the accoutrements of things American—a big house, a swimming pool, English horse prints, suggesting an Anglican history that was not ours. When the busy noise of assimilation is in full gear, what a great silence there is about one's own history.

A 1996 exhibit at the Jewish Museum in New York called "too Jewish: Challenging Traditional Identities" reminded me poignantly of him. In one piece, artist Elaine Reichek explores the idea of décor as a means of Americanizing, of "passing" and of "connecting people to a past they wished was their own."[1] In the piece, "A Postcolonial Kinderhood," Reichek recreates her childhood room. The tableau includes a colonial style bed, washstand, rocking chair, floor lamp, and hooked rug, "a whole-sale purchase of the American dream through the colonial-style trappings signifying American culture."[2]

In the midst of this restrained décor is a zinger: On the beautiful hand towels hanging on an antique-spooled rack, the initials "J. E. W." are monogrammed. It is as if the letters scream, unleashing a storm in the room's serene milieu. These towels depict how anxious Jews were to work their way into the fine points, even the monogramming, of the establishment culture. And once they were there, how unable they were, really, to be properly contained and girded in. In short, Jews are indelibly "too Jewish."

How familiar this was to me. There we were with our noses pressed against the glass, right up against Protestant culture. When I was growing up, quotas were still in place for Jews in private schools and the best colleges. That was the route to the apex of America. That was belonging. Yet my father was paradoxical; no matter what he acquired, what he achieved, what we achieved, he always felt like an outsider. It was as if he clung to it. That too was part of my legacy.

The exhibit struck a deep chord. It touched in funny and poignant ways how Jews of the '50s chiseled themselves in order to fit in. Nose? Too Jewish. Name? Too Jewish. The way you talk? Too Jewish. Loud? Oh yes, too Jewish. Money? Definitely too Jewish. And that curly hair must be flattened and tamed. In all ways hone and tone down the boisterous Jew. Always present was this stringent internal measure: How would it look to the goyim? Oh, how I knew the hot emotionality that was at the molten core of my family and how it would never fit.

Orthodox? Hasidic? That was the ultimate of too Jewish. They were the antithesis of modern, of being accepted as American. We were barreling forward in all of our astonishing success, leaving this far behind. We were not in a drift away from Orthodoxy. We were in flight. It had the tinge of antireligion.

The "too Jewish" that we were had to be reshaped and remolded, even stamped out and made to disappear. And somehow all this would make us acceptable. If we blended in then the Jewish caricatures of hooked nose and money-changer, the Jewish slurs and accusation of Christ-killer would disappear. Somehow, magically, antisemitism would too.

Oh, what naïve thinking. Yet I do not believe our attachment to Jewishness was any less. Jewishness, over thousands of years and many difficult conditions, would not have survived without developing some elasticity in order to adapt to different conditions. And all of this success that Jews were attaining was indeed a different condition. Like the Jews of Spain, we took on this crypto quality. Outwardly, we created an aura of invisibility, holding our Jewishness even from ourselves.

How things have changed. For one, the so-called establishment hardly has the grip it once had on setting standards of decorum. Today, styles, looks, and ways of life are created, mass marketed, and sold in every mall or magazine under the name brands of Martha Stewart or Williams Sonoma. There are no gatekeepers. All you need is money. For another, so many other groups, far more visible than Jews, are clamoring to have a piece of the pie.

My parents came of age smack into a one-two punch: The Depression, then off in the distance, like a drum roll, the Holocaust. How difficult to be them: young, talented, educated, to be in America, and be able to do anything. Then the Holocaust materialized at their rear flank, emanating from Germany, where the Jewish life they so emulated had been lived. Then the snuffing out of Jewish life spread across eastern Europe and Russia, till they were no longer from somewhere, from a culture that actually existed. I think about the dissonance they must have felt and buried.

Jews now are 20 percent of the enrollment of Ivy League colleges. A Jew ran for vice-president. Suddenly, the fundamental premises of the world my parents lived in and passed on to me had melted away. Assimilation, once so prized, was now a dirty word.

And so what was my heritage? Both my parents were assimilators, pas-
sionately so, and they both were not with equal passion. They both could
be stopped dead in their tracks by their own contradictions. At one moment, the gates of freedom and American opportunity were wide open and
they were chasing me through. To go through was both Jewish obligation
and fulfillment of Jewish destiny. They were all for obliterating any trace
of a line, a boundary, between Jewish and American. America was the
Promised Land.

Then in a flash, those same gates were shut tight. Be a Jew; stay with
your own kind! That was the duality of my childhood, the complex and
contradictory messages that hobbled, inspired, and confounded me. For
years I saw their messages as hypocrisy, their free-floating double standard
that they would clamp down on me without notice. Later it became simply what they handed me, rich in perplexity.

My parents lived on a turf between two cultures, a not unfamiliar place
for Jews. It made for this duality, for parts of self that were inconsistent.
How to bring together antisemitism that is "fixed like the stars" with the
infinite promise of America. Or wed the stiffness of temple with the vi-
brancy and intimacy of Yiddish culture and its proximity, in my household
with the revolutionary rights of humankind.

Despite the urgency of both of my parents to belong, they stood apart,
somewhat by their own design. It was a version of being a Jew: "A people
apart" has a long and potent history. This was what came to me from
Jewish history, funneled through the particular prisms of my parents.

But as surely as night follows day, I, or rather my father and I, became en-
snared by these contradictions. When I was seventeen and still attending
my egalitarian boarding school, I brought home a boyfriend whom I was
quite mad for who was a Gentile.

This pushed my father over the edge. It was not that he dwelled on
Jewish persecution. But in certain circumstances, this pool of fear and bitterness that he held within would burst forth fresh and undigested. This
was one of them.

It was 1960. I wasn't getting married. But the issue for my father was
intermarriage. I was not to cross this line. I was not to consort with the
enemy. Suddenly all the centuries of antisemitism that had faced Jews
faced me. The ghetto walls rose. The enemy had been brought into his

home in the guise of love, the most potent weapon of all. It was a fifth col-umn. I had made my father helpless.

He invoked the Holocaust. His words, poignant and pragmatic, came to me—I believe were meant to come to me—as a prophecy from a wrath-ful God. As Hitler tore Jews away from their non-Jewish spouses, so too it would be for you.

I would like to be able to say that I raged at him, that I was able to go with the liberal, we-are-one sensibility of my own heart and my own gen-eration. I would like to be able to say I ran off with my love. I did not. My father silenced me. I fell back into the fold. I too for a time was no longer a person of many strains. The boyfriend knew none of this. But he disap-peared from my life. I was unable to cross my father. The incident stayed in me like dead weight. He had transplanted his fear to me.

But one did not stay still in the '60s. Idealism burst forth and I was not only caught in its flow, I had my own deep well of it. The Holocaust was wonderfully absent from the mood. As generations are wont to do, we planted ourselves quite separately.

I had what I considered to be larger issues of justice on my mind than Jewish justice, which ironically was too overwhelming for me anyway. The tortured Jewish story was submerged by ROTC recruiter cars getting turned over to protest the Vietnam War. The struggles of the '60s were compelling and they were a way to put my own aside. I lived for many years as if my ethnicity and religion had been vaporized.

Several years after my father died, I married. My husband's maternal grandfather was an Orthodox rabbi; his father was from a German Lutheran family, although his religion was strict intellectual. This family has it own complicated issues about Jewish identity.

When the furor over the high rate of intermarriage arose a few years ago, I found myself looking on with curiosity from the sidelines: There it was again. A part of me had been an early casualty of this war. Only now I could see beyond the poignancy of my father's fears to the dilemma. Assimilation is real, the bonds are weakened, consciousness diminished, Jewish identity thinned. Yet was this trajectory of assimilation inevitable?

I decided to go New York's Lower East Side, where Jewish life from eastern Europe began in America in the 1880s. I wanted to delve into this history to feel the richness of where I'd come from.

I met my guide, Philip Schoenberg, at Schapiro's Wine Cellars on Rivington Street. I couldn't miss him—he was wearing a kitschy "New York Talks and Walks" T-shirt, his pants hiked high. A New York City social studies teacher, historian, nostalgia maven, he did it right; we began with a glass of kosher wine alongside Schapiro's wooden wine barrels, an establishment that opened its doors in 1899.

We walked the narrow, crowded streets of New York's Lower East Side. What I saw were the archeological layers, each a people in motion, on the way to getting a foothold in America. My grandparents came as part of one huge emigration: We are in the midst of another. An elementary school is now a Hispanic cultural center. Storefronts, once Jewish or Italian, are now the San Jose grocery or Mojo Café. Alluring Spanish music was in the air.

The tenements are five to seven stories, usually walk-up, a mosaic of ornate landings and fire escapes. In 1900, "Dr. Phil" told me, five hundred thousand people lived in two square miles. One family to a room, it is said to have been denser than Calcutta.

We were surrounded by today's immigrants—Asians, Dominicans, Senegalese, but we still visited the Tenement Museum to learn about the immigrants of another era. The museum has a model of how German, Jewish and Italian families lived, outhouses and all. After World War II, three hundred thousand left, fanning out, across the Williamsburg Bridge to Brooklyn, or to Long Island, to more space, more air—to move up.

I thought of the Jewish neighborhood I grew up in, Pittsburgh's Squirrel Hill. It was the second neighborhood for Jews, the one Jews moved up to. That was what my father's family did after they gained a foothold. What a different positioning from the first, the Hill District. Newcomers of every origin made that superhuman effort to climb out of it and not look back. My father attended Letsche School in the Hill, which still stands. But the Lower Hill was demolished and replaced with the Civic Arena, luxury apartments, and spaghetti strings of highway extinguishing it as a neighborhood.

Class, when you are at the bottom as my father's family was, was the identity to shed—obliterate—like the neighborhood itself. What stigma is added to race, ethnicity, or religion when tangled up with being poor. I understood the impulse, perhaps the imperative, to leave much of it behind.

The Lower East Side is dotted with Jewish artifacts of the famous and historic, gastronomic and religious—Streit's Matzo Factory, Guss' Pickle vats of the movie *Crossing Delancey,* the high school attended by Zero Mostel and Walter Matthau.

On East Broadway was the building where the *Jewish Daily Forward* was published. Founded it 1897, it had a circulation of 250,000. In its heyday it was must-reading for Yiddish speaking immigrants. I. B. Singer wrote for it the '30s, Elie Wiesel in the '50s. In the 1970s it moved to 45 East Thirty-third Street. The small *Yiddish Forward* serves a dwindling population. The English edition, with a circulation of 26,000, has superb coverage of current Jewish culture. And the political debates are still lively and reflect today's issues, such as a recent one between a part owner who is connected to its socialist labor roots and a neo-conservative editor who has since been ousted.[3]

The majestic Norfolk Street Synagogue was making a comeback. The Gothic style temple, built by German Jews in 1850, was the first Reform congregation in the country. The congregation eventually moved uptown to become that of Temple Emanuel. The building was abandoned in 1974, then bought in 1986 by Angel Orensanz, a Spanish Jew who planned to use it for his sculpture studio. Now it has blossomed into a cultural center, very popular for weddings. "People kill to marry here," Orensanz's brother told me. And for performers of all kinds, like Mandy Patinkin singing "Mamaloshen" (mother tongue), a program of Yiddish songs.

As for the gastronomic, Russ and Daughters has an incomparable fish counter: nova, sable, white fish, sturgeon, herring, chubs. Here I feel an actual physical wave of nostalgia for creamed herring, which, as a child, I ate right from the jar.

Orchard Street, the bargain district, was populated with Pakistanis and Chinese selling wares on the street. I was reminded of the mismatched rubber boots my parents bought from a Lower East Side pushcart on a trip to New York to see Yiddish theater.

With all the movement of peoples, the Lower East Side has a Jewish presence and persistence. Schoenberg said about 20 percent are Jewish, on the upswing with a recent influx of Orthodox Jews from Brooklyn, moving in to the huge Cooperative Village.

I passed a store that looked like a shoemaker's. I peered in. An old man with a long beard was sitting behind the counter repairing the thin leather straps of tefillin. Orthodox men wrap tefillin around their foreheads and left arms and fingers for morning prayers. The straps are attached to small boxes containing bits of scripture. I was reminded of the tefillin of my father's father that I had and kept in its embroidered Russian bag. I don't recall how I wound up with them.

And so in this "foothold" neighborhood, I saw the restless movement of the Jewish people in the flow of all people in this diverse and restless land; into the suburbs, uptown, into the entertainment industry; back again in the revival of a temple, the return of observant Jews. It seemed a continuous cycle of shedding and recovering. Yet some things stay put, in family, in faith, and in memory: An old man repairing tefillin, a pungent fish counter.

NOTES

1. Norman L. Kleebatt, ed., *too Jewish?: Challenging Traditional Identities* (Piscataway, N.J.: Rutgers University Press, 1996), 26.
2. Ibid.
3. "Editor of Jewish Weekly Faces Ouster," *The New York Times*, April 8, 2000.

F O O D

One day in the newsroom, before I began this project, the food editor handed me a new book, Claudia Roden's *The Book of Jewish Food: An Odyssey from Samarkand to New York.*

Jewish cooking, as I knew it, was usually cloaked in female and Jewish invisibility. What was it doing in the slick marketplace? Were my mother's kugel, my Aunt Izzie's tsimmis, and gefilte fish becoming a cuisine? Such was the time we lived in. It tickled me.

A good part of my life, especially when my children were home, was lived on the domestic plane, taken up with the quotidian of laundry, cooking, and daily child rearing. But ironically, it was in Roden's recipes that I caught this first glimpse of the scope of Jewish history. In dishes from Italy to Egypt to India, I could imagine women over their stoves cooking for their families. In the food, I could see the complex and concrete way that Jewish culture is mediated—the ability of Jews and Judaism to adapt and yet stay the same. I felt more drawn to this book than the contentious newsroom discourses on assimilation and multiculturalism.

Among the disparaging things that have been said about assimilating American Jews is to refer to them as "food Jews," as if a corned beef sandwich is all that is left. It may be true for some, but such dismissal misses something significant: How important food is to the culture, to the sense of peoplehood that is Jewish. By food I mean the recipes handed down, the shopping in the markets for the special ingredients and spices, the pots and pans for preparation, the special holiday dishes and serving pieces tucked away in cupboards. All this activity, for everyday or holidays, is centered in the privacy of the home. It is where the powerful bonds of family and community are forged and passed from one generation to another. Yet the entire enterprise is largely invisible to many who write about matters like Jewish continuity because, I believe, it is a largely female enterprise.

The rules of *kashrut*, or kosher, have been a bulwark for thousands of years that have preserved Jewish separation and distinctiveness. Food is how we come together. It can also be how to remain apart. When you break bread together, you see the Other. Remove food from relationships and you are left with thin gruel. Jews were resented even before Christianity because of their refusal not only to intermarry and worship, but eat with others.[1]

Roden's book is divided into Ashkenazic and Sephardic. Her view of Ashkenazic cooking gave me a new perspective on the roots of my place in the Jewish cultural landscape. "Ashkenazi cooking . . . was of a people closed in on itself with little contact with the non-Jewish population and the outside world," writes Roden.[2]

I found those recipes the least interesting. On the other hand, the Sephardi recipes excited me. "Sephardi cooking developed in communities whose people had an intimate contact with and were deeply influenced by the world they lived in. Sephardi life was characterized by an openness which was the result of generations of living at ease with their neighbors," Roden writes.[3]

For Rosh Hashanah, I tried a new dish, concia di zucchine (marinated zucchini) from Italy. This is a Sicilian dish brought to northern cities by Jews fleeing the Inquisition, says Roden. So some Jews wound up in Italy following the Spanish Inquisition. The zucchini is sliced thin on the diagonal, fried in olive oil, marinated in wine vinegar, with basil and mint on top.

After the expulsion, most Jews went to the Ottoman Empire, which became the center of the Sephardi world. And they were welcomed. North

Africa had the largest population; half were in Morocco. Istanbul was the second largest Jewish community in the Ottoman Empire. Salonika was the most important Sephardi city there ever was. These communities declined in the eighteenth and nineteenth centuries.

I got out a map and followed the routes of the recipes. A smaller number of Jews went a northern route after the expulsions and wound up in Amsterdam, London, Bordeaux, and Hamburg, where they benefited from expanding trade and the religious tolerance that came with the Protestant Reformation. Some Sephardic Jews arrived in the New World as early as the 1650s.

Cooking was how Jews, women at least, got grounding. It was how they integrated where they had come from with where they were. Each holiday I tried a different recipe. One was chittarnee—sweet and sour chicken in onion sauce, of the Bene Israel community in India. This dish is from the Baghdadi Indian community. It calls for a variety of exotic spices I had never cooked with before, like turmeric, coriander, and cardamon. For Passover I tried an almond cake. This is *the* Passover cake of Istanbul, says Roden. I also made the haroset of the Jews in Egypt. They were all delicious.

Trying these foods made me realize in a new way the variety of Jews there are, and were, beyond what I knew in my small community of Squirrel Hill in Pittsburgh where I grew up. Food was a big part of our culture too. Lower Murray had a pungent Jewish air. As a child with my mother, we did the triangle; first to Polonsky's, the deli for corned beef and rye, chopped liver for a Friday night, fish—chubs or sable—blintzes for a Sunday brunch. Then up the street to Silberberg's Bakery—they made the best nut horns. My mother would hold her number in line, running into everyone she knew, chatting, and at the same time making sure no one got in front of her. There we put change in the blue cans for Israel on the bakery counter. Then she shepherded us across the narrow street, crossing in the middle, weaving in and out of traffic. People waved, yelled, and stopped to talk, holding up traffic. After all, this wasn't just shopping. It was hearing news, gossip. It was community, even in the middle of street.

On the other side was the fruit and vegetable store, Engel's. Already laden with bags, my mother would point—sometimes she would taste—and Mr. Engel would bag tomatoes, melons, cherries, peaches. Food was a way we inhaled, ingested, Jewish. In selecting cheese Danish and pastrami, we greeted our neighbors, then in breaking bread with each other, we understood who we were.

I wrote a story for my newspaper once about a gefilte fish demonstration at a local fish store done by the mother of the owner. I thought that the audience would be made up of younger women like me, trying to figure out how to carry on this old-country tradition. But no, they were all older women who already knew how to make gefilte fish. They spent as much time talking to each other as watching the demonstration. It was not so much how Mrs. Benkovitz made it, but how *they* did. One used a pinch of sugar, another a bit of paprika, another a different blend of fish. Each variation told something of where their people were from in eastern Europe.

Food is part of Jews' incredible mechanism of survival, how they have both stayed the same and adapted. This often porous boundary has allowed Jews to be enriched by and enrich others and still not lose who they are.

In America now we have this mixing or fusion of cuisines, so much so that it seems all cultures may lose their distinctiveness. Some foods now seem to have become virtual property of the mass culture—pizza, the taco, the bagel. It is a testament to the fluidity of our cultural boundaries or maybe more so to the marketing strength of diversity.

In hard times, food customs in the privacy of the home may be all that is left. Even after converting to Catholicism, Spain's crypto-Jews held onto their vestigial traditions. In fact it was the way they were discovered and brought before the Inquisition. The Inquisitors charged that women lighted candles and wore clean clothes on the Sabbath. They did not eat pork or seafood and did not mix milk and meat. They salted their meat and cooked on Friday for Saturday. They made matzos at Passover and fasted on Yom Kippur. Keeping food customs kept their Jewishness alive.

At a more basic level, food is survival. In the extreme conditions in the Terezin concentration camp, the women prisoners wrote down their recipes, as they ate their bread and thin soup. It was the way they kept their Jewish Czech German culture and traditions alive. The women did not survive the war but their written recipes did. The book *In Memory's Kitchen* is a compilation of them. It is hardly an ordinary cookbook. From memory, the women wrote down their recipes for various kinds of strudel; flaky, chocolate, or plum, which "should be high and beautiful." There are recipes for macaroons—with a "bisschen Milch"—a little milk, for onion and potato kuchen and Maseloksch, a flourless cake made with layers of matzo and almond and cinnamon likely for Passover.

"They dared to think of food to dwell on what they were missing—pots and pans, a kitchen, home, family guests, meals, entertainment." The book itself has been called "an act of psychological resistance, forceful testimony to the power of food to sustain us, not just physically but spiritually."[3]

They too as women formed community in the metier of food.

NOTES

1. Jasper Griffin, "Their Jewish Problem," review of Peter Schafer's *Judaeophobia: Attitudes toward the Jews in the Ancient World*, in *The New York Review of Books*, December 18, 1997, 57–59.

2. Claudia Roden, *The Book of Jewish Food: An Odyssey from Samarkand to New York* (New York: Alfred A. Knopf, 1996), 213.

3. Ibid.

4. Cara De Silva, ed., *In Memory's Kitchen: A Legacy from the Women of Terezin* (Northvale, N.J.: Jason Aronson, 1996), xv (introduction by Michael Berenbaum).

YIDDISH CULTURE

The assassination of Yiddish killed not just a language but a cultural universe, a way of being in the world that is Jewish without being automatically religious.

—Alain Finkielkraut, *The Imaginary Jew*

To my surprise, the language, literature, and music of Yiddish culture, lost to me, was emerging in the receptive climate of multicultural America.

A group calling itself the New Orleans Klezmer All Stars was playing at Wilbert's, a local bar with live music. They blend a strong New Orleans flavor of jazz, some country, funk, and rock with the contagious klezmer sounds. Band leader Glenn Hartman calls their sound "ethnic grunge."

"Klezmer is never lukewarm, it's always high energy," said Hartman, twenty-nine, the band leader and the accordionist who did his master's degree on klezmer at Tulane University.

Klezmer, the Jewish music of eastern Europe and Sephardic countries, is growing in popularity. Presumed to have disappeared in the Holocaust, it seemed that not long ago the only place to glimpse a klezmer musician was floating in a Marc Chagall painting. Now klezmer has found its place in today's multicultural spectrum of Irish dance, Cajun, and reggae.

The piercing sounds of the clarinet and violin have a way of intertwining the ecstatic and the mournful. This peculiarly Jewish sound opens my heart, conjuring up images of weddings from Poland to Ukraine. Yet it also fills me with pathos. Was klezmer always so tinged with sadness or is it because it is now overlaid with the tragedy of the Holocaust?

Only two in the seven-member band were Jewish, which is not that different from the bands of a hundred years ago in eastern Europe. They were often made up of itinerant musicians, Jews and Gentiles and gypsies. Originally, the groups included in their repertoire Hungarian, Romanian, or Polish folk sounds.

"My grandfather was a short Jewish man," Hartman, who grew up a Reform Jew in California, explained. "My father is a doctor. Now in the United States we are culturally awash. People are looking for things. Reggae is not mine. Klezmer hits me—it's mine."

That was the brutal bargain, what the short Jewish man forfeited to have a son who is a doctor, and what the doctor's son wants back. "At first I would not say I was playing Jewish music," he said. "I was uncomfortable. Now I say it. We have learned to embrace the Jewish community."

I understood his trajectory. I lived with the same discomfort.

So it's a klezmer comeback. The Klezmatics are nationally known, the Metropolitan Klezmers are a women's band, there's KlezKamp in New York and even Yitzhak Perlman has made a klezmer recording. "There are hundreds of klezmer bands in the United States," Hartman said, "and as many in Berlin."

There is something of a Yiddish cultural revival going on. I heard a local klezmer group at a Jewish wedding at a Reform Temple. Following the ceremony, the high whiny sounds of the clarinet whipped up a turbulence of celebration as the bride and groom each, in turn, carried high on chairs, were danced around, everyone else whirling with the music in abandon. Klezmer does, indeed, loosen the restraint of Reform celebration.

"Ashkenaz" is Toronto's biannual sprawling weeklong Festival of New Yiddish Culture at the Harborfront. "Yiddishkayt Los Angeles" is a similar event blending Yiddish themes with art, contemporary dance, and acts such as that of Sara Felder, who describes herself as a lesbian American Jewish juggler.

Yiddish was long declared dead between assimilation and the ascendency of Hebrew. Now classes are springing up, in Jewish Community Centers and in degree programs in at least eight U.S. universities. The resurgence of Yiddish is due to the opening up of eastern Europe and the rise of ethnic studies. The interest is particularly strong among young people. "They know it was the language of their families," Tom Freudenheim, a former director of the YIVO told me in an interview. "They feel a need to retrieve a personal past. It also has to do with the culture we live in that now makes ethnic identity valid."

The YIVO offers summer classes in conjunction with Columbia University, as does McGill, Oxford, and the University of Vilnius in Lithuania. Even in Israel, where Hebrew is supreme, Hebrew University and the Rena Costa Center at Bar Ilan University offer Yiddish. Some twenty-three summer Yiddish programs or festivals are offered, some with klezmer, in such varied places as Ukraine, Alsace, St. Petersburg, Tel Aviv, Brussels, and Munich.[1] Even the playwright Tony Kushner has become a fan of Yiddish.

But none compare with what Aaron Lansky is striving for at the National Yiddish Book Center in Amherst, Massachusetts.

If ever there was a *mensh* (person of good character) to the elderly vestige of Yiddish speakers in this country it is Lansky, the ultimate *zamler* (book collector). He is charming and attracts many cheek-pinching women; he is rescuing their world, which had nearly disappeared.

When Lansky was a twenty-four-year-old Yiddish literature student at McGill University more than twenty years ago, he caught this vision of a culture vanishing before him. The last of the Yiddish-speaking generation in America were moving from their homes or dying. Their homes, like mine, were lined with Yiddish books. Their children did not know what to do with them—they couldn't read them—so they were heaving them out by the thousands.

Lansky, with a band of volunteers, began gathering them up. They rescued books from garages, basements, and attics. Once they rescued eight thousand books from a dumpster on Sixteenth Street in New York after getting a call at 2 A.M. that they were there. "At first we estimated (collecting) seventy thousand books in North America," Lansky said in an interview. A couple of years ago they had 1.4 million books and were still getting more.

The center opened in 1997 in its new building in the midst of a ten-acre apple orchard on the Hampshire College campus. Its wood shingle rooftops are intentionally reminiscent of an eastern European shtetl or village. Part library, part cultural center, and part museum, it is a place where Yiddish literature is being reconstituted.

Lansky is collecting a definable Yiddish literature, 45,000 titles that were published from 1864 to 1939. The first book published was *The Little Man* by Mendele Moykher Sforim. The literature includes Sholem Aleichem, I. L. Peretz, and later, Isaac Bashevis Singer in the United States.

The flowering of this literature came at a time when Jewish life in eastern Europe was opening up to the outside world. It addresses both the dilemmas and opportunities raised in the 150 years of Jewish Enlightenment, the *haskalah*, from the French Revolution to the Holocaust.

"It was the most concentrated outpouring in all of Jewish history," Lansky told me. "Much there is relevant about how to live as a Jew in the modern world."

The center's library serves as a resource for scholars, libraries, colleges, and universities. Books have replenished Yiddish collections at more than four hundred libraries.

So Yiddish lives! The urge to pinch the cheek of Lansky is more than understandable. Against all odds, he is bringing back a dying generation's language, literature, and culture, long declared dead. But Lansky is about far more than pleasing elderly ladies with his ingathering of dusty Yiddish books.

Lansky has made his own assessment of American Jewish identity and he finds it ailing. "When Jews arrived, they checked their culture at the door in exchange for membership in the larger American polity. It was not a bad deal. It was the first time in history we belonged. Yet we lost a sense of ourselves," he said.

What he sees is a Jewish community overwhelmed by and lost in American culture. He sees American Jewish identity as washed-out, dilute, near-invisible. He understands well what he calls kids' anemic view of Jewish life. "At thirteen, I was expelled from Hebrew school. In 1968 there was so much more that was compelling," he told me.

But his remedy is not for Jews to close themselves off behind a wall of religiosity. "Throughout history, Jews' give-and-take with the non-Jewish world did not threaten but strengthened Jewish culture, challenging and refreshing an ancient tradition with a constant flow of new forms, new food, new ideas," Lansky wrote in *Pakn Trager,* the center's literary magazine.[2]

"Yiddish literature is where Jewish culture met the modern world. European Jews lived separate but were not separated. They did not live in a social isolation but in a cultural specificity and richness. Jews were always surrounded by non-Jewish populations without being subsumed by them," he told me.

He touched something I was searching for. We were lost in America, made so by our own success. I didn't know if Yiddish literature was what I was after, but Lansky was offering ground to stand on. He was calling for space for Jewish life that is not sealed off, not solely religious, and that is engaged with the outside world, without loss, an engagement that is mutually enriching.

Yiddish is a fusion of Middle High German, Romance and Slavic languages, Hebrew, and Aramaic. Before the Holocaust it was the mother tongue of eleven million Jews, its literature a hallmark of secular Jewish culture. Now, ironically, it is spoken mainly by Jews who are ultra-Orthodox.

Lansky's aim is to encourage and revive a Jewish literature. It is a project no less ambitious than reviving a Jewish life. He is inviting us to become grounded again in Jewish culture of eastern Europe, a world that was literary, spiritual, political, and filled with humor. It is the past of most American Jews. And in the process, he invites us to find a greater sense of ourselves.

"We are not about nostalgia or sentimentality," Lansky told me. "We are looking to connect to a cultural identity that arises from an historical sense. Before the war 80 percent of the world Jews spoke Yiddish. We were European—those answers lie with that culture. You have to know where you came from."

I peered down from the balcony level of the center to the large room below. It was the library. Young women were busy cataloging books from boxes or stacked on carts. Momentarily, I was stunned by the power of the image of those books, this beleaguered literature. The Nazis burned them. The Soviets purged their writers and stamped them out in the name of banishing the evils of religion. And those were only the enemies!

The Israelis turned their backs on what was the mother tongue of eastern European Jews for a thousand years and proudly adopted Hebrew, the ancient and holy language of the Jews. As for us, the assimilated children and grandchildren of eastern European Jews, we do not know much more Yiddish than the *kvetch* or *chutzpah* uttered by any average American. I wondered guiltily what happened to the books on the shelves of my mother's library. I had no idea.

Yet looking down I saw the young interns answering fax requests from libraries and scholars around the world for copies of Yiddish books. "Yiddish has not spoken its last word," said Isaac Bashevis Singer when he received the Nobel Prize in 1978. Indeed. Today it is Yiddish by fax.

Lansky's aim is to delve into that culture that was grotesquely interrupted by the Holocaust. The center produced a collection called "Jewish Short Stories from Eastern Europe and Beyond" for National Public Radio. It is thirty-one stories read by twenty-nine Hollywood actors: Jeff Goldblum reads Isaac Babel's "The King," Rhea Perlman reads Grace

Paley's "The Loudest Voice," Claire Bloom reads Cynthia Ozick's "The Shawl." As we crisscross from the Russian Pale to a New York public school Christmas play, to Auschwitz, one can grasp the continuity of Jewish experience from eastern Europe to America that Lansky is aiming for. What comes through too is how much Jewish culture is woven into this country—in the writers, humor and sensibility, actors and actresses—although often not labeled as such.

He is bringing professors of Jewish history, a discipline that has grown up in the past thirty years, to the center for conferences. These historians place Jewish life in a broader social and cultural context to provide insights into the past that are essential to understanding where we are today.

What was surprising to me was that I hardly heard anything about Israel or the Holocaust at the center, the two pillars upon which many say American Jewish identity has been built. The bookstore has almost no books on either subject. Neither is part of the mission or the discourse. Lansky is picking up and moving on from the space of nothingness left by the Holocaust.

"Through Israel, we live our Jewishness vicariously," Lansky told me. "It is to be a Jew by proxy. They do it for us. As for the Holocaust, it is not an identity."

I now understood his words even more clearly. We have an origin that disappeared. A new homeland was created that is more foreign to us than our own. We are cut off, rootless and searching for a connection to a past that cannot be found.

What Lansky sees is that his center is about something alive, not dead, that is here and not thousands of miles away. It is about us, American Jews. We are a new kind of Jew, who is not a victim of European antisemitism and not Israeli. His search is for a nascent American Jewish identity. It is about making Jewish life, distinctly American, flourish.

My Jewish sense of myself was stifled by the Holocaust and worn away by assimilation. Lansky was throwing open these books in ways both real and symbolic. Yes, it was a literature to read. But he was also constructing a way to reach across to the past. I was taking him up on his enticing offer to let history's currents grab and revitalize me.

NOTES

1. Raphael Fink of the University of Kentucky keeps a web site of Yiddish programs: http://www.cs.engr.uky.edu/~raphael/yiddish.html

2. Aaron Lansky, "Back on the High Wire Again," *Pakn Treger* (summer 1997), 48. *Pakn Treger* means one who traveled from shtetl to shtetl in eastern Europe bringing books and news of the outside world.

NAMES

When my father came of age, he changed his name from Malitovsky to Mallet. The new name was shorter, sleeker, and more American. It gave him, I'm sure, the anonymity and freedom of movement he seemed to desire.

Other than occasionally being asked if I was French, the name gave me the same invisibility as to ethnicity and religion as my father. Yet I was never completely comfortable with Mallet, or rather my father's name change. It had an ersatz quality; it wasn't the real thing. Yet the real thing, at least growing up, was somehow dreaded. There was a certain stigma to a Jewish name.

When I married I changed my name to my husband's—Bergholz. I liked having what I considered a more Jewish sounding name, albeit with an odd spelling (it's actually German).

Names can be complicated. Later, when I became a writer, I went back to Mallet. As a woman I am attuned to names, how fluid they can be, with marriage, career, and divorce. Perhaps I am attuned to names even more because I am a Jew. I am practiced at hiding in the mystery of a name.

I am not alone. In my readings on Jewish history, I came across many name changers.

Name changing can be a kind of camouflage. Writer Gini Alhadeff describes her father's name change from Shalom to Carlo that way.[1] They were Sephardic Jews, with roots that went back to Andalusia, Spain, before the Inquisition.

Those in the public eye have often sought the disguise of name change. Take the French socialist Leon Blum, who was vilified as a Jew when he was elected French prime minister in 1936. Not long ago the Larrouse dictionary printed that Blum was originally named Fulkenstein. The family threatened to sue and had the edition confiscated. "To state in France that a political figure is in reality nothing but a foreign Jew disguised as a Frenchman is to disqualify him objectively in the eyes of the majority of Frenchmen," wrote the French writer Albert Memmi.[2]

The famous painter Marc Chagall began his life as Moisei Segal, in the Belarus town of Vitebsk. But name changing in France didn't reach its peak until the aftermath of the Nazi period. Historian Paula Hyman found that "of the name changes that occurred between 1803 and 1957, a startling 85% took place between 1945 and 1957."[3]

Names are interwoven with identity and identity itself evolves, is fluid over a lifetime. We are always in the process of becoming. One can, at times, feel discomfort, ambiguity about who one is. So too, as life circumstances change, so can a name. For Jews name changing can reflect a need to dilute, even obliterate Jewishness in order to fit in, gain acceptance, or get ahead. When someone shrinks from a Jewish name, it may reflect an environment that prefers to be without Jews.

American Jews were hardly exempt, especially in the entertainment industry. "No one was more careful to expunge his or her Jewishness than Jews who were in the public eye," wrote Charles Silberman. Sixties songwriter Bob Dylan changed his name from Zimmerman; the father of Linda Eastman, wife of Paul McCartney, was born Epstein; Peter Lorre was Laszlo Lowenstein; Jill St. John was Jill Lowenstein; Lauren Bacall was Betty Joan Perske; Tony Curtis was Bernard Schwartz. Celebrities "acknowledged their Jewishness in subtle ways, evident to other Jews but invisible to Gentiles," Silberman said.[4]

So, too, Jack Benny was Benjamin Kubelsky; Eddie Cantor was Israel Iskowitz; George Burns was Nathan Birnbaum. Even Woody Allen, who brought Jewish shtick and Jewish angst into mainstream American culture, began life as Allen Stewart Konigsberg in a small neighborhood south of Flatbush.[5]

Hollywood was not the only place where there was extensive change of names. Some big figures in academia also did: Anthropologist Ashley Montague began life as Israel Ehrenberg, sociologist Robert Merton as Meyer Schloknich. This invisibility was a technique of Jewish survival.[6]

And Erik Erikson, the man who invented the concept of identity, was a name-changer too. The name Erikson was his own invention when he came to America: He began his life as Erik Salomensen, then later changed his surname to Homburger, the name of his adopted father.

The famed architect Frank Gehry was born Frank Goldberg in 1929 in Toronto. And Ralph Lauren was Lifshitz.

Name changing was and perhaps still is an imperative in Russia. Leon Trotsky, the Menshevik revolutionary and second in command to Lenin, was Leo Davidovitch Bronstein. He not only played down his Jewish up-bringing, he was a contributor to the revolution's destruction of established Jewish institutions.[7]

Grigory Evseevich Zinoviev, longtime president of the Third International, was born Radomilsky; Litvinov, who was in charge of foreign affairs for the Soviet state, was Maxim Wallach; Karl Radek, who reorganized the Russian press, was Sobelsohn.[8] And Yevgeny Primakov, the Russian foreign minister under Yeltsin, was born Finkelstein.[9]

Name changing is not limited to celebrities and political leaders. Sometimes the change happened at Ellis Island and sometimes later. Even in my generation, a classmate Paul Schwartz became Paul Scott.

Name change is one kind of camouflage. Conversion was another, especially in Europe before the Holocaust as the noose of antisemitism tightened. Alhadeff did not know of her Jewish heritage until she was twenty. Her parents converted to Catholicism when their first son was born, which was also when her father's brother Nissim was sent to Auschwitz. She remarked acerbically about her heritage: "We knew only that they must have left (Spain) following the Decree of Catholic Laws, refusing to convert so that my father could do so, canceling out in one stroke a millennium of dogged devotion."[10]

But then expulsion is not the same as the threat of extermination. At another time she observes, "Jews are famous for their powers of adaptation, but famous too for wanting to remain among themselves separate from those who are not them."[11] She sees her father's conversion as another of his adaptations, perhaps like the conversos of Spain.

Among the famous are some notable conversions: The German poet Heinrich Heine; Karl Marx's father; Madeleine Albright's parents; and Edith Stein, who died in the Holocaust and on whom the Vatican is about to bestow sainthood. I don't know whether these converts reached for Christian theology or for a disguise to get through the antisemitic times in which they lived.

Franz Kafka, a Czech Jew, who wrote in German, perhaps best captures the unease of the alienated Jew even though in his writings he did not refer to Jews. *The Trial* tells the story of man uncomfortable with himself, for whom it is not possible to fit in. Things happen to him that he cannot control or understand. Kafka's fiction preceded the Holocaust.

By the time of the Holocaust, reaching for invisibility with a simple name change or even conversion wouldn't do. There was no place to hide. The movie *Sunshine* is about three generations of a Jewish family in Hungary in the tightening grip of Hungarian, German, Nazi, and Soviet antisemitism. The first generation changed their names, the second converted to Catholicism. But such maneuvers were scant camouflage by the time of the Holocaust.

Israeli fiction writer and Holocaust survivor Aharon Appelfeld gives us a picture of an Austria inebriated, pickled in antisemitism and its byproduct, Jewish self-hatred. He describes the catastrophe closing in and crushing Jews psychologically, even before the physical destruction. In the novel *The Age of Wonder,* a thirteen-year-old boy tracks every mood shift of his parents in the days before the deportation. It depicts lives breaking apart. "In the bitter days of the last year, before the deportations—in the terrible confusion when people were exchanging their religion, selling their shops, abandoning their wives," writes Appelfeld, the father becomes an antisemite and blames the Jews. Aunt Theresa, taken care of by nuns, converts. His mother frantically does good, taking in orphans in some strange helpless reversal.[12] The story is haunted by a palpable sense of impending loss.[13]

Some whom the Holocaust did not eliminate carried out self-obliteration, not of their Jewish names or their Judaism, but of themselves: suicide.[14]

Hermann Wallich was cofounder of Deutsche Bank, one of the world's powerful banks today. Married to a Gentile, he was a believer in assimilation. But after Kristallnacht, the Gestapo came to arrest him at his home in Potsdam. His wife called him at the bank and warned him not to come home. He decided to commit suicide. "There is no place in Germany for me," he wrote in one of the notes he left. "I am no longer interested in trying to start a new life elsewhere." He made this astonishing statement in a final line to his lawyer: "It is my assumption that a dead Jew is no longer a Jew." He believed his death opened the way for his children to assimilate fully.[15]

Israelis regard names as most important identifiers. They left the diaspora behind and that meant shedding their diaspora names, those crippling names and crippled identities. They became whole by taking Hebrew names, remaking and fortifying the outer rind. No more diluted or camouflaged Jew. No, they cloaked themselves in a bulwark, the imagined invincibility of a Hebrew name.

And many of the names had a message. Zionism was about transformation. Ahad Ha'am was a cultural Zionist: His name means "One of the People," the pen name for Asher Zevi Ginzberg born in 1856 to a wealthy Hasidic family in Ukraine. His aim was to translate Jewish faith to a secular culture and for the land of Palestine to become a spiritual center.

Israeli writer Amos Oz was born with the name Klausner. He changed it in 1954 at the age of fourteen when he left his home in Jerusalem to study, live, and work on Kibbutz Hulda. His name means courage or strength. Israel's first prime minister, David Ben Gurion, was born Gruen; his name means lion cub. Ehud Barak took a new name too; Barak means lightning.

Eliezer Ben Yehuda, a Russian Jewish philologist born Eliezer Perlman, moved to Palestine in 1881 at the age of twenty-three. He devoted his life to the revival of Hebrew as a modern spoken language. Ben Yehuda means son of Judas, or the Jews.

The family of Hebrew University political science professor Yaron Ezrahi, author of the recent book *Rubber Bullets,* also came to Palestine from Ukraine. His grandfather, Mordechai Krichevsky, changed his name to Ezrahi, which means citizen. A Hebrew scholar, educator, and socialist Zionist, Krichevsky had been arrested in Russia for his political activity.

The Israeli poet Yehuda Amichai wrote:

One man's parents gave him an old-fashioned name from the Diaspora.
These days only very old, very praying Jews still go by such a name.
His friends gave him a wild name, because he grew up to be
a big brave paratrooper, raised horses out in the world
and came back to raise them in the hills of the Galilee.
His parents own a shop of women's undergarments,
corsets for the stout ones, lightweight bras and little silk panties for the lean ones.

And whoever laughs at the story of a generation gap like that,
whoever even cracks a smile, doesn't know a thing about

Wild horses or names of the land of Canaan or Diaspora names
or the hills of Galilee or women, or women's garments, either under or over,

Or the land of Israel, or the history of the people of Israel.[16]

Amichai, who died recently, is considered the national poet of Israel. He changed his name in 1946. Amichai means "My nation lives!" You can almost hear the band playing, see the flag waving.

The Israelis may have remade themselves with their Hebrew names, but they also remember what happened in the diaspora. On the walls of Yad Vashem, the Holocaust memorial in Jerusalem, are the names of 1.5 million Jewish children. Yad Vashem means monument of names.

NOTES

1. Gini Alhadeff, *The Sun at Midday: Tales of a Mediterranean Family* (New York: Pantheon, 1997), 52.

2. Albert Memmi, *The Liberation of the Jew* (New York: Orion Press, 1966), 119–20.

3. Paula E. Hyman, *The Jews of Modern France* (Berkeley: University of California Press, 1998), 190.

4. Charles E. Silberman, *A Certain People: American Jews and Their Lives Today* (New York: Summit Books, 1985), 60.

5. *The Jerusalem Report* (June 5, 2000), 46.

6. Lawrence J. Friedman, *Identity's Architect: A Biography of Erik Erikson* (New York: Scribner, 1999), 144.

7. Salo W. Baron, *The Russian Jew under the Tsars and Soviets* (New York: MacMillan, 1976), chapter titled "Era of Revolution."

8. Ibid.

9. William Safire, "Russia's Pols," *The New York Times*, July 30, 1998, A23.

10. Alhadeff, *The Sun at Midday*, 64.

11. Ibid., 15.

12. Aharon Appelfeld, *The Age of Wonders* (Boston: David R. Godine, 1981), 201.

13. Appelfeld himself escaped from a labor camp at eight when his mother was killed. Then he wandered in the woods for three years. He was picked up by the Red Army and served in field kitchens in Ukraine. He went to Palestine in 1946 at the age of fourteen.

14. Some German Jewish writers who committed suicide during the Nazi period are: Kurt Tucholsky in Sweden in 1935; Ernst Toller in a New York hotel room in 1939; Ernst Weiss in Paris in June 1940; Walter Hasenclever in a French

internment camp on the eve of rescue in June 1940; Walter Benjamin on the Spanish frontier in September 1940; Carl Einstein in Paris in July 1941; Stefan Zweig in Brazil in 1942; Alfred Wolfenstein in Paris early in 1945. Peter Gay, *Freud, Jews and Other Germans: Masters and Victims in Modern Culture* (New York: Oxford University Press, 1978), 163.

Writer Cynthia Ozick, in *Metaphor and Memory* (New York: Alfred A. Knopf, 1989) discusses the suicide of Italian writer and Auschwitz survivor Primo Levi in April 1987 and adds these names: Tadeusz Borowski, who lived through Auschwitz and wrote "This Way for Gas Ladies and Gentleman," turned on the household gas three days before the birth of his daughter; the poet Paul Celan; the Austrian born philosopher Hans Mayer, who was in Auschwitz with Levi. Mayer changed his name to Jean Amery by scrambling the letters into a French anagram.

15. Katie Hafner, *The House at the Bridge: A Story of Modern Germany* (New York: Scribner, 1995), 46–49.

16. Yehuda Amichai, "Names, Names in Other Days and in Our Time," *Open Closed Open* (New York: Harcourt, 2000), 131.

Part Two

❧

I S R A E L

10

OPENING UP JEWISH

When my older son, Lou, graduated from college he wanted to travel. He wanted an adventure. He applied to the Peace Corps.

"Why not go to Israel," I said to him, I'm sure more than once. We had been to Israel before as a family. It had been, in fact, the year Lou turned thirteen, a kind of Bar Mitzvah trip. Looking back on that time after his college graduation, it was as though I was trying to crack open a door and coax him through.

He went. He found a program called Project Otzma. He lived and worked on a kibbutz for three months and studied Hebrew intensively. He spent the rest of the year working with immigrant children from the former Soviet Union and Ethiopia.

Then Lou went back another year and worked as a counselor for Otzma. He became a fluent Hebrew speaker. Living in Israel for those two years, he drank up Jewish life. He was on the Israeli streets Friday mornings as people rushed to buy bread and flowers in preparation for Shabbat. And he felt the quiet descend at dusk. He lived in Jewish time and space, in a way that he, and I, had never done. And he has made this observance part of his life.

Jewishness was flooding into our lives. Around the same time my other son, Max, was taking classes in Jewish studies in college. One summer when Lou was in Israel, Max lived with him for four months in Jerusalem and studied Hebrew. David and I visited and drank up Israel too.

One evening, we were walking on the beach in Netanya, watching the beautiful sunset, and our two sons asked my husband and me a question something like this: We're Jewish; in what form did you hand it down to us? It wasn't an angry question, just uncomprehending.

David felt less on the spot than I did, with his mixed background, his mother Jewish, his father not. He feels a deep bond with Israel, but he is indifferent to organized religion. But I caught a glimpse of how my relationship to Judaism must have appeared to Lou and Max. I was a person who had not grappled with my legacy. The best I had to offer was passivity. I had put forth a lot of talk about passion and values, a sense of the weight of Jewish survival and subliminal messages about ways to hide. But we had given them few particulars.

They wanted more from us. They looked out and saw a rich Jewish life in which they had not been invited to partake. They had arrived at young adulthood as forthright Jews. They wanted to know why they had grown up lacking Jewish content. Where was the Jewish paraphernalia in our lives? A mezuzah by the door, a fast on Yom Kippur, celebration for Shabbat, a Star of David worn around the neck. Why did we not know the prayers, the language, and the history? These were all things we were somehow too American for. And these symbols, rituals, and subjects of study carried none of the static and ambivalence for them that they did for me.

I don't think it was happenstance that Lou found Israel and Max followed suit. What they were impatient for was to step into their religious heritage. And they weren't burdened by the tortured Jewish issue of not belonging. For example, both were successful athletes; Lou had even played soccer at an Ivy League College. It would never have occurred to them that being Jewish would hold them back or dictate their life choices. What would they know or care about the stilted ghetto habits of the eastern European Jew? It was, it seemed, a new world indeed. Was this not in a sense, the normalization that Theodor Herzl, who called for a Jewish state, had striven for? And why not? My children were reaching for a

Judaism they could touch, feel, see, and be. Lou carries his own *kipa* (Hebrew for skullcap) to Shabbat. They fill their mouths with Hebrew words, wear Stars of David around their necks. What they wanted was the age-old capacity in Judaism to nurture and embrace. And they wanted to know—why have you kept us from it?

I began to catch a glimpse of the Judaism they were reaching for. And also how I had held it at some distance from myself. David and I had grown up in a time when the universal and the particular seemed somehow mutually exclusive. And so to belong, we went with the universals, hid in them actually, and gave our sons only the bare skeleton of the particulars. And now they were saying, sure, the universals are good: they have firm values about freedom, justice, rights, and reaching out to the less fortunate. But why not the particulars, too? If the universal is good, isn't the universal and the particular better? Indeed, why not?

Perhaps this is what multiculturalism has opened the door to. Being particular does not mean you have to be a poor Jew behind the ghetto walls. It could mean being a successful Jew out in the world.

So I decided to go to Israel, as both of my sons had done. They had experienced something powerful there. I was following in their footsteps. I would be in Israel for close to eight weeks, the first six on my own. Then David was coming for a week. The last week my two sons would arrive. That was the way everyone's schedules had worked out and the various configurations were fine with me. Our family's journey into Jewishness was both individual and collective. I was glad for the time on my own as well as with them.

A day or so before I was to leave, I looked at my packed things on the floor—suitcase, laptop, carry-on with a book to read, passport in my purse. That would be my universe. I felt light and exhilarated. How appealing it was, the idea of feeling this powerful sense of myself, tested in this new place and new culture both foreign and intimately familiar.

I would be living in the same neighborhood my sons had. I would be studying Hebrew at the same *ulpan* (intensive Hebrew school). I would not only walk the same streets but my journey, like theirs, was a search for a Jewish identity. The arc of my Jewish evolution, dormant for so long, was now set on a fast track. Israel was a way to reach into the richness of Jewish life. I would step out of my family, out of English, and out of my crimped

American way of being Jewish. I would immerse myself in Hebrew, experience Shabbat, and most of all from this faraway place, mull over and try to integrate all that I had been absorbing of Jewish history.

But in the dark of night during those days before I felt pure anxiety. Years of habit and routine that I was suddenly breaking added to my disquiet, but caution is also my nature. How hard it was to go forth. I'd never been much of a risk-taker. I'm inclined more to look inward than outward to expansive new horizons. One could say, too, I am a typical second child, holding back, watching others take chances, an observer. Journalism in this respect is not only a profession, it is a way of life that comes naturally.

Sometimes I wonder if what I'm doing now in my fifties has a tinge of the puerile, my missed adventure of adolescence. After college I took a job in my hometown for the summer and lived at home. I was to move away to an exciting job in the fall. But the job at home turned out to be challenging and they asked me to stay. I liked it and never did go away. A few years later I married and soon after had children. It was not until I was forty-six that I joined that great American rite of passage and moved away from my hometown to another city. And that was because my husband was offered a new job.

I've been the one left at home rather than the one doing the leaving. Whether it was a husband traveling or children going off to school, I can feel each tooth in the grinding gear of such transitions.

Now it seemed I had galvanized in a new way. I was going somewhere under my own steam. It was not a child's interest, a husband's job, or my own job sending me. I was putting myself in a new place.

I was not going with the power of a news organization behind me. I would be on my own and I would have the time to dally. I was going with good tools: my journalist self, an observer, able to ask questions, figure things out. I believed that my curiosity would serve me well.

David took the day off to take me to the airport and Max drove up to see me off. Dressed in my new blue travel suit, I kept looking back as I inched forward in the line into the plane. My tall son was waving, his arm around his father. "I love you; I'll miss you," we all said. And suddenly we were apart. A moment before I was telling them how to warm the brisket and make a vegetable for dinner. Like that, I was out of the cocoon. I was in this universe of one.

ENTERING

Israel gave our parents a pleasure whose taste they'd forgotten:
the pleasure of being Jewish. No more excuses, dissimulations, or
hidden fits of self-contempt. Israel let them live again, in public,
in loving union with their image of Jewish destiny.

—Alain Finkielkraut, a Frenchman and son
  of Holocaust survivors in *The Imaginary Jew*

I forgot to mention my other baggage. The bag, laptop, carry-on, and purse don't begin to tell you about all the baggage I was going with.

I was going to the Jewish homeland, you see. I loved the fantasy of it, even the sound of it. It resonated deep inside. This was no nostalgic connection to an old country, to stories buried in memory. It was a new country, this foreign place, where they speak not the mother tongue, Yiddish, but that of the father, Hebrew. It was a place that grew up side by side, with us, like a faraway fellow orphan. We believed that we, in America, were one part of a reconstituted Jewish story; they, Israelis, unknown as they have been to us, were quite another.

Indeed, as I walked the short distance in the Newark airport from Continental to the space of El Al airlines, I could feel the culture shift from universal secular America to particular Jewish Israel. As I approached the line for the stringent El Al security check, I felt twinges, layers of identity, usually quite dormant, galvanizing, coming into play for me, potent and confusing. I lined up with a tour group of African American church women; black hatted men with their wives, hair covered, shepherding their children along; secular Israelis glancing over their Hebrew newspapers.

How to explain this shift in climate? For Jews, certain words have particularly deep meaning and are powerfully evocative. Survival and rescue, exile and diaspora, return and homeland are such words for me. So, too, are assimilation and extinction, persecution and extermination, and perhaps the most powerful: Remember. When such words come up for me, a flashing red light goes on. Perhaps it is "Jewish sensitivity," hypersensitivity, even paranoia. The Jewish narrative has come into play.

Here's a piece of the Jewish narrative. When I was growing up, an article appeared in the paper about a teenager, a Jewish teenager. He had held someone up with a gun and taken off in a stolen car. This news sent a shudder through our house. He was a Jew! Jews didn't steal! Jews were held to a higher ethical standard. And, of course, our concomitant reaction —what shame, what public humiliation for us. There was perhaps even a grain of this vestigial fear—would a pogrom follow?

So, too, growing up we had to be perfect. You know the vaunted Jewish family. Bad things simply didn't go on—except antisemitism. We were doctors, lawyers, businessmen, fighters for political justice. No drinkers, druggies, wife and child beaters, teen girls who got pregnant, traffickers in pornography or prostitution were to be found. Never mind that this sometimes involved denial of considerable proportion. Only now is the Jewish community acknowledging and dealing with its own domestic violence.

On November 1, 1998, the *New York Times* ran a page one story about the white slave trade. A twenty-one-year-old woman from Ukraine got off a tour boat and took a job dancing on tabletops. Her boss burned her passport and made her work in a brothel. When she refused "she was beaten and raped before she succumbed," the article said.

The city was Haifa, Israel. While the article was about prostitution worldwide, Israel figured prominently. "Israel is a fairly typical destination.

Prostitution is not illegal here, although brothels are, and with 250,000 foreign male workers—most of whom are single or are here without their wives—the demand is great. Police officials estimate that there are 15,000 paid sexual transactions every day. Brothels are ubiquitous." They are also frequented by Israeli soldiers, business executives, and tourists, the article said.

I felt stricken reading this. To me, it was not an article about the slave trade; it was about Israel. I had a kind of throwback reaction, a kind of old world reflex. What would it mean for the Jews? But aren't Jews made of the same flesh as others?

No, Israel, the one of the mind's eye, had to be perfect, had to be some Jewish ideal. It was the Israel of strong boys, girls with braids, picking oranges in the sunshine on a kibbutz, defending their borders, building the new just society, "a beacon to others."

The Zionists, those secular miracle-makers, not only created a country, they created new Jews. Israel was where the feeble, persecuted diaspora Jew, the starved, ragged remnant of the Holocaust, was transformed into the healthy Jew, physically and spiritually. If the diaspora Jew was weak and soft, the new one was strong and muscular. If the diaspora Jew was manipulative and wily, the new Jew was straightforward and direct. If the diaspora Jew was a huckster or middleman, the new Jew was a peasant farmer or efficient technocrat.[1]

Not that our lives weren't good, we were here, after all, in this other Promised Land, but Israel was an ideal, something more than we were. Israel allowed us to stand taller. It was a love object, a repository for our Jewishness, a part of keeping our Jewishness intact, as we were swirled around in this melting pot. We were connected to it in some organic, symbiotic way.

This connection made us cling not so much to the real, corporeal Israel but to Israel the Good, the little Israel, Israel the victim, defending its sanctioned boundaries, not Israel the occupier, Israel of the Intifada, Israel with its own assassin of its own esteemed political leader.

It was the David and Goliath Israel of the raid on Entebbe, not of Israel retreating from the Lebanon. It was Israel right or wrong. We were not about to have the love object defiled. We were not to criticize. It was Israel out of history and its consequences and into the realm of an epic story—the end of exile, the Return to the Land.

Because, you see, Israel was doing something important for us. Its military exploits helped us all recover from two thousand years of victimhood.

Just being the Jewish state made us feel good about being Jewish. And we didn't have to carve out such a definitive place for Jewishness in our own lives: We were free to make our way here, in all the pull and tug of ecumenism, pluralism, multiculturalism, or whatever it is now called.

The first encounter with Jewish authority came with the wall of El Al security that faced me even before I had my ticket checked. "Did you pack your own bag? Has it been in your possession at all times? Did anyone give you a package to give to someone else? The reason I am asking you these questions is that someone could be using you."

El Al's unsmiling young interrogators carry out their meticulous scrutiny. They are the new Jew; competent, serious, purposeful, humorless, macho even if female. Yet I found this encounter not in the least off-putting. I, a Vietnam dove, felt this surge of Jewish chauvinism. Here were my people in the act of defending themselves. I, too, felt the transforming effect.

I was suddenly aware of my own deep imprint of defenselessness, insecurity borne of my father's fear. I felt the absence of a powerful outer rind of my own, so palpable in Israeli officialdom.

Of course, all airlines have come far closer to El Al these days in terms of security, even for domestic flights. But El Al was among the first and probably still the most vigilant because Israel is such a frequent target of terrorism.

"What will you be doing in Israel? Visiting family? Business?" I was struck by the intensity with which they inquired, actually profiled each passenger. For we who luxuriate in the safety of secular America—at least before September 11, 2001—it's a sharp reminder that Israel may have made the new Jew, but it's still not safe to be a Jew, especially in the Jewish state. Israel, that haven for the Jewish people, who were in such peril in Europe, is a very high security place. Israel does not have settled boundaries and has continued to build settlements in the West Bank. The Palestinians have no state of their own and potent voices on both sides have not accepted the existence of the other. And since September 11, 2001, matters have become worse. Antagonism toward Israel across the Arab world and in Europe has heightened.

As I settled into the plane I noticed that the attendants wore the uniforms of the national airline, spoke Hebrew, and had names like Dorot and Yitzhak. Enveloped here in nationality, I felt the tangibility and power of statehood.

So, too, I entered the force field of Jewish history. I could feel my time orientation shift from an American's short view to the Jewish one that spans thousands of years; from Moses and the laws needed to govern ourselves in the diaspora to David and the power it took to conquer and defend Jerusalem.

If Israel is a repository for our Jewishness, this relationship goes both ways: We too are actors in Israel's narrative, its epic ingathering of the Jewish people. To them, my life in America is actually one of exile. America, the superpower watchdog of democracy around the globe, this polyglot nation, is not a center, as we like to think of it. It is the diaspora, a part of that two-thousand-year scattering of the Jewish people. We, as Jews, live in this polarity, which makes for a certain tension, a pull to the center, which is Jerusalem.

"Next year in Jerusalem," we say at the Passover seder, metaphorically to denote our longing for freedom. This state of unfulfillment is part of the tension of Jewish existence, perhaps of human existence, a perpetual state of longing, of not quite being there.[2] And then suddenly there was Israel, a tangible place of promised fulfillment. I think of the many young Israeli friends who say to my son Lou: "So when are you moving here?" That's the expectation. It's no ordinary immigration but called "making *aliyah*," which means "going up," "ascending," a holy meaning as in going up to read from the Torah. Israel may disappoint as a love object, as a repository of Jewishness, but we have disappointed too. American Jews have not joined their ingathering in significant numbers. The largest Jewish community in the world is still in the United States: 5.7 million.[3] The Jewish population in Israel is 4.9 million.[4]

All this baggage, raising such complicated questions for me about belonging. It is hard to grasp what belonging means anymore in our increasingly mobile societies and cultural amalgams. It was the dream of Zionism's founder Theodor Herzl that the Jewish people, by gaining their own state, would be normal, would belong and thus be like every other nation. Has that happened, in Israel or in America?

And here I am on this paradoxical adventure going to this foreign land to find, in a sense, home. Or perhaps to find a way to assuage the hurts of the Jewish past and achieve an inner sense of belonging, or peace. Perhaps this trip is to repair these discomforts that estrange me.

On the airplane sat ultrareligious men in black hats and women with their heads covered. I, wearing a pants suit, my hair loose, felt stripped of the privacy of my beliefs. My appearance said I was secular, that is, not Orthodox or ultrareligious.

Before I began this project, I would have felt defensive and judged by these visibly religious Jews. But a year of study and thought about the tributaries to Jewishness made me appreciate the breadth of Judaism, from the secular Jews who founded Israel, to the Hasidic Jews of Poland before the Holocaust, to the Sephardic Jews of the Ottoman Empire. I came to see the whole spectrum as a kind of biodiversity. And this diversity in Judaism, often so contentious, may in itself be a powerful force for survival. So I felt more accepting, of them and of myself. I may be at one end, but I am a legitimate part of this Jewish continuum.

Half dozing, I watched a strange movie about a music manager, a magician, and a prostitute from Chernobyl who perform at the summer festival at Arad. I slept for a while, then woke up as if in a dream. I looked to the back of the plane and glimpsed men praying in a soft white florescent light. I had no idea what the time was but they did. They were wrapping themselves in *talit* (prayer shawls) and wearing their tefillin. They were reciting morning prayers. I noticed another man standing in the middle of the center row of seats, as others slept on each side, doing the same in his Yonkers T-shirt and khaki shorts, kipa and prayer shawl.

I watched for a long time. I was suddenly deeply aware of my alienation from religion, including my own. We had, in fact, a strain of antireligion. For my mother, Orthodoxy was backward. She believed that as one became more educated one became less religious. She felt it appealed to some irrational part of human nature that could be overcome. And she saw it in some opposition to progress, getting an education, being modern.

Certainly, learning has long been a Jewish value, especially yeshiva study for boys. Yet out of the Enlightenment values of reason and progress, religion and secular education had become polar opposites, at least in my family. Reform Judaism with all its rationality was fine. But divine revelation, following *halakha*, or Jewish law, keeping kosher or adhering to certain kinds of dress—no way. My parents were part of this eons-old crusade to bring about the acceptability of the Jewish people. And they believed such differences, such setting ourselves apart, would impede acceptance.

At one time I would have looked at the men praying in the back of the plane and felt the intrusion of religion into my space, even of *my* religion. Religion, I believed, was something that should be kept private, out of the public space.

But what I caught a glimpse of while watching those strangers pray, was not only the obedience to rules and ritual that I was always so quick to question, but the succor they seemed to get. I was startled to realize that that was something never offered me. Religion was not portrayed to us as something that could protect or nourish. It was not there as a membrane of support. It was more something *we* were expected to protect. Judaism was in much more jeopardy than we were. We better be strong because we were its only defense. And my mother had given me the prototype; it was so much like my obligation, my need to protect her, than the reverse.

So, you see, I carried a lot of baggage to open, examine, and ruminate upon. Some I was sure I would leave behind, some would come back with me transformed, and who knew what entirely new things I would find.

NOTES

1. Paula E. Hyman, *Gender and Assimilation in Modern Jewish History: The Roles and Representation of Women* (Seattle: University of Washington Press, 1995), 142.

2. Arnold M. Eisen, *Galut: Modern Jewish Reflection on Homelessness and Homecoming* (Bloomington: Indiana University Press, 1986), 18.

3. 2000 National Jewish Population Survey, Council of Jewish Federations, New York.

4. World Jewish Congress, *Jewish Communities of the World*, 1996.

12

ISRAEL ON THE GROUND

Immediately upon arriving in Israel, I felt enveloped by the heat, sun, and stony arid landscape. It filled me with a certain bleakness. But I soon settled into the small apartment I had rented and over the next days began to get to know my neighborhood. My adventure began to pick up stride. First, the necessities—in one direction was a tiny corner grocery store, in the other, a bakery. Across Bezalel was the *shuk*, the big open market. A café was down one street and down another was a lovely restaurant with outdoor eating.

Like a cat, I expanded my territory in widening circles. I lived in an area of Jerusalem called Rehavia. Tel Aviv is home to the stock exchange, the national labor group, and the army general staff. But Rehavia in Jerusalem is the intellectual and political center of the country.[1] The old Knesset or parliament building, now the tourism ministry, was just a few blocks from me. The new Knesset and Supreme Court were not far away, as was the president's house.

Rehavia is considered an elite area. Later, I heard that Mizrachim—what Jews from eastern countries are called—charged that the education they got was a far cry from that of kids from Rehavia. Although my immediate area was not upscale by American standards, it was homey. And the longer I was there the more familiar it became.

The sound of someone practicing the piano often streamed out of the second floor of the adjacent building. On the other side was a teacher training institute and teachers walked in and out all day. Across the street was Raymond, a shoemaker. He worked in his kiosk, his name written out front in Russian. When I would return home, I would peer in and catch a glimpse of him working on a pair of shoes.

I have often wondered in this exploration, how is a Jew imprinted and why is that imprint so deep? One way is Jewish space. In America and especially for secular Jews, Jewish space is wedged into crevices. We enter it in the temple, at holidays or through Jewish organizations. But Israel is different. Israel is Jewish space.

Israel on the ground was electrifying for me. The customs agent was a Jew, as was the taxi driver, the shopkeeper, the newscaster, and the mayor. The newspaper stand, dress shops, and beauty salon were Jewish. Walking the streets I felt as though for the first time I was stretched out fully in my own skin. With every sense, I felt connected to all that surrounded me.

I became fascinated by what people wore: the black hats, and baseball caps; the black coats and spandex pants; sleeves below the elbow and no sleeves at all. A kipa-wearing boy ran down the street sucking a popsicle, the juice running on his white shirt.

The hair of the religious women was covered but the long masses of curls of the secular ran free. I, who spent so many years taming curly hair, found one wild mane of female hair more beautiful than the next. I decided to let mine grow and be one of them. And I was dazzled by the chutzpah of religious Jews, to simply be Jews, pray and study in their own world. Unlike us, they do not hurl themselves at this gargantuan task of making the world safe. In their black clothes they thumb their noses at Jewish invisibility, they say, here I am, take it or leave it. Jew is like a skin color, worn on the outside.

I had always held my Jewishness inside. Israel transformed me. Now it was as though my Jewishness filled the air. I had not realized that I had lived by that over-developed Jewish capacity to function in space not my own. There, I felt that the air I breathed was Jewish and it was intoxicating.

Every day I awakened early and I was ready for adventure. The sun always shone, the sky was blue and the light was captivating. I loved life on the street and felt open to it all. I was in fact in love with the Jerusalem air, attuned to its diurnal cycle. How fresh it was in the morning and, as the summer went on, how hot in the afternoon. Then in late afternoon, the coolness began. I loved going to Hebrew class in the evening, to come out again at night, after a day's work. I sometimes went out for dinner with people after class and would sit outside at a Jerusalem restaurant till late, giving myself over to soft laughter in the Mediterranean night.

Each day was my own creation. I was doing what I loved, being a reporter, observing, soaking up, ruminating. Only now I was not only trying to understand the lives of others, but also my own.

I became fascinated with street names. Walking out of the door of my apartment was like stepping right into all the history I was trying to make sense of. Going left and walking to the corner I came to Ussishkin Street. Ussishkin? That would be Menahem Mendel Ussishkin, a Russian Zionist born in 1863. A stocky bull of a man, he vehemently opposed and helped to defeat a proposal that came before the Sixth Zionist Congress in 1903 that the Jews make their homeland in a colony in African Uganda.[2] Yes indeed, Ussishkin is an Israeli hero.

If I went right on Ussishkin, I would come to the busy boulevard Bezalel. Now I was in the neighborhood of Nachlaot with its charming stone alleyways and cobbled courtyards. My sons had lived on Bezalel. At the end of the street was the Bezalel Art Gallery, the first arts institution in pre-state Palestine. It's an Arab style structure and has a café courtyard. The name Bezalel is taken from the Torah. He was the biblical craftsman Bezalel ben Uri who constructed the Holy Tabernacle and Ark of the Covenant in Sinai.[3]

Each name excited and tantalized me. Each was a mystery to be solved. Like Narkiss, the narrow one-way street I lived on a block over from Bezalel. Who was Narkiss? I found out months after I left Israel. He was Mordechai Narkiss, who came to Palestine from Poland in 1920. Narkiss was the right-hand man and successor to Boris Schatz, who founded the Bezalel School. The art Narkiss collected became the nascent collection of the Israel Museum.

As I walked Jerusalem's streets, these names became a window into the history that Israel has put together for itself. Each name was part of the monumental job of giving coherence and wholeness of identity to this fractured people. I got a sense of what a complicated stew Jewish history is—the many strands that have fed it. It was forged out of the thousands of fractures made by the movement of Jews across the world, over thousands of years. Israel sifted through it and decided who—with the honor of a street name—had been part of the flow of making this state.

On the ground in Israel, I got a sense of Jewish wholeness I had not had before. Just as I had not known I did not breathe Jewish air, I did not know I lived in a fractured history. Israel put the pieces together. It was Israel's story and I wanted to learn it. It was part of putting together my own story. It was a way to be healed.

Walk to the right on Narkiss out of my building and there was King George, a nod to the British and their troubled time of the mandate; a jog to the left was that famous intersection of King George and Ben Yehuda. Eliezer Ben Yehuda was the creator of the modern Hebrew language.

There were streets named for figures of or important to the Jewish diaspora, like the great Yiddish writer, Sholem Aleichem. His character Tevye the Dairyman wrings his hands as he witnesses the breakdown of traditional eastern European Jewish life as it was faced with modernity.

So, too, a street was named for the French writer Emile Zola, who wrote "J'Accuse," an impassioned defense of the Jewish captain and accused spy Alfred Dreyfus. "J'Accuse" was written in the storm of antisemitism that followed Dreyfus's arrest and later exoneration.

From Great Britain we have early twentieth-century statesmen, David Lloyd George and Arthur James Balfour, the backers of the idea of a Jewish homeland. From Germany there is Martin Buber, the philosopher who escaped the Holocaust and emigrated to Israel; and Schocken, a street at the Mt. Scopus campus of Hebrew University. Schocken was a Jewish publisher in Germany, shut down by the Nazis in the 1930s. The publishing house then opened in Jerusalem and New York. It is now back in Germany and was purchased recently by the German firm Bertelsmann, which has recently apologized for its Nazi ties.

There is a street called Harav Kook that is for Avraham Yitzhak Kook, a religious Zionist who became the first chief Ashkenazi rabbi of Palestine in 1921.

These names grounded me in the history of Israel, rather the history of Zionism, or more accurately, the history of Jews viewed through a Zionist lens. In those names I found the heroes, the suffering, the religious passion, the intellectual muscle, the artistic creativity. I saw the poets of Spain and military heroes, state builders and Yiddish writers. Even the heroes of American democracy Washington and Lincoln were honored with small streets.

Every day I walked and felt there was this giant puzzle before me—the mystery of Jewish history. I was trying to put it together, in fact I felt I must put it together, if I was to get my own sense of being a Jew on solid ground. Fleshing out the people behind those names was one of my ways in. And I wondered too, how I, an educated, aware, curious person had lived so long with such a fuzzy understanding of all of this.

Back in my neighborhood, Ussishkin crosses Alharizi Street named for Yehudah al-Harizi, and Solomon Ibn Gavril Street.[4] Both were also twelfth-century Spanish poets of the golden age.

The Zionists of course have a certain prominence: Ruppin Street winds its way around the Knesset, the Israeli parliament, and other government buildings. German-born Arthur Ruppin went to Palestine in 1908 to work in the Zionist organization. He published the first journal of demographics of Jews and then became the first professor of sociology at Hebrew University.

There is a street for Odessa-born Ze'ev Jabotinsky, the charismatic Zionist who advocated militarism in Palestine. And of course there is a street for Herzl, which winds its way to the mountain summit where Theodor Herzl, the founder of modern Zionism, is buried.

I was dizzy with the number of figures in Jewish history that come together in these street names. It was as if Israel was saying to all those who traveled there: know who we are, the complex historical ground we stand on. We had no land, no mountains or rivers to remember. But we had something else that was powerful, thinkers and doers who, if we remember them, give us coherence. Know what brought us to this land, and know who has made it possible for us to stay. On every street I sensed this fresh new nationalism, both filled with and unsure of itself.

And the Holocaust is never far away. The street Saloniki was named for the thriving Greek port city with a rich Jewish culture before the war. Now called Thessaloniki, 96 percent of its 56,000 Jews were killed at Auschwitz.

In fact, one of the reasons Israel feels so intense is, I think, because being there is to experience in some literal fashion the death-to-life, Holocaust-to-Israel paradigm of my generation. Whether there was a cause and effect relationship or not, the birth of the state of Israel followed the Holocaust. It was the triumph of the generation of Jews who lived after the Holocaust. The Holocaust endowed the Jewish state with the deeper meaning of Jewish survival.

The Holocaust may be inexplicable, but Israel is not. In Israel, ordinary Jews do ordinary things—work, eat, argue on the streets, drive too fast, raise children. Israel is real and tangible. To enter this Jewish space, to feel the quickened pace of life on the streets, made me want to hold onto it as if it were life itself. Israel is both the reality and symbol of Jewish survival, that bulwark against every Jewish persecution in all of history, including the most recent near-extermination. It makes it hard for Israel and Jews everywhere to let go of this struggle. It is part of the Jewish story.

The fact that Israel exists in a hostile surround only amplifies this echo of survival. No event is simply what it is. It echoes to the whole history of Jewish survival.

A few streets have Arabic names; Azza (Gaza), Hebron, Yeriho (Jericho), but most are of the victors. To name, to honor one's dead, are the spoils of war. "The act of renaming places is crucial to the enterprise of conquest: 'Drawing a map and determining names are [acts] of taking possession, of creating a new reality,'" writes Susan Slyomovics in her searing critique of the Israeli attempt to obliterate Palestinians.[5]

Jerusalem, it doesn't take long to see, is about layers of conquest and reconquest over centuries. There is always something that went before, even ancient layers of one's own.

Jews are an old people with a long history and so there are many to remember who in some way enhanced Jewish survival, dignity, or regeneration. But how different this seemed. Usually it is the losses and the persecutions that are remembered, as in American Holocaust culture. Here it is the celebrations and victories.

I marvel at this ambitious attempt to give coherence to the Jewish past that existed for centuries without land and a common everyday language. I felt as though they were saying to me, our history, however fractured and far flung it may have been, is central to who we are, to Jewish identity. We stand on this physical ground, but we are also defining a narrative that reaches deep into the past.

While Jews were often victims of European nationalism, they are relatively new to their own.[6] Even though the state is over fifty years old, it has been a contentious half-century with five wars and an ongoing battle with Palestinians. With all of Israel's militarism, its legitimacy is not secure. And so as I walked the streets of Jerusalem I felt a joy with each piece of the puzzle I had solved. I felt pride in being part of this Jewish history. And I also felt a shadow of that old Jewish insecurity, even pathos.

I have a hard time seeing Israel from the outside, whatever its problems. I am viscerally connected, like to a member of my family. I hear critiques of Israel, understand and even agree with some of them, but never with distance or dispassion. This thirst for Jewish space, for air to breathe that is Jewish, for Jewish survival made me myopic for many years to the other parts of Israel on the ground: the Palestinians, the territories.

NOTES

1. Tom Segev, *The Seventh Million: The Israelis and the Holocaust* (New York: Hill and Wang, 1993), 256.

2. Salo W. Baron, *The Russian Jew under Tsars and Soviets* (New York: Macmillan, 1976), 148.

3. *Tanakh*, Exodus 31, 1–6.

4. Ismar Schorsch, *From Text to Context: The Turn to History in Modern Judaism* (Waltham, Mass.: Brandeis University Press/University Press of New England, 1994), 82.

5. Susan Slyomovics, *The Object of Memory: Arab and Jew Narrate the Palestinian Village* (Philadelphia: University of Pennsylvania Press, 1998), 66.

6. Arnold M. Eisen, *Galut: Modern Jewish Reflection on Homelessness and Home-coming* (Bloomington: Indiana University Press, 1986), 191.

13

*I was born in 1939, shortly before the outbreak of war, when it
became clear to my parents that they were not going back. They may have
dreamed in Yiddish, spoken to each other in Russian and Polish,
and read mainly in German and English, but they brought me up
speaking one language only: Hebrew.*

—Amoz Oz, *Under This Blazing Light*

When my mother read Hebrew, she
would run her index finger under the strange letters, right to left, and the
words would effortlessly come out of her mouth. Then she would an-
nounce, "You know, I don't understand anything it said!"

She was proud of her accomplishment yet she also had disdain for this
gross defect in her Jewish education. She had been made to learn to read
this ancient tongue, yet was not taught any of its meaning. It was no wonder she had a lifelong dislike for rote learning.

She didn't make the same mistake with her children. The temple we
went to was Reform: We studied no Hebrew. It was antiquated, indeci-

pherable, the dead language of the closed religion we left behind because we were modern.

Not only has Hebrew survived, it has had an amazing rebirth. "The most significant event is the revival of Hebrew, even the state is less of a miracle," said Israeli writer Amos Oz. "The language was the sleeping beauty. For 1800 years it was not spoken in the intimacy of the bedroom, nursery or yard. It was not an everyday prosaic, flesh and blood language."[1]

Hebrew, as a modern spoken language, is still developing. A teacher told us about the web site for the Academy of the Hebrew Language.[2] There you can see the new words that are still being adopted in Hebrew for modern usage, like video clip, sitcom, roller blades, logo, jet lag, or lozenge.

Hebrew also has found its way into other languages. The word "maven" (or "mavin") is a Hebrew word, now in the English dictionary. It found its way into Yiddish first in Europe, then immigrants brought it here where it later became part of English. I had thought it had come originally from Yiddish. I didn't know that many words in Yiddish—about four thousand, one teacher told us—had come from Hebrew. Even seichel, a word I remember my father saying meaning good sense or judgement, came from Hebrew.

When Jews arrived in Palestine, Hebrew, the language of prayer for all Jews, was what Ashkenazic Jews who spoke Yiddish and Sephardic Jews who spoke Ladino had in common. And Hebrew, the language of the fathers, was appropriate for a society that would now defend itself with force.

When I went to college, I studied Russian with the mistaken idea that it had something to do with my heritage, when in fact it had little. My grandparents may have lived in the Russian Pale but their world was Jewish, their language Yiddish.

Yiddish was the living language of my family, even though it faded quickly to the sidelines for the imperial ascendancy of perfectly spoken English. Yiddish had an evocative power and an intimacy. It was what they spoke when they didn't want us to understand. And it was funny and rich both in the way it sounded and in the concrete ways it captured human foibles. I hear wisps of its cadences in American humor. Its view of the world has been a rich vein for comedians. "You can't dance your *tuchis* (rear end) at two weddings," describes a man having an affair. When your heart pounds in fear it is like a *tup lokshun*, a pot of boiling noodles. And the word for busy body is *kochleffl*, stirring spoon, one who stirs the pot.

Yet Israel is what is new, Israel is where my children were drawn, and Hebrew is the language. Hebrew is the language of the Jewish people, the entrée to the religion, culture, history, and of course to Israel. So I took it up, the Jewish language of prayer that in my lifetime has become the language of everyday: "What's up?" "computer," "pass the pepper," and "where's the bathroom." I set out, as my sons had done, to speak Hebrew.

It is all talk, in fact, until you sit your tuchis down in a Hebrew class. The teacher Yemima pointed with her index finger to her mouth. She touched her throat for the "resh" to show how deep down the "rr" sound begins and then pointed to her mouth to how the sound comes out.

Look and listen. It is primitive and elemental in a way I am not used to. Yes, the mouth is where language comes out. I think of language as communication, even culture. But first of all it is physical. Look, listen, and imitate.

It was my first day of ulpan, or Hebrew school in Israel. I started in the beginners' class. Yemima's hair was tucked under a straw hat with a small rolled brim. It framed her warm face, made more radiant with vivid eye makeup, red lipstick, and earrings. She wore stylish suits with long skirts and long fitted jackets. I wondered about her a little like a child with a dazzling young new teacher. What was she, religious, or is she a model?

Amazingly, the first day was all in Hebrew, but then why not? There was no other common language among us. When Yemima had to, she spoke French to Sylvia, who was Jordanian, who then translated into Arabic for the two teenage boys from the Armenian Quarter of the Old City.

You may be wondering, what kind of class was this in the heart of west Jerusalem? To enter this class was to be thrown into an astonishing diversity, a microcosm of the movement and searching of people today. Irene, from Korea, attended a Christian Bible college in Jerusalem. She was a true beginner: She didn't know the alphabet. She was a true believer as well. I told her I was working on a manuscript about Jewish identity and the next day she put a book on my desk on messianic Judaism, about how Jews can be Christians too.

Kudi was a black woman from England; Esther and Yonaton were a Korean couple who gave themselves Hebrew names for the duration and were in a teacher training program in Israel; Gitte and Inge were from Denmark. Inge had been a kibbutz and hospital volunteer for the past two years and had an Israeli boyfriend. Jefferson was from Brazil; Letitia was from France, as was Joelle, a social worker whose parents were from Algeria and long before that Spain. Her sister lived in Israel and she is seeing if she too might want to emigrate; Andrea was from Costa Rica.

And several Americans—John, from Chicago, Ari, a medical student from Philadelphia whose father is Israeli. And there was Anton, twenty-six, from the Urals in Russia, who has a wife and three children.

"Beautiful!" "Excellent!" "Bravo!" said Yemima beaming her beautiful smile. She glowed with each of our responses. I felt like a toddler basking in her praise, which seemed essential to venturing forth with these foreign sounds. Even as she corrected mistakes, she would repeat and smile.

She pointed to her chin, ear, and throat. "I read, you repeat." Language was drama to her, the unfolding of each word. Each sound, each meaning was wondrous. She wanted us to own it, make it a mother tongue. "Aleph," she said the first letter of the alphabet. "The words that begin with it are powerful and fruitful: Love, people, you, I, God."

The class met four times a week, three hours at a time. Often I studied in the mornings. I sat at a little table by the window in my first floor apartment. The cool Jerusalem air, the sounds of the street came through the window. Each morning, an elderly Ethiopian man swept the drive. And most mornings a chirping little boy was out on his balcony a couple of floors up from me to greet him. He was two-and-a-half-year-old Rafaela.

"*Shalom*," (hello) called out Rafaela, who had a full head of blonde curls.

"Shalom," answered the man from below. Rafaela was bold and had a big voice.

"How are you?" asked the man, who must have learned to speak Hebrew later in life.

"How are you?" answered Rafaela. They babbled back and forth, a rhythmic repetition. I wanted to be Rafaela, king of his Hebrew. He does not, as I do, struggle with verbs in the past tense. I wanted to join their very public, very special Hebrew class.

Instead I moved up to the next level at school, yet I wasn't sure I belonged there. I could barely hang on. Anton moved up too. This class was different. These were not people on the outside of Israeli society peering in, the tourist or visitor caught up in the glow and wonder of discovering Israel. These were people who lived, worked in Israel. Some were Palestinian. Some had made *aliyah*. Language was not an adventure but a necessity. They were trying to make their way in the uphill struggle to understand and be understood. Many, like Anton, spoke enough Hebrew to get along, but they didn't know the grammar and couldn't read and write. Shlomit, a young Ethiopian woman, worked at a grocery store, and South African Denise ran a chic restaurant with an Israeli. Anwar was a young Palestinian who lived in the mixed Arab-Jewish neighborhood of Abu Tor.

Most in the class were young, gaining the language skills they needed for the futures they wanted. Israel was a foreign land. Even though many Israelis speak English, without Hebrew, Jew or not, you do not enter this society. Without it, you are always an outsider.

The teachers Ayelet and Michal were young, hip, secular Israelis, fun, but demanding. My first night I met Ennis. She asked me if I had read the popular book *Emotional Intelligence* by Daniel Goleman. I presumed she was from some European capital. It turned out, to my surprise, that she and her sister Samech were young Palestinians who worked in Jerusalem, one an engineer, the other a health care administrator. I felt this initial flush of a friendship that might blossom, made more so perhaps by the chasm between us. But a wall was there; my overtures of friendship were politely declined.

Then there was Simone, a fount of Palestinian rage toward Israel, although he was Italian, married to a Palestinian. He and his wife were architects working on restoration and reconstruction projects in the West Bank cities of Bethlehem, Nablus, Jericho, and Ramallah. He was learning Hebrew but his wife, he said, simply couldn't bring herself to learn the language of the oppressor. He was affable, talkative, and hated Israel. He told anyone who would listen about the horror of coming through the Israeli security checkpoints or dealing with Israeli officialdom. "I consider Jerusalem an occupied territory," he ranted. "We don't recognize the municipality for deciding changes in sewer lines or where to put the schools."

Hebrew is an ersatz language, he said, it is not authentic; so many modern words are made up. He saw Israel as Serbia, the Palestinians as the Kosovars.

His political talk upset me. Was he challenging Israel as occupier or Israel's legitimacy? I could never tell and I'm not sure he made the distinction. Most unnerving was the venomous way he said it. He reminded me of the Black Power radicals of the '60s.

His presence had the effect of driving a wedge between the Palestinians and Jews in the class. There was an invisible wall between us that I did not find surmountable, much as I wanted to. We were in the same class, just not together. But it was naïve of me to think that Simone had made the wall. We each carried our histories, which were to harden even more in the new Intifada that broke out a year later. In time came the actual wall, on the ground and visible.

NOTES

1. Amos Oz, "Where will Israel be 50 years from now," lecture at the Cleveland College of Jewish Studies, May, 10, 1998.
2. http://hebrew-academy.huji.ac.il/english.html

14

ISRAELI

In the movie *Voyages* by the French filmmaker Emmanuel Finkiel, a young Russian family, caught up in the flow to the "homeland," decides to immigrate to Israel. They ask their neighbor, an old woman, if she wants to go too and she does. Once in Israel, the old woman finds herself alone in this entirely foreign place. Amid the buses and traffic in the summer heat, she searches for a cousin who turns out to be in a nursing home.

"It's nothing like the way my husband used to talk about it," she says to a woman who befriends her. "No one even speaks Yiddish." That Israel, of course, the one her husband described, was the one of the mind's eye, the Promised Land, that object of longing. "It seems there are no more Jews in Israel, only Israelis," she remarks wistfully.

Israelis, indeed. What a riot of color, patchwork of ethnicity, shadings of class, spectrum of religiosity Israel is, a veritable panoply bursting at the seams. A young Russian woman plays her violin on the street corner, the case open for change. Ethiopian teenage boys hang out on Ben Yehuda Street wearing their turquoise jewelry and pencil thin braids. Ultra-Orthodox Jews walk the streets on Shabbat in their fur hats and silk jackets. The young hip women wear their tiny black tops with thin spaghetti straps and different color bra straps showing. And the macho guys with their short hair or shaved heads and close fitting T-shirts and jeans are savvy about computers, the ways of war, and pop culture.

I had gone there worried about my Jewish identity, with the Israel of my mind's eye as the repository. But the reality is that Jewish Israelis are not only simply Jews, just as we are not of one dimension. Yes, it is the Jewish state but there are so many other pressing matters of identity to deal with. And I am not even talking about the serious concerns of Palestinian Israelis, Bedouin, Thai, and Christians who also make Israel their home.

In the broadest sense, Jewish Israel is an east-west fault line. It is where Ashkenazic and Sephardic Jews have integrated for more than half a century. It is in the Levant, of the Levant, yet European Jews brought with them and planted their western way of life and their western sense of superiority toward the East, even though *their* position in Europe was often tenuous.

In Israel, all Ashkenazim are thrown together in a single pot, whether they are of German, Polish, or Russian origin. Each of course, has their special story, their own place in the pecking order. The German refugees coming in the '30s, for example, were called "Yekkes" and were made fun of for trying to re-create their cultured lives of books and pianos.

The Sephardim, Jews originally from Spain or Portugal before the expulsions in the late 1400s and early 1500s, are also thrown together with other Jews from the Middle East under the term "Mizrachim," which means east. They include Jews from Morocco, Tunisia, Yemen, Iran, Iraq, and Egypt. They also include Jews from Turkey and Greece, even though those countries are considered western in some circles, and Bulgaria and Yugoslavia, which are southern European.

Each group within the Mizrachim brought with them a different cultural heritage and a Jewishness that was intact and traditional. It had not been rocked and frayed by the struggles for emancipation and drive for modernization that fractured Judaism for so many in the west.

While many Mizrachim are well-integrated into Israel, they have their grievances, many dating back to the stringent demands made of them to assimilate when they came in the '50s and '60s. "They were considered from primitive countries," Ishak Saporta, a professor of business at Tel Aviv University, whose family was originally from Turkey, told me. "The thinking was—we have to civilize them. They were tracked into vocational schools and lived in public housing. Saporta is part of a group called Keshet, which deals with issues of economic equality such as the right of Mizrachim to buy apartments as they have become privatized.

What Mizrachim see today, and with some resentment, Saporta said, are Russians coming in and being celebrated. They are well educated and skating ahead of many Israelis who have been in the country for several generations. Indeed, Russians have a presence in Israel. In a decade, they added 20 percent to the population and have their own political party. Many do not Hebraize their names. Two newspapers in Russian are on the stands on Fridays. Airlines had busy flight schedules to many former Soviet Union cities. Their sheer numbers and level of education will make them an increasingly dominant strain in Israeli life.

The Ethiopian immigration, Saporta says, more closely resembles that of Jews who came from Arab countries in the '60s. The younger generation is assimilating and becoming Israeli. At a special showing of the movie *Endurance*, about the Ethiopian runner Hailie Gebrselassie, the audience, all young, well-dressed Ethiopians getting their foothold in Israel, cheered wildly for him. What pride they felt as Ethiopians, as Gebrselassie, an Ethiopian Christian, won a gold medal at the 1996 Olympics in Atlanta. How complicated it is to weave together these strains of identity. How familiar this complexity, this multifaceted identity, is to an American eye.

These strands of identity change from generation to generation as well. My husband and I visited his cousin who lives on a kibbutz. She is of the socialist Zionist generation. Her son, a regional manager of a large water and sewage treatment plant outside of Haifa, is a hard line nationalist, opposed to Israel relinquishing any land. His fifteen-year-old daughter half-listened to our conversation, a ring in her pierced navel.

Other issues of identity press to be heard in this small country. At the Gay Rights March in Tel Aviv a man said me: "I live in Tel Aviv, where it is easier to be gay. I work in a big place. My mother and sister accept me. But in small towns, it's almost impossible to be different, even a different ethnic group. There's a lot of intolerance."

Orthodox women press for greater equality in Jewish law in regard to divorce. In the newspaper each week were stories of ultra-Orthodox Jews blocking streets on Shabbat so cars cannot drive on them.

And of course there is the ubiquitous American who does not emigrate but has infiltrated with music, fast food, clothes, television shows, ideas of individuality and equality, mass culture, and philanthropy. These marks are all over the Israeli cultural amalgam. There are even deeper marks made by the American military, ideas of free enterprise and private ownership and American style electioneering—James Carville was a consultant to Ehud Barak. The political landscape is shaded as well by the efforts of American presidents who have tried to shepherd a peace process.

Israel is also full of the signatures of Jews from all over the world. Every tree, garden, square, bench, art museum, or cultural center has a plaque on it, making Israel the keeper of some faraway person's Jewishness.

Israel has many problems—dirty streets, rapists and child molesters, stray cats, and political corruption at the highest levels. And it has the massive challenge of achieving peace with the Palestinians. But it is brimming over with richness as well. It has music, literature, parks to relax in, cafes, lush fields, housing going up, a democratic government, courteous bus drivers, movie theaters, markets with dazzling arrays of fruits and vegetables, and an exploding computer industry, albeit tamped down some by the second Intifada.

Israel is a complex place indeed. Hebrew University political scientist Yaron Ezrahi describes Israel as a society bursting at the seams, dying to take a breath and expand. But since its inception, Israelis have been locked into the nation's three overarching narratives: Judaism, Zionism, and socialism.

The enormous accomplishment of restoring Jewish sovereignty, Ezrahi writes, has generated three encompassing communal narratives. One is Orthodox religious Zionism that says returning to the land is a divine mission. Another is national Zionism, which Ezrahi says was drawn from European secular Zionism. At its core is the tenet that Jews are not safe: The nation, with an army to defend it, replaces God. The third is socialist Zionism, which said that the Jewish return to the land will be in the form of a socialist community.[1]

These narratives have had a powerful hold on Israeli society and are magnified by the backdrop of the Holocaust and the many Israeli wars. Israel has not had the opportunity to share in what Jews of western countries have so prized; liberal thinking that places such a high value on the individual and individual rights.

Ezrahi calls Israel "an impoverished culture of selfhood." In the years prior to the new Intifada when there was hope of peace with the Palestinians, the hold of these powerful narratives had weakened and Israeli individualism had begun to emerge. It was a "polyphony of voices," diverse narratives of ethnicity, religion, and class. It was increasingly possible for each individual to have "a distinct voice with its own sensibilities and moral agency."[2]

Ezrahi writes that this shift to the personal, to the idea that each person narrates a unique story, questions and challenges the society's long held notions about power and war.[3] And the grip of those wider societal epics had loosened sufficiently to allow Israel to comprehend the Palestinian narrative of national liberation. Ezrahi calls it "the beginning of a liberal post-epic era in Israeli democracy."[4]

One of the ways Israel became real to me was through its own struggle with these identities. Yes, it is the Jewish state, but when I stood on the street and looked around, what I saw was that it was full of complicated Israelis.

I felt closer to Israel and at the same time more separate. I also realized that with all my freedom to form my own identity, if I want Jewishness, I will have to find ways to put it into my life.

Now with the second Intifada, Israel has hunkered down again to war. The blossoming of individuality that Ezrahi described has constricted. "Palestinian terror has pushed Israel back into the Zionist womb," wrote historian Tom Segev.[5]

"Does anyone still remember how we lived just two years ago," wrote Doron Rosenblum on August 3, 2002, in the local newspaper, *Ha'aretz*. "What it was like to get up in the morning without asking where the next terrorist attack will occur and what 'action' will follow it, in an endless cycle? Within just a few months, terrorism, ostracism and siege became the principal definers of our identity: no longer the free, resourceful and life-seeking Israeli nation we used to be. We are now a Jewish community that is being bitterly persecuted, besieged in an armed ghetto."

NOTES

1. Yaron Ezrahi, *Rubber Bullets: Power and Conscience in Modern Israel* (New York: Farrar, Straus and Giroux, 1997), 80–83.

2. Ibid., 79.

3. Ibid., 6–7.

4. Ibid., 16.

5. Tom Segev, *Elvis in Jerusalem: Post-Zionism and the Americanization of Israel* (New York: Metropolitan Books, 2002), 161.

SHABBAT

Six days you work, on the seventh, you rest.

—Exodus 34:21

*Of all the holy days, the Shabbat alone is included in the
Ten Commandments. In the Book of Exodus, Shabbat is linked
to the creation of the world and the divine rest that completes it.*

—Rabbi Irving Greenberg, *The Jewish Way: Living the Holidays*

On my first Thursday in Israel, I was already worried about Shabbat. Shabbat is a time for connecting and I had no one to connect with. The arrival of David and my sons was weeks away. This first Shabbat would test my solo venture.

I thought of my mother when I was a child, sporadically lighting the candles on a Friday night and saying, "Good Shabbas" all around, that warm English-Yiddish Sabbath greeting. But for the most part, acknowledging this day in my childhood was vestigial: It faded as my mother got older. As an adult, I did not observe Shabbat: Like most Americans, Friday was the day to gear down, to be done with work, the day to start the weekend.

Then after my son Lou returned from a year in Israel, I would get this "Shabbat Shalom," the Hebrew greeting, late Friday afternoons on the voicemail. Shabbat had become part of his life. He bends the American rhythm.

Then I was in Israel enveloped in Jewish time and space. Jewish time? In my first Hebrew course in the States, the teacher wrote on the board, 20 Adar, 5759. Presto, there we were in Jewish time. The year was 5759.

"If God gave Moses the Ten Commandments at Sinai in 1280 B.C.E., then what is 5759?" I naïvely asked one day. It seemed I had never quite thought this through.

"That is the beginning of Genesis, that is Adam and Eve, the beginning of the Torah," the teacher said. Now it may not fit with evolution, but that is where the Jewish story begins, the beginning of Jewish time.

The Jewish calendar is different too, lunar not solar; the month Adar falls in February–March. Daily business life in Israel, of course, runs on the Gregorian calendar as the rest of the world. But the months, Jewish or secular, are filled with the cycle of holidays and observances. And of course each week is Shabbat. The Hebrew word for Saturday, in fact, is Shabbat; the day and the observance are fused. It is that time each week when the rhythm changes, you rest, roll back from your life, and are renewed. For people who are religious, the renewal comes by being in touch with God in his creation of the world in six days and his rest on the seventh.

One way that Jews are imprinted so deeply is through Jewish time. The rhythm of time becomes part of the organism. In Jerusalem, as the week comes to an end, you can feel the city move to Shabbat.

If I was worried on Thursday, by Friday I was a little panicky. Everything would be closed. There would be no buses. How dependent I was on knowing there was a place to buy a cup of coffee. Shabbat is the time to fold into something else. And I was keenly aware that I had nothing to fold into—no family or friends, no one to cook for me or for me to cook for. Yet I tamped down these flutters of panic. I was in this mode of being on my own. I was comfortable with the idea of folding into myself. Is that not Shabbat too?

Friday morning I set about on my errands. The streets of my neighborhood had been transformed. The corner stores displayed no fewer than fifteen newspapers, the fat weekend editions. Flowers spilled out of shops onto the streets. The plaza at Ben Yehuda and King George was filled with activity. A man there must have had thirty buckets filled with gorgeous flowers. Women, men, children were rushing in all directions, their arms filled with packages.

People rushing with bags. That's how you know Shabbat is near. It is something to behold—the determined shoppers. I could only imagine the festival of food. What a tremendous amount of work there was to make this day of rest.

I was reminded of Murray Avenue, the street of Jewish shops, this smidgen of Jewish space, where I grew up, now both more and less Jewish with an influx of Russian immigrants and Orthodox families, restaurants and butchers as well as a plethora of Asian restaurants and graduate students. How it bustled with people, especially on Fridays. How my parents were drawn to it, and me too. Nothing at all like the sanitized supermarket.

First I went to a butcher. "Two chicken breasts," I pointed and gave my prepared phrase in Hebrew. I wound up with two whole breasts, rather than one split. I realized my mistake but I was not quick enough to make the change. So there would be abundance. It was Shabbat, after all.

Then I went to the grocery store. It was busy now, like the day before Thanksgiving or Christmas at home. I had been warned about Israeli rudeness. But I found everyone quite helpful, certainly no brusquer than in my grocery at home. I bought potatoes and onions. You know when you buy these hearty items you are not a tourist, you are living somewhere.

I made a chicken casserole with potatoes, onions and tomato, a warm Shabbat family meal for six—or one for a week. It was delicious. How connected food is to renewal. I was warmed by it enough so that I was not lonely for home but in tune with the country retreating into the warmth and quiet of Shabbat.

At about ten the next morning I was drawn outside by the sound of men singing coming through my open window. I walked in the direction of the voices and found they were coming from a building at my corner. The Shabbat singing was streaming out of the open second floor window above the small corner grocery and the laundry.

I sat on a bench on a spit of park across the street and soaked up the sound, the cool air and the warm sun. There were no buses, few cars. Birds were twittering. The sun was bright and trees and bushes softly fluttered in the Jerusalem air. It was a peace like no other. I was thrown back on myself. When the buzz and forward motion of daily life slowed down so radically, how easy it was to put everything aside.

In front of me, on foot a group of young Thais in T-shirts walked down the street speaking Hebrew to each other. Religious men in their finery paraded past, talit, prayer shawls, like grand capes were draped around their shoulders and down their backs. One man wore a silk jacket, a wide regal fur hat, knee socks, as if he had stepped right out of medieval Poland. He had elegant long side curls and a long beard and carried his prayer book.

Large families walked together: women dressed in long skirts and hats, baby strollers, small boys in their *kipot*, girls in their starched dresses. What a picture of family togetherness, and what labor, I thought, to get everyone turned out this way, and each week. I thought of the dresses my sisters and I wore as children to temple. They had the same wide collars, full-skirted small prints with sashes in the back. And my mother, with her firm hand, pulling the brush through my tangled curls which she then gathered tightly in a barrette.

So, too, people in ordinary informal clothes were out with their dogs. Others, with their children, carried soccer balls down to Sacher Park. It was such a mixture of people parading by, perhaps because this street was the border between a secular and religious neighborhood. Everyone was enveloped in the warm quietude of Shabbat. No one broke the spell. It offered a peace so missing in my life. I have lived as a modern woman, working long hours, raising two children. And part of me was spent, depleted. I was drawn to this ancient cycle of restoration.

I sat for a long time. After a while a religious teenager appeared and sat at the bench farthest from me. He made no acknowledgement or eye contact. He wore a black hat, *tzitzi* or fringe at the waist, and his white shirt was hanging out. He was disheveled and he hunched over on the bench biting his fingernails. Like me, he watched the passersby. For some reason, like me, he, at this moment, sat apart from this seamless life.

As Shabbat drew to a close, it was astonishing to watch activity resume with a flourish. It was as if people had rested and now they were poised. Israelis go out after Shabbat ends, even though the workweek begins on Sunday. Suddenly buses are careening around the narrow corners and the outdoor cafes are bustling with people.

That first "after Shabbat" I went to a dance performance at the elegant Jerusalem Theater that began at 10:30 P.M. The Israel Festival was underway, a month-long lineup of music, theater, and dance. I went early, bought a glass of wine at the café in the lobby, where one after another, jazz, folk, and rock groups played.

This was very civilized, I thought looking around, me and sophisticated Israelis perched around our small tables, smoking, drinking, laughing, and talking. It could be an event at the Museum of Modern Art in New York. Women wore jeans—tight was de rigueur—high-heeled, spiky sandals, hair masses of curl. For young girls the uniform was tight and black. The older women like me were in their loose linens and simple jewelry. The young men had short hair, perhaps the current style or their proximity to army service. Soldiers—another whole class of people—stood erect, strong, and purposeful, even though they were not the official security at this social occasion. Neither the men nor women had their heads covered for religious purposes.

I went downstairs to the theater for the dance performance. In this lobby hung a photo exhibit of near nude and nude female dancers jumping from water into the air. The artist Moshe Berkovich said of his work: "The decision to defy gravity to float to the skies and dance among the clouds, then dive down to the watery depths, inspired me to create this exhibit. The skies are the ceiling the waters the stage floor."

I didn't get as sumptuous again as that surfeit of chicken breasts that first week. But I would go to the shuk, the big open market that would reach a kind of frenzied madness by late on Friday. The sellers yelled their prices like auctioneers, grapes, melons, whatever they were offering, hoping to sell all by the end of the day. "Four shekels, (one dollar) for ten pita!" A man hustled a tray of them, steaming hot, carried on his head, to the stand in the middle of the walkway in the outdoor area. Two shekels for luscious looking parsley. Oh, what sensuousness food has. I wanted to buy it all.

I was planning what I wanted to cook when my husband and children would arrive. I honed a "shuk soup," a fine mixture of what looked good at the market on Friday tempered only by what I could carry. It went something like this: orange lentils sold right from the burlap bag; tomatoes, onion, garlic, potato, carrot, zucchini, and whatever else appealed to me from the heaps of vegetables at the stalls.

As the weeks went on, I was invited to Shabbat dinner a few times. Israelis have this spontaneous Shabbat hospitality. It is family dining, not a "dinner party" even with a new acquaintance. One family who invited me to their home were secular Jews but they followed tradition, ritually lighting the candles and blessing the bread. There was good conversation and hearty food.

I got used to the rhythm of Shabbat. I would spend part of the day in my apartment, quiet, resting, and studying Hebrew. Then I would go for a long walk. I explored the intimate narrow streets of the Shaarey Chessid neighborhood, where, on Shabbat, blockades prevented cars from coming through. The houses were of old Jerusalem stone and the red tile roofs caught the sun. Flowering bushes and vines twining into trees exploded in a riot of fuchsia, pink, red, and purple.

On the other side of Shaarey Chessid was the park where late in the day men and kids played soccer, families sat under trees in the shade with picnic baskets, and Palestinian women in their long garb pushed their babies in strollers. All took place in the tranquility of Shabbat.

I was amazed at how quiet the children in my building were. In the early evening, the first sign of Shabbat ending was the sound of children playing games again outside.

At times I struggled: Who was I in relation to Shabbat? My worry was about more than that I would be alone. It was that I would feel apart, be unable to partake. I was a Jew, I was there, and yet I might be unable to put a toe in the water of this central Jewish and Israeli experience. Like my father, I would be perpetually outside my group that is already on the outside.

So I was poised to feel negatively. I was amazed at how easy it was for me to go with the flow. I took pleasure in my openness to this experience. If I lived there I would embrace Shabbat. I love cooking for people and the warmth of family and friends gathering. Yet I felt no imperative to be more religious, to be anything other than what I was.

Living there on that street I seemed to be suspended from my long-held oppositional categories—religion and me—me in the trench for the separation of church and state. It was ironic because Israeli society is contentious to an extreme over religion. But I was an outsider, in an interlude in which I felt free of the need to take up those struggles. What I found in myself was a smooth flowing continuum of Jewish identity, secular to religious. It felt much like this border area I lived in between a secular and religious neighborhood where people flowed back and forth. It was a smooth seam, not a chasm.

Each time I walked down my street, I heard the sounds of children's voices coming from behind a wall. One day I ventured through the gate and peered in. I had some trepidation, as schools are heavily guarded against intruders. I saw an enclosed playground, deeply shaded by trees to protect children from the Jerusalem sun. It was for the nursery school of Har-El, a Reform synagogue. Their sign out front said it was the first Reform Synagogue in Israel and that Shabbat services were held on Friday at 6 P.M. I decided to go.

The synagogue was small, unlike the grand Reform Temples in the States. Outside was a beautiful shaded garden. Inside, the sanctuary was a plain room. It was so quiet, the sun was setting, and the warm Jerusalem air was coming through the open windows. Again, I felt the Shabbat peace.

The prayers were read. I was astonished at how different they sounded from the services I grew up with. The Hebrew of the service was the same language the congregation conversed in! The language of prayer has always been so foreign, stilted, so outside my experience. Now I could even pick out words and meaning. How intimate and personal. This was connected to life, not apart from it. The singing here was beautiful, too.

My mind wandered. I thought of Leo Baeck, the chief rabbi of Berlin who presided over the end of a thousand years of Jewish life in Germany. I, of this Holocaust generation, find, where Judaism is concerned, that I am never far from these matters of survival and existence.

After Kristallnacht on November 8, 1938, Leo Baeck said, "Many can remember how they stood in the street that night. . . . It was a dark night and it seemed to them to say in invisible handwriting . . . 'God has numbered the days of your kingdom and brought it to an end'" (Book of Daniel).[1]

Yet there I sat in Israel, where the Holocaust is never far from the surface, in this simple synagogue, of German origin in fact, this place of gathering for song, prayer, and peace. It is a place where Judaism lives and breathes and is passed on. How thin the Jewish membrane had become in me. How fortifying I found this. I thought again of the Israeli poet Yehuda Amichai, and that his name means "My nation lives!"

NOTES

1. Leonard Baker, *Days of Sorrow and Pain: Leo Baeck and the Berlin Jews* (New York: Macmillan, 1978), 229–30.

16

FEMALE

One day I took the bus to go to a conference about women at Bar Ilan University, a little more than an hour from Jerusalem.

Traveling by public bus in Israel is a world unto itself. Soldiers clatter on, their guns slung over their shoulders. Usually the driver has the radio on. The music alternates between American and Israeli soft rock. Then when the news comes on, the whole tenor changes. Everyone, it seems, perks up and listens. Often the driver turns up the volume. Since I was in Israel in a quiet interlude, I could only imagine what frantic dialing and ringing of cell phones there must be when the radio spews forth news of an attack.

As I boarded, a woman sitting in the first row spoke right up: "You're going to Bar Ilan?" I was surprised by her boldness. I was used to being ignored by Orthodox Jews.

The woman's name was Frieda. She was wearing a black hat pulled down tightly over her hair and an orange dress. Her eleven-year-old son sat next to her. He would stay with her sister, she told me, who lived in the nearby religious neighborhood of Bnei Brak, while she attended the conference.

We talked, bonding instantly as the comfortable cool Mercedes bus wound its way through the narrow city streets and then onto the highway, which descended the Jerusalem hills. Out the window, townhouses, poised in semicircles on hilltops, looked like teeth. An Arab village nestled between the hills, a cluster of low square houses with the tall mosque at center.

The conference was organized to discuss the inequality between men and women in Jewish divorce law. At the time, there were two hundred thousand *agunot* among Israeli women. "Agunot" translates as chained; these are women who want a divorce but are not able to get one under Jewish law, although their husbands may divorce and remarry.

I don't recall exactly how Frieda and I started. She simply came out with her life, what brought her to this meeting. Her need was great, as was mine to reach across, at least from appearances, a great divide. It took eight years for her ex-husband, the father of her son, to agree to give the "get," the consent to divorce under Jewish law. She was very bitter. That was her second marriage. Her first husband was severely brain damaged in the '67 war. She has a daughter from that marriage.

Orthodoxy and feminism may seem an oxymoron, but in recent years, issues of justice had been getting a lot of attention among observant women in the United States. Orthodox feminist Blu Greenberg has spoken widely on the subject. She says that, yes, feminism may contribute to intermarriage and a lower birthrate, both crucial Jewish concerns. But still, Judaism and feminism have a deep bond—they both stand for justice.[1]

To some extent, in Israel, feminism is another American import like gay rights, teen violence, or Toys "R" Us. Conference organizer Tova Cohen told me this conference was similar to those that have been held in the United States in recent years, which have sparked the interest of Orthodox women in Israel.

Frieda and I got off the bus in what seemed the middle of the highway, then went through a security gate, and we were on the Bar Ilan campus. As we made our way through the maze of buildings, passing the law school, where Yigal Amir, Prime Minister Yitzhak Rabin's assassin, attended, I listened to Frieda. What I heard was so familiar: the grinding injustice and muffled rage of being female. She was so hungry to hear a message to affirm what she has lived and felt and kept inside for so long. I could hear my own voice in her from years ago, and that of many women I knew at the beginning of the women's movement. She yearned for justice. She yearned to be heard. She was propelling herself into feminism.

Listening to Frieda, I recalled when I thought my own anger would paralyze me. My father's double message was not only about Judaism, but about being female as well. By all means, be all you can be, he'd say, but you must also marry and not be too aggressive or opinionated—in other words, play the proscriptive role of a woman. Women are made invisible, except of course when it comes to sexuality and then one is at times too visible. Perhaps I will always be too finely attuned to women's second-class status.

How odd to return to the Jewish turf of my childhood where I as a woman was held at the fringes. It was the men who gathered at my grandfather's Russian shul. My much younger brother was Bar Mitzvah; the Bat Mitzvah for girls did not exist then. It was the men who handled the precious objects, the Torah and its cover at the ark of my temple. See this world, but don't touch. It is not of you.

The question is always debated, what does it mean to be a Jew, writes Gail Shulman. "For a feminist, why bother to ask the question at all." The mother keeps kosher; the father goes to the *minyan* (the ten men required to conduct Jewish prayer). "We watched while they did." Women were unclean and even evil.[2]

Writer Cynthia Ozick writes of her traditional synagogue: "When my rabbi says, 'a Jew is called to the Torah,' he never means me or any other living Jewish woman. . . . My own synagogue is the only place in the world where I am not named Jew."[3]

In 1964, I sat with the women upstairs at an Orthodox synagogue in Moscow. The men prayed loudly down below and the women talked about their children, the market, and the intriguing sandals of the American girl in their midst. It was almost as if, held to the sidelines, the everyday chatter was a kind of revenge on the piety they were held from.

In *Bread Givers*, Anzia Yezierska's, searing portrayal of an immigrant family, it is the mother who must deal with the real world concern of putting bread on the table. She would like to lease a room in their apartment so they can pay the rent. But the front room is where the tyrannical father studies Talmud and Torah. So it may not even be considered.[4]

Susannah Heschel says of Yezierska and also writer Mary Antin that their heroines repaired their lives "through education and careers or financial independence but invariably without assistance from family or community. Liberation was achieved only by breaking off and struggling alone."[5]

I considered Frieda's life as we walked across the campus, how unequal women are in Orthodox Judaism. Susannah Heschel argues, "It is not feminism which poses the threat to Judaism, but the denominations' own inability to come to terms with the challenges posed by modernity."[6]

As we walked I had to wonder how much the treatment of women figured into my argument with Judaism. Probably not much, as Orthodoxy had fallen away from my family long before the recent rise of feminism.

I am admiring of the women in the religious fold who stayed and fought for changes. The non-Orthodox Jewish world is speckled with women rabbis and cantors who made places for themselves. I am always moved by the sight of women at the pulpit in kipot (skullcaps) and talit (prayer shawls). I love hearing the voice of a female cantor. I was deeply moved by the woman rabbi at a funeral who spoke of tears as the only fluid given off by the body that deals with the healing of emotional pain.

But for me, being female and Jewish made for a deafening amplification, another layer of nonbelonging to a group that already did not belong. Wanting a family, wanting to be myself in my family, made gender the more immediate and pressing struggle.

Yet I have no doubt that the value Judaism puts on justice, equality, and freedom are the wellspring for feminism for me, for Frieda, and many others.

Shulman also writes that her Jewishness is at the root of her feminism— a compassion for the oppressed, a sense of history and community.[7] Perhaps it is no accident that leaders of the women's movement such as Betty Friedan, Gloria Steinem, and Letty Pogrebin were Jewish or of Jewish origin.

"To be a feminist, one had to have had an experience of being an outsider more extreme than merely being a woman . . ." writes Carolyn Heilbrun in "Becoming a Woman."[8]

But stepping away from my Jewishness did not exempt me from coming to terms with the feeling of being an outsider among outsiders. Staying or leaving does not shield one from the vulnerability embedded in the past.

Frieda and I talked for a couple of hours, reaching across the religious/secular divide that was not actually so enormous. We walked arm in arm across the campus, each there for different reasons. For me it was a step into the foreign land of Orthodoxy: For Frieda, the not-so-foreign land of feminism.

She was the revolutionary seeking justice. I had the more conservative aim: Making another pass at subduing the vulnerable outsider in me that is both woman and Jew.

NOTES

1. Blu Greenberg speaking at Congregation Beth Am, Cleveland Heights, Ohio, February 12, 1999.

2. Gail Shulman, "A Feminist Path to Judaism, in *On Being a Jewish Feminist: A Reader,* ed. Susannah Heschel (New York: Schocken Books, 1983 and 1995), 105–109.

3. Cynthia Ozick, "Notes Toward Finding the Right Answer," in Heschel, *On Being a Jewish Feminist,* 125.

4. Anzia G. Yezierska, *Bread Givers: A Struggle Between the Father of the Old World and a Daughter of the New* (New York: G. Braziller, 1975).

5. Heschel, *On Being a Jewish Feminist,* xiv–xv.

6. Ibid., xxx–xxxi.

7. Shulman, "A Feminist Path to Judaism," in Heschel, *On Being a Jewish Feminist,* 105–109.

8. Carol Heilbrun, "Becoming a Woman," in Heschel, *On Being a Jewish Feminist,* 117.

17

L O S S

There were three people I wanted to see in Israel—the aunt of an elementary school friend; the niece of a Russian family I had helped when they immigrated to America; and an Israeli rock star. They were unconnected to each other, from three different generations and three parts of the world—Germany, Russia, and Greece. But they all, I found, had something in common. In each of their families the Holocaust had cut its swath, leaving many dead and the survivors with potent family stories.

A few months before leaving for Israel I visited my sister in New York. A number of years earlier, she had run into a woman whom had I gone to elementary school with. So while I was visiting, my sister invited Susannah over and I told her about my upcoming trip. She replied that a few years before she had attended an amazing family reunion in Jerusalem. There she had met all of these relatives, now with children and grandchildren, whom her family had helped out of Germany and to find asylum in Palestine in the 1930s when they were teens.

I was astonished to learn about Susannah's background. As a child, what I saw in Susannah was the ultimate assimilated Jew. Of German origin, she and her family were important members of the same Reform Temple we attended. Her father, as I recall, was the first and for many years the only Jew in an exclusive Protestant club in Pittsburgh. In those years this well-off family was held up as both the symbol of and battering ram for Jewish acceptance. Yet how much had been obscured by this veneer of assimilation.

By the time I met Susannah, her father was in a second marriage. Susannah's mother lived in Israel. It turns out that she, her father, and her brother had been active in rescuing family members from Germany.

One of the people they helped to leave Germany was Hanan Sonneborn, who changed his name to Aynor in Israel and went on to serve as an Israeli ambassador to Mexico, Senegal, and Ethiopia. I met Aynor's widow Sarah in her Jerusalem apartment. Sarah, an intelligent and dignified woman likely in her seventies, has set up a scholarship for graduate education for Ethiopians in Israel to promote their upward mobility.

Sarah met Hanan while working in displaced persons (DP) camps in France after the war. He was born in 1916 in Frankfurt. He left Germany in 1935 when he was kicked out of school because he was a Jew. He arrived in Palestine two years later and joined Kibbutz Ashdot Yaacov.

Sarah unfurled an intricate family tree across the dining room table. It was the Sonneborn family, once of Germany, now scattered to the United States, Israel, and England. It looked like a huge willow tree with hundreds of wavy lines, only the wisps went up rather than down. As I studied the tree, I saw that each line had a box with a person's name and each generation was drawn in a different color.

I counted nine family members who, like Hanan, were able to leave Germany and go to Palestine through Youth Aliyah. Youth Aliyah was a program for teenagers to train in agriculture and then immigrate to Palestine. And I saw the families that sprang forth from those who emigrated. Most of these teens were born by 1921. The Sonneborns who were born in 1925–26 couldn't participate in Youth Aliyah and were killed in the Holocaust. I did a quick count: thirty-three.

Sarah and Susannah's sister Ellen made this tree for the family reunion in 1994 and also a book with interviews from all the surviving members. It is a work of art, a piecing together of that which had been shattered, an attempt at family healing.

It was Sigmund Sonneborn, Susannah's maternal grandfather, who helped these young people get involved with Youth Aliyah. He had emigrated to the United States and worked in clothing manufacturing in Baltimore. He could not sleep over worry about relatives still in Germany. "Now is the time for us to do something," he said in the book put together about the family. "We will send our family's children to Israel, later the parents will follow." He sent his son Rudolph to find out about what could be done.

The Sonneborns' history in Germany dates back to 1735 to a town called Breidenbach. One Sonneborn was a kosher butcher; others were in horse and cattle trading.

At the family reunion that Susannah had attended, they went to Yad Vashem, Israel's memorial to the Holocaust, and lit candles together. Sarah said the ceremony was very moving. Those who attended from Israel are now grandparents. They did not know when they left Germany as boys that they would never see their families again. They never had the chance to say good-bye, Sarah said to me. The losses they endured are embedded in their lives even though they were fortunate to survive the Holocaust. At Yad Vashem the town of Breidenbach is listed as a disappeared community.

Genia Svechinsky was nineteen years old when we met, a quiet, poised, serious young woman with dark curly hair who planned to enter the Bezalel Art School in Jerusalem. She came to Israel immediately after her seventeenth birthday and is fluent now in Hebrew and English. Her parents, both doctors, live in Russia. We had coffee together at Aroma coffee shop in Jerusalem, walked, and visited an art museum.

Genia and I were meeting at the end of the century in Israel, as our families might have at the beginning of the century in Kiev. She is the niece of Michael Maryamchik, the father in the family I adopted when they came to America in the wave of emigration of Russian Jews in the early 1990s. When Michael became a U.S. citizen, I attended the ceremony with him. After, we went out for a celebratory lunch and he told me his family's story.

Before World War II, the Maryamchiks lived in Kiev. When the German invasion of the Soviet Union began in June 1941, his mother, Sophia, was fifteen, living with her parents. One day in September, Sophia's mother was going to work and met a friend she knew from the Komsomol. He was political, a party boss. "You know I am leaving; my family is being evacuated within hours," Michael related that the man said to her. "I can get a place on this train for you. It is the last option. Take your children and leave. It is a matter of life and death."

Most people had no idea what was about to happen, Michael said. Adults in Ukraine remembered the conditions under German occupation in World War I as much better than the later Russian occupation—the best army that ever occupied Kiev, so the ironic expression went, he said.

Michael's grandmother gathered up her two children and housekeeper and took that train. His grandfather had been enlisted to dig trenches around the city. His grandmother didn't know his location so she sent telegrams and letters at train stations along the way so he would know what direction they had gone. Later, he found them in Chelyadinsk, in the Ural Mountains, and met up with them.

The day after Michael's maternal grandmother left on that train, the German army surrounded Kiev and occupied it. Shortly after, the roundup of Jews began. More than 33,000 were slaughtered in a ravine outside the city at a site known as Babi Yar. It was three months after the German invasion of the Soviet Union had begun.[1]

Michael's father, Joseph, was also from Kiev and was living with his mother and two brothers when he joined the Red Army in the summer of 1941 at the age of nineteen, a few weeks before the German invasion began. He served as a radio technician on airplanes for the entire war, ending up near Berlin in 1945. Joseph's mother and two brothers were killed at Babi Yar. His father had died before he was born and so the war left him with no family.

Michael's mother, Sophia, finished school in Chelyadinsk and started studying at the medical university there. After war the family came back to Kiev and she finished her medical training. His father became a boiler engineer.

Now in the new wave of immigration, the Maryamchik family, like the Sonneborns, is far-flung; Michael and his family are in the United States, his mother, sister, and her husband are in Russia, and their daughter Genia is in Israel. Another branch of the family has immigrated to Munich.

The third person I wanted to see in Israel was rock singer Yehuda Poliker. One day, I read in the paper that he would perform at the Gay Pride March in Tel Aviv. I decided to go.

I first discovered Poliker in the sack of CDs my son Lou brought back from Israel two years before. Sounds of Israeli singers Shlomo Artzi, Rami Kleinstein, and Poliker would filter through the house. I was drawn to them, even though I didn't understand a word of the lyrics. For my birthday, Lou made me a mix to play in the car.

With Lou's translation and my improving Hebrew, I was shocked to find that Poliker often sings about the Holocaust. His songs are mournful, such as "Dust and Ashes," the title song of one of his CDs, and "The Small Station Called Treblinka." I had trouble imagining the Holocaust in popular culture, in the music of a top rock star. But there it was. The song goes like this:

And there isn't even a ticket office
And there isn't a ticket officer
And in a million passings
You will never receive a return ticket
And no man is waiting at the station
And no one is waving a handkerchief . . .
Because here is the Treblinka Station . . ."[2]

In Israel, I found, the Holocaust permeates the lives of many. It fills museums and memorials. It amplifies Zionist history and adds an aggressive, edgy tone to the public discourse about security. The music of Poliker and lyricist Yaacov Gilad assuages a wide audience.

Poliker, also a composer, sings about longing for Salonika, that once thriving Jewish city in Greece (now called Thessoloniki) where his father and his large family lived. His music has a plaintive sound, a Greek pathos perhaps, of loneliness and of loss and pain. I knew nothing about Sephardic Jews, how some of them got to Greece or what happened to them in the Holocaust. But Poliker's music got me interested in finding out more about this branch of Jewish history.

When the Jews were expelled from Spain in 1492 and Portugal in 1497, the Ottoman Empire welcomed them. And the port city of Salonika was one of the places Jews settled. They were citizens of Turkey, a predominantly Muslim society. Then in the Balkan wars of 1912–13 the Greek army took Salonika from the Turks. Ten years later a population exchange took place; the Turks left and about a hundred thousand Greeks returned after 450 years.

A film at the Diaspora Museum in Tel Aviv captures Jewish life in Salonika before the Holocaust when one-third of the population was Jewish. They worked as seamen and stevedores, in the wineries and as weavers of silks and woolens; in law and medicine; as tailors, salesmen, and common laborers. Ladino, the language of Sephardic Jews, was spoken on the streets.[3] The Jews learned Greek but spoke with an accent that made them identifiable. And that became a catastrophe for them in the Holocaust.[4]

Jewish life in Salonika ended on August 18, 1943, when the last of nineteen transport trains over five months left the city. Many Jews were near death after the two-week train trip with almost no food, water, or heat. Most were killed within hours after their arrival at Birkenau Auschwitz, 56,000 people or 96 percent of the Jews of Salonika, the end of this once thriving Jewish community.

For the Sephardic Jews who survived in places like Rumania, Bulgaria, and Yugoslavia, Jewish history became tragically bracketed by the Spanish expulsion on one side, the Holocaust on the other.

In Israel that day, I found that a friend of a friend was driving to the Gay Pride March. I met her the next morning in front of the Jerusalem Theater, the designated place for gays and lesbians to meet and drive caravan-style to Tel Aviv. In an hour or so, about thirty-five people were busy taping streamers to the sides of their cars and pink posters to their hoods that read, "Without Pride There Is No Hope."

We drove. Keeping a caravan of cars together on Israeli highways and city streets was no small feat, with drivers making frequent high-speed lane changes. But the caravan stayed together more or less. By the time we got to Tel Aviv the streamers were shredded and bedraggled.

The parade was underway when we arrived. More and more people were joining or gathering to watch along the sidewalks. Skinny girls in their tight yellow and green Wrigley outfits were passing out Doublemint and Juicy Fruit gum. It was a Tel Aviv party, sponsored by the city, in the June heat. The floats, with pumping music, came into view. Girls in feathers, another bare-breasted in the noonday sun, danced on a float of Noah's Ark. Male dancers and drag queens were flamboyant.

Once at the march, I found a spot of shade and began chatting with Shlomo, an affable man, gray at the temples, like anyone's sweet father. He was cynical about the march. There have always been gays and lesbians among Jews, he said, yet the march is not grassroots Israeli, but a direct import from the United States. Gay rights was brought here in the '70s and '80s by Israelis who had lived in the States. Gay victims of the Holocaust are not given proper recognition, he said. As for the Holocaust, yes, he is the child of a survivor. Even though Israel gave his family a haven from the Holocaust, he, as a gay man, does not have a full sense of belonging here. Then he told me the long and complicated story of his family in the Holocaust. They were from Poland, his mother was in a labor camp, and his father did not survive. As a second-generation Holocaust survivor, he would like to write their story.

I had to return to Jerusalem before the buses stopped running for Shabbat, so I didn't have a chance to hear Poliker perform. But when I got back to the States, I found out more about him. He began his musical career in a rock band in Haifa. Later, Poliker teamed up with Yaacov Gilad and they found they both were second generation Holocaust survivors. Gilad's mother is from Poland and also a survivor of Auschwitz.

In the movie *Because of That War*, the two musicians, with stubble beards and wearing black T-shirts, talk about the difficulties growing up as children of survivors—the insecurity, the fear of loss, the high expectations. Theirs are poignant stories of how the Holocaust damaged people's lives and how that damage is passed on. Poliker and Gilad have brought these experiences into their music.

Poliker's father, Jocko, spent two years in Auschwitz. He was the only survivor in a family of fifty. His pregnant wife was gassed and his two-year-old son Mordechai was trampled in the panic on the transport train. He witnessed his wife's father being "dragged like a dog." He went to Israel after the war, where he met his wife Sara in a home for immigrants. Yehuda was named for one of his father's brothers.

Yehuda Poliker lived at home till he was thirty. "He would not let me out of his sight," he said of his father. "He used to come to school: 'Are you there? Ok, fine, just checking.' School trips were out of the question. The only trip was to Caesarea and he accompanied me."

Poliker, who speaks haltingly, describes how his stutter began. "I was five or six years old; my father and mother were going to a Bar Mitzvah in Tiberias. My father was getting something to eat. He would eat bread whole—from the Holocaust. He could not stop doing it. He took a huge hunk and swallowed it whole. It got stuck. He started to choke and turned blue. I ran to the neighbor, who was a doctor. 'When I get back, will he be alive?' I felt I would have no father. He would be dead."

Gilad's mother, Halina Birnbaum, was ten when the Nazis came to Warsaw, thirteen when she was deported to the Madjanek labor camp. They left from the Treblinka station. As a child, she said, she never realized it was a place. "Those who were hunted were sent to this station. I imagined it as this ultimate end from where you never returned. I would hear the train whistle, like a cutting knife. When will they show up?"

Gilad said, "If I did not do well in school or misbehaved, (she would say) 'I got out of there for this?' I had to justify her life. . . . I now think that if the dead don't mean more than the living, at least they mean as much."

In the film, Halina meets with a group of schoolchildren to tell her story. "People were piled on top of each other in the train," she said. "People fell, I too. Someone fell on my face and I was choking. I tore myself free and I reached the window and I could breathe.

"'Where's my mother,' I asked.

"'I am your mother now,' my sister-in-law said. It was as if an axe broke my body." Later she spent two years in Auschwitz. She was eighteen when she arrived in Israel as an illegal immigrant.

"I became a different person, I changed language, sometimes it seemed as if I came from stone, as if I was not born like everyone else. It is not history (the Holocaust), it will never be history for me, it can never even be the past for me," she says as the rapt schoolchildren try to make sense of what she is saying.

I looked at these children's faces in the film and saw the Holocaust being implanted in the minds of this new generation of Jewish Israelis, just as it marks Israeli soldiers on their mandatory visits to Yad Vashem.

Other children of survivors have made films about their parents' experiences, such as *Children of Chabannes,* about children sheltered in a village in France, and *Into the Arms of Strangers,* about the ten thousand Jewish children who were taken in by families in England. Like Poliker and Gilad, these artists are able to articulate the way family relationships were severed and show how even today those wounds are still being mended.

NOTES

1. Daniel J. Goldhagen, in *Hitler's Willing Executioners* (New York: Alfred A. Knopf, 1996), 154, cites a sample of German slaughters following the German invasion of the Soviet Union: 23,600 in Kamenets-Podolski on August 27–28 1941; 33,000 over two days at Babi Yar in September 1941; 21,000 in Rovno on November 7–8, 1941; over 25,000 near Riga on November 30 and December 8–9 1942; 10,000–20,000 in Kharkov in January 1942.

2. "The Small Station Called Treblinka," written by Victor Schlengel, translated to Hebrew by Halina Birnbaum. Music by Yehuda Poliker.

3. Exhibit on the Jews of Salonika at Beit Hatfetfuzot, the Diaspora Museum in Tel Aviv.

4. Hahom Dr. Solomon Gaon and Dr. M. Mitchell Serels, eds., *Del Fuego: Sephardim and the Holocaust* (New York: Sepher-Hermon Press, 1995), 94.

MODERNITY

I got off the bus on Derech Hebron in the mixed Arab–Jewish neighborhood of Abu Tor. In the midday heat, I climbed up a steep hill. On one side were beautiful homes in the Arab style of architecture, some under renovation. I recalled that Anwar from my Hebrew class lived in Abu Tor and I wondered if his house was nearby.

I was going to see Avraham Infeld, president of Melitz, one of many groups in Israel concerned with fostering Jewish identity, both in Israel and abroad. Infeld sat behind his desk in a small cluttered office, an older man who looked and spoke to this audience of one with the rhetorical skills of an ancient rabbi.

How do we tell our story? What is the past one can connect to that explains where we are today and that allows us to carry Judaism forward in a way that is positive and animating? Those were the questions that were on my mind. We have been told that the paradigm of our generation is the Holocaust and Israel. Infeld takes a contrary view. He believes the most challenging historical event for Jews is the advent of modernity and what was brought with it—the fracturing of Jewish life.

"The big revolution in Jewish life since Sinai is not the Holocaust and not Israel. It happened two hundred years ago when the Jewish people moved into modernity. It totally disrupted what had been very, very clear. Anywhere you went in the Jewish world you got the same answer about what it meant to be a Jew.

"Jews were a people, slaves in Egypt, who walked through the desert, came to Mt. Sinai, met with God, signed a covenant, and God looked after them. And they kept God's commandments. We sinned and so we were scattered among the nations. Our role was to keep ourselves distinct as a people, keep God's commandments, and hope God would forgive us and return us to Israel.

"That was the self-understanding. It wasn't non-Jews who put us in exile. Jews put themselves there. The hope was that God would send the Messiah and return to us to the land of Israel.

"Then came the French Revolution, nationalism, modernity, and laws. The larger world said to Jews, 'Stop being different. Come out of the ghetto. Become one of us.' Everything we are dealing with today is because of how we have responded to that invitation."

It is hard indeed to imagine the Jewish world before modernity. Historian Jacob Katz argues that in the profound changes brought on by the French Revolution, for Jews "the change seems to have gone deeper, transmuting the very nature of their social existence."[1]

Europe was a Christian society and strove for religious unity. The Jew was a stranger and in exile. But "the Jewish nation was to be preserved in a suppressed state in order to testify to the truth of Christianity."[2] The Jews had no legal claim to acceptance or toleration. If they were permitted to live in a given locality, it was because of a contract between the Jewish community as an entity and relevant political authority.[3]

That acceptance was subject to changing political circumstances. The contract could be terminated at any time. A wave of expulsions swept across Europe: Germany in 1182, England in 1290, the kingdoms of France in 1306 and 1394, Austria in 1421, Spain in 1492, Portugal in 1496. Even later, Jews were expelled from Vienna in 1670, from Prague in 1744 and from Dresden as late as 1777 when Moses Mendelssohn intervened. Jews were "utterly dependent on local authority for the right to reside anywhere."[4]

The result was a general movement of Jews eastward beginning in the sixteenth century to the Polish lands, which later became the Russian Pale, and to the Ottoman Empire. Later, beginning in the 1880s, Jews migrated again from the lands of the Pale westward in Europe and to the New World.

With the rise of rationalistic ideas, the separation of church and state and the secular nation state, Jews gained citizenship in the wider polity. "It was only when a sphere of life divorced from religion evolved that a situation was created for Jews to be included on a comparatively equal footing with Gentiles in a single social and political unit."[5]

There were Jews living under French rule, but not French Jews, said Paula Hyman in describing the situation in France before the Revolution. "As yet there existed no social space for the construction of a French Jewish identity."[6]

It is easy to see why Jewish commitment to separation of church and state was and continues to be so passionate; it made life possible for them in the wider world.

In France, Jews were granted rights by the Constituent Assembly in 1791, two years after the Revolution. "To the Jews as a Nation, nothing; to the Jews as individuals, everything," was the famous phrase of Count Stanislas de Clermont-Tonnerre at the time.[7] The Jews gained citizenship but lost communal autonomy. The institutions of Jewish self-government, such as the rabbinic courts, declined precipitously.

Citizenship now was derived from the state and not from membership in Jewish community. The process of assimilation was set into motion. As Jews began to be educated in secular schools, they learned the language of the wider culture. At this time, Sephardic Jews in Amsterdam, Frankfurt, or Bordeaux were far ahead of Ashkenazic Jews in terms of partaking of the wider economic and political life.

While Jews continued to be Jews, over the next one hundred and fifty years the powerful process of assimilation "would transform the descendents of Yiddish speaking village peddlers into comfortable members of the urban French bourgeoisie."[8]

This French model became the pattern of citizenship and assimilation across western Europe. As for the wider society, nothing short of total assimilation—Christianization—was expected in return for the gift of citizenship.

The Yiddish writer Sholem Aleichem in *Tevye the Milkman and Other Stories* depicts the same forces of social change at work at the beginning of twentieth-century Russia.

When Tevye's first daughter Tsatl insists on marrying for love, he says to her intended, Motl, "At once when can you be the matchmaker, the father-in-law, and the groom all rolled into one? I suppose you want to be the bandleader too? I never in all my life heard of a young man making matches for himself."[9] The next daughter marries a young man imbued with the ideas of revolution, and a third a non-Jew.

Sholem Aleichem's stories are characterized by intimacy with family, the reader, with every life situation, but most of all with God. At one point Tevye laments, "[I] asked God an old question about an old old story: What did poor Job ever do to You, dear Lord, to make You hound him day and night? Couldn't You find any other Jews to pick on?"

Sholem Aleichem's stories became part of popular American culture when *Fiddler on the Roof* debuted in the 1960s. It was a nostalgic view of shtetl life at a time when Jews here were rushing headlong into assimilation, gaining acceptance in institutions of higher education, the professions, and the business world.

Modernity brought about a fracturing of Jewish life. Jews and Judaism would never be the same. The events of the Holocaust and the founding of Israel may be seen as part of the response of the larger community to the advancement of Jews politically and economically as well as the Jewish reaction to modernity. Some Jews have said "no" to full participation in a larger polity, Infeld told me. They do not give up the wholeness of that closed Jewish world. They are waiting for the Messiah. They raise the walls higher. They are 20 percent of the Knesset (the Israeli parliament). They fill the neighborhood of Bnei Brak outside of Tel Aviv and Williamsburg, New York.

Some say the opposite, Infeld continued. "He (the Messiah) isn't coming. The larger society has invited me to stop being different. Why not assimilate? I embrace emancipation. The best is to be universal. I am one of you—Jews can stop being Jews."

Then there is the majority—"We will accept becoming like you. But we do not accept your God. We are just like you but a different religion."

"So Judaism became a religion," Infeld said. "Before it was a religious culture of a people."

Judaism was retrofitted to be a religion. That is how Jews and Judaism became legible and understandable to the larger Christian society in the west. At the same time, Jewishness as an ethnic identity was submerged. Jews lived in nation states with single ethnicities such as French, German, or Dutch that did not accept difference. At times life for Jews was tense, at other times the antisemitism was untenable.

Reform and Conservative Judaism evolved as adaptations of the religion to the demands of modern life. Reconstructionist and Modern Orthodoxy were even later adaptations.

But this understanding of the Judeo-Christian tradition did not do away with the virulence and malice that lay in the history. The charge of deicide, that the Jews killed Christ, would emerge again and again, regardless of how much Jews were integrated in the larger society.

In the east, large empires, such as the Russian and Ottoman, ruled over multiethnic populations. Jewishness was defined, made legible, in Russia as an ethnic group and Jews retained their traditionalism. In Russia, both the religious and political institutions of the majority were too brittle to reform. Among some Jews, more radical solutions were envisioned, such as dropping religion all together in favor of socialist or communist ideology, or advocating for Jewish nationalism: Zionism. Jews did not achieve civic equality until the Russian Revolution in 1917.

"Also," Infeld said, "many tried to assimilate and did not succeed. The law and the next door neighbor said no." So there was yet another solution, one that said, "If I can't become like you, I will become like you in another way." That solution was nationalism and the creation of a state. In that sense Zionism and Israel are a product of the nineteenth-century building of the nation state.

In the United States, unlike in western or eastern Europe, Jews are hard to categorize. With our fervor for religion, preoccupation with race, and new emphasis on multiculturalism, being Jewish is seen as something of a blend of both ethnicity and religion.

Infeld believes that Jews respond in one of these four ways to the challenges of modernity: Ultra-Orthodox maintain separation from non-Jews; others assimilate and discard Judaism; others have thrown their lot with the state of Israel; yet others remain as Jews and still function as part of a larger society.

So how are we to understand our story? In thinking about Jewish history on top of this hill in Israel in the mixed Arab Jewish neighborhood of Abu Tor, I saw with greater clarity where I had come from. In a sense, I am a prime example of an assimilated American Jew. But that would be too facile. I have much to draw on, much that is latent. The Holocaust was like a lava spill. It blew up and coated everything. Yet enormous change, resulting from the Jewish encounter with modernity, had been set in motion 150 years before.

At the deepest level, I was formed in the Russian Pale. Jewishness as a religious culture and Yiddish culture permeates my values and way of seeing and being in the world. Transposed into the American culture, I was fit into the religious solution of Reform Judaism. Yes, a great deal was lost through assimilation. At the same time, some of my Jewish identity is in the nation state of Israel. I am now looking for ways in the American environment to make all this more defined in my life.

NOTES

1. Jacob Katz, *Out of the Ghetto: The Social Background of Jewish Emancipation 1770–1870* (New York: Schocken Books, 1973 and 1978), 1.

2. Ibid., 14.

3. Ibid., 6.

4. Ibid., 17.

5. Ibid., 38.

6. Paula Hyman, *The Jews of Modern France* (Berkeley: University of California Press, 1998), 15.

7. Ibid., 27.

8. Ibid., 53.

9. Sholem Aleichem, *Tevye the Dairyman and the Railroad Stories* (New York: Schocken Books, 1987), 48.

19

LINES

The three sisters of Franz Kafka were killed in the Holocaust. So were Dolfi, Mitzi, Rosa, and Pauli, sisters of Sigmund Freud. Madeleine Levy, the granddaughter of Captain Alfred Dreyfus, was killed at Auschwitz. The sister of Theodor Herzl died at Theresienstadt. So did Frieda, Lisa, Anna, and Rose, the four sisters of chief Berlin Rabbi Leo Baeck.[1]

Stored in my memory, embodied perhaps in my socialist grandfather, was the idea that the early part of the century in eastern Europe was this yeasty, exciting time. My image, formed in childhood, was that Jews were actively engaged in the events of the day in debating the various current ideologies of socialism, Zionism, communism, democracy. That debate was brought to America and gave many Jewish households here an intense political flavor that carried into my generation.

Yet what I have come to understand is that all that fervent political activity did not come from just an inspired idealism, but from the ominous and growing desperation of the times. Some Jews in Europe may have been financially successful, but in parts of Europe antisemitism was rising: Opportunities to earn a living were shrinking. This period that I had thought of as one of great political ferment had a large component of fear. The Jews of Europe were looking for solutions. They were desperately searching for an economic and political climate in which they could exist.

During the nineteenth century, the Jews of Europe, east and west, underwent a population explosion greater than the non-Jewish population. In 1825, there were 2.75 million; by 1900 that number had increased to 8.5 million. In 1897, 5.2 million Jews lived under the Russian Empire in the Pale of Settlement.[2]

Many made a living as middlemen in commerce between the rural areas and urban centers. But that began to break down in the late 1800s with the development of the railroad and competition that came with the freeing of the serfs. Jews found it increasingly difficult to make a living.

Within Europe, Jews moved from shtetl life to the cities. Jewish life was becoming increasingly urban and impoverished. The population of Berlin increased twelve times in the nineteenth century: the number of Jews, twenty-seven times. In the decade 1860–70 the Jews of Warsaw grew from 25 to 33 percent of the population.[3] It was their increasing impoverishment that was a major impetus for migration from eastern to western Europe and to the United States.

Yiddish emerged as a literary language and a vital secular culture. In 1886 there were three Yiddish dailies. Shalom Jacob Abramovich, whose pen name was Mendele Mokher Seforim (1836–1917), published *The Little Man* in 1864. It is considered the first book of modern Jewish literature and Abramovich is considered its father. Yiddish writers helped unite the ghetto community with the larger world. These writers "articulated the unconscious strivings of a growing number of Jews who sought ways out of the narrow confines of their traditional life."[4]

Political parties and movements proliferated: Zionists, Bundists (members of a Jewish labor organization in eastern Europe), assimilationists, liberals, religious revivalists, social revolutionaries. Much of this fracturing was in response to an increasing sense of powerlessness and impoverishment of European Jews. No one could be indifferent.[5] This alienation became known as the Jewish question: how would Jews find a way to live in Europe? And its concomitant: How would others find a way to live with

Jews? Antisemitism was in the air. All the while, a segment of Jewish life stayed in traditional Orthodoxy.

In France, in October 1894 Captain Alfred Dreyfus was arrested and accused of treason. It was the number one news with the critical adjective, *Jewish* officer.[6]

The Dreyfus family owned a mill in Alsace, a region of France recently conquered from Germany, making him doubly suspect. The case brought about an outburst of antisemitism from a coalition of clericals, neoroyalists, nationalists, and antisemites that challenged the legacy of the revolution of one hundred years before.

Dreyfus was found guilty and made to go through a humiliating public ceremony called "degradation" in which the braids and brass buttons of his uniform were ripped off and his sword broken. An angry mob surrounded him and shouted, "Traitor!" and "Death to the Jews!" Dreyfus never questioned his superiors and maintained his belief in French justice and the fatherland. He felt the rights of Jews and the separation of church and state were among the great achievements of the Enlightenment.

The French writer Emile Zola was among those who defended Dreyfus. He wrote his famous defense "J'Accuse" in the newspaper *L'Aurore*, on display at the Jewish museum in Paris.

Dreyfus was found guilty and served five years on Devil's Island. Then in another trial he was found guilty again and given ten years detention. But he was a scapegoat for antisemitism. In 1906 he received a presidential pardon, twelve years from the time the ordeal began. The verdict was annulled and he was reinstated in the army, going on to serve in World War I.

A young Jewish journalist from the leading newspaper in Vienna was in Paris to cover the Dreyfus trial and witnessed the angry mob shouting antisemitic epithets at him. He was Theodor Herzl. "If religious tolerance and racial harmony were impossible in France, the home of the Rights of Man, they were, Herzl was now convinced, impossible everywhere."[7]

Herzl wrote his slim seventy-three-page tract *The Jewish State: An Attempt at a Modern Solution of the Jewish Question* in the summer of 1895 at the age of thirty-six. It was published in London the following year.

When Herzl wrote the tract, he was in a heightened state. "He dashed down his thoughts on scraps of paper, walking, standing, lying down, on the street at the table, in the night—as if under unceasing command."[8]

"The idea which I have developed in this pamphlet is a very old one," it begins: "it is the restoration of the Jewish State. The world resounds with outcries against the Jews and these outcries have awakened the slumbering idea."[9] He said he was not proposing Utopia, but a solution to the grave situation in many countries.

It has been called an Enlightenment tract. Why, Herzl reasoned, couldn't Jews benefit as well from progress? "I believe in the ascent of man to higher and yet higher grades of civilization: but I consider this ascent to be desperately slow."[10]

Yet he also believed in the inevitability of antisemitism. "Wherever Jews exist, antisemitism exists. . . . It is a national question which can only be solved by making it a political world question to be discussed and settled by the civilized nations of the world in council."[11] We are a people—one people. Herzl called for the founding of a Jewish state, setting off the movement for political Zionism. The first Zionist Congress was held in Basel, Switzerland in 1897.

For these Jews, Zionism was the Jewish revolution, as the French revolution and other revolutions of national self-determination had been.[12] It was a coming together of equal citizenship and nationality, the right of a people to a homeland. Jews may have entered European societies as citizens, but they could not fully fit into or partake in the nation states of Europe that were defined by single ethnicities. The Zionists saw diaspora Jews as politically impotent and passive. They set out to remake Jewish life.

In that arc of 1881 to 1914, Jews traveled north to south in the Pale and east to west from the Pale to escape grinding poverty. In that time, 2.5 million Jews came to the United States. Writer Mary Antin came here in 1891. She spent her youth in Plotsk, Russia. "America was in everybody's mouth," she wrote of the time before she emigrated. "Businessmen talked of it over their accounts; the market women made up their quarrels that they might discuss it from stall to stall; people who had relatives in the famous land went around reading their letters for the enlightenment of less fortunate folks; children played at emigrating . . ."[13]

Emigration was accelerated by the pogroms of 1881 and the May Laws of 1882, which established Jewish quotas in schools and limited movement of Jews outside the Pale. More pogroms followed, in Kishinev in 1903 and again after the revolution in 1905.

In 1895, the tsar's secret service agents circulated a story that a conspiracy was afoot among Jews to take over the world. In 1905 the story was printed on the tsar's presses and disseminated as the *Protocols of the Elders of Zion*. It has been proven to be a forgery in a court of law but the *Protocols* have had staying power. They are still in circulation and may be found in Arab countries today and on the Internet.

Some Jews stayed put and sought solutions in Europe. The Bund, the union of Jewish workers, was established in 1897 in Vilna. It attempted to combine Jewish identity with class struggle and sought an alliance with Polish workers. By the turn of the century many Jewish workers looked to the Bund rather than rabbis for political leadership, an indication of how far Jews had secularized.

The situation in Russia was deteriorating. Among a new radical element of Jewish youth, the idea of fighting it out with the reactionary regime gained ground.[14] Some became communists.

A week after the Russian Revolution in October 1917, Britain issued the Balfour Declaration, which promised the Jews a homeland in Palestine. The problem was that the British promised the Arabs of Palestine independence too.[15]

And in Germany? The Jews achieved emancipation under Bismarck in 1871. They moved rapidly into the middle class by taking hold in the developing capitalist economy and in the creation of culture. "It was one of most brilliant Jewish communities anywhere."[16]

The Wilhelmine era, argues Peter Gay, was the period of the German Jewish symbiosis. Educated Jews were woven into the fabric of German culture and acted like Germans. . . . Jews were entering the cultural market in striking numbers. There was a kind of explosion of Jewish talent in drama and art, among critics, book and art dealers, publishers and editors.[17]

But for many Germans, the infusion of Jews was not a pleasing sight. The true German was so by race, the narrowest definition of nation state.[18] The term antisemitism was first used in the 1870s by the German journalist Wilhelm Marr. It was an ethnic racial designation rather than a religious one, to describe the negative German reaction to Jewish citizenship and entrance into mainstream society. The depression of the 1870s fueled the wave of antisemitism into the 1880s. In Germany, antisemitism rose alongside Jewish success. The "Jewish question" was no longer one of religion but of cultural invasion.[19]

Yet at the turn of the century the Holocaust could hardly have been anticipated in Germany. "When German Jews worried over truly vicious antisemitism in the Wilhelminian epoch, they looked to the Dreyfus case in France and the pogroms in eastern Europe."[20]

The ferment that characterized the last years of the nineteenth century was a time of contradictory trends. They included both growing desperation and new opportunities.

Sometimes when I imagine Jews at the turn into the twentieth century, they are in lines, long snaky lines moving slowly, always leading somewhere. Jews were in lines to come here, to make revolution, to go to Palestine, to change their place of residence or their place in the social order, or to change *the* social order, or to create a new identity. Some lines reaped the fruits of assimilation and the dangers of assimilation too—the rise of antisemitism. Later the lines were of naked bodies going to gas chambers. What a century it has been, of movement, of long lines, to a land of opportunity, to the opportunity to build the land, and for some to nowhere. They were all Tevye's grandchildren.

At the end of the century, there were many containers for Judaism. Jewish identity fractured and multiplied, each shaped by time and place. Some were containers of disguise, making Jewishness invisible. Others transmuted into ideologies that were funneled and infused into the mainstream. Another was to make Jewishness more defined and more legible.

One hundred years ago the Jews of Europe faced many crossroads. I come out of this stew—of ideology, of emigration, of the dream of statehood, of the darkness of obliteration.

The later twentieth century brought new changes. Political sovereignty was achieved. The birth of the Jewish state set off new migrations to Israel of Jews from eastern countries. So did the fall of communism in the late 1980s. Exile ended although it is still deeply imprinted in Jewish memory. All these changes have made for an incredible diversity in Jewish life.

And sometimes when I imagine Jews in lines, it is simply through life, from birth to death, trying to make sense of this small, persistently distinct and fractured people. That is the journey I am on.

NOTES

1. Aharon Appelfeld, "The Kafka Connection," *The New Yorker* (July 23, 2001), 38. Freud Exhibition, Library of Congress, Washington, D.C., summer 1998. Michael Burns, *Dreyfus: A Family Affair 1789–1945* (New York: HarperCollins, 1991), 483. Ernst Pawel, *The Labyrinth of Exile: A Life of Theodor Herzl* (New York,: Farrar, Straus and Giroux, 1989), 537. Leonard Baker, *Days of Sorrow and Pain: Leo Baeck and the Berlin Jews* (New York: MacMillan, 1978), 280.

2. David Biale, *Power and Powerlessness in Jewish History* (New York: Schocken Books, 1986), 120.

3. Ibid.

4. Salo W. Baron, *The Russian Jew under Tsars and Soviets* (New York: Macmillan, 1976), 129.

5. Biale, *Power and Powerlessness,* 118.

6. Michael Burns, *Dreyfus: A Family Affair 1789–1945,* (New York: HarperCollins, 1991), 112.

7 Ibid., 263.

8. Theodor Herzl, *The Jewish State: An Attempt at a Modern Solution of the Jewish Question* (New York: Dover Publications, 1988), 12.

9. Ibid., 69.

10. Ibid., 74.

11. Ibid., 75–76.

12. Others more recently have argued that Zionism was part of western colonialism in the Middle East or an arm of world imperialism and that the Palestinians are part of the Third World struggle against it.

13. Baron, *The Russian Jew,* 71.

14. Ibid., 72.

15. Tom Segev, *One Palestine Complete: Jews and Arabs under the British Mandate* (New York: Metropolitan Books, 2000), 46.

16. Leonard B. Glick, *Ashkenazic Jews in European History,* four lectures on tape at the National Yiddish Book Center's 1995 summer program in Yiddish culture, Amherst, Mass.

17. Peter Gay, *Freud, Jews and Other Germans: Masters and Victims in Modern Culture,* (New York: Oxford University Press, 1978), 154.

18. Glick, *Ashkenazic Jews.*

19. Ibid.

20. Gay, *Freud, Jews and Other Germans,* 166.

KIBBUTZ DEGANIA

Israel on the ground is a vast array—
the dense, sometimes poor neighborhoods in Tel Aviv, the new settlements
built in the Jerusalem hills, the Arab villages and Bedouin tents, the huge
apartment complexes for recent immigrants and the burgeoning string of
computer companies on the north coast.

But I had my eye out for another Israel, the one that offered a healthy
life in the countryside—picking oranges on a kibbutz. This Israel resonated
to my idealistic strain, to this utopian view of communal life. It was handed
down to me from my mother and she, I believe, learned of it from her father.

My mother never lived this life, mind you, nor likely did her father, but
she had this certainty that the health of the individual was drawn from the
vitality of the small intimate community. Perhaps my mother had nostalgia for shtetl or village life left behind long ago. She believed in the socialist ideal of equality forged in the radical and desperate politics of the
Russian Pale. She had a longing for a Jewish life, a turf that rapidly disap-

peared with assimilation. And finally, she felt that community was a potent antidote to the experience of many Jews as outsiders.

These strands were part of Zionism in the early part of the century and connected me to it. So in Israel, when the chance came to visit Degania, the first kibbutz in Israel, I jumped at it.

When Lou had been in Israel before, he became a friend of Gil Haran, who is a member of Degania. Gil invited us to visit, so when Lou and Max arrived we drove up to the Galilee where Degania is located on the bank of Lake Kinneret at the foot of the Golan Heights.

Gil, Lou, Max, and I sat on a stone wall in a bit of shade at the kibbutz. Nearby were the lush, well-tended fields of red and yellow dates, oranges, grapes, and bananas. An ancient olive tree, cut down and started over, stood in front of us, its silvery leaves flickering in the breeze. As I looked out over the fields and hillsides it was as if I could feel the Zionist stirrings from early in the century; work the land, construct a community of equals, put physical labor into Jewish life, build a Jewish homeland. Kibbutz life, like at this outpost here, was a small, but important Jewish stream of this century.

"They came for the Zionist socialist dream," Gil told us. "They did not want to be owners. They wanted to be farmers."

Gil's wife, Yael, grew up on Degania and her father, mother, brothers, and grandmother, who is in her eighties, still live there. Gil worked in the factory while he finished his university degree and Yael was a teacher in one of the children's groups. They have two children.

Degania was founded in 1910 in what was then Palestine. The entrance today is just across from the road that winds around Lake Kinneret. The Jewish Agency bought the land in 1905 from an Arab sheik who lived in Lebanon. About fifty Arab families of the village of Um Juni had worked the land. Degania, which means cornflower, now has six hundred members.

Kibbutz Degania came out of the Second Aliyah, or second wave of Jewish immigration to Palestine. It began in 1905 coming out of the political ferment in Russia and eastern Europe set off by the pogroms and the first Russian Revolution the same year.

About thirty-five thousand came in the Second Aliyah but only a small number stayed. Still, it has a special place in Zionist history. Decidedly secular, the ideals of socialism, return, and working the land flowered, forming an ideological backbone for Zionism. S. Y. Agnon's novel *Only Yesterday* is set in this period. Agnon is the only Israeli to win a Nobel Prize. Today, Israel's new Russian theater, called Gesher (which means bridge), idealizes the village life of the Second Aliyah in their acclaimed production of the play *Kfar* (village).

At the time of the Second Aliyah the population of Palestine was six hundred thousand Arabs, forty to fifty thousand Jews, ten to fifteen thousand Christians. "Most Jews lived in Jaffa, Sfat, Acco, and Tiberias," Gil told us. "The rest lived in small villages that were owned by sheiks or the Turkish government."

The first to settle Degania were a small group of ten: sixteen- to nineteen-years old, nonreligious, Zionist, and most of all socialist. The Jewish Agency asked them to work the fields to keep the land from reverting to the Turkish government. They lived in the mud huts left by the Arabs when the land was sold. "The experiment was a grim ordeal; the Jordan Valley was an inferno, and malaria took a heavy toll on the little group."[1]

The kibbutz museum has a photo of seven men and two women of the original group. The father of one of the women, Miriam, was the chief rabbi of Poland. He was so disapproving of her decision to make aliyah that he sat shiva—mourning for the dead—for her. Women were added to the group for the housework but when the first work schedule was made up and Miriam was told the women would cook, she said, no, she would take care of the cows. That, in fact, was her job until she was eighty-five years old. "Ever since, women choose any job and work any hours," Gil said. "Today, 90 percent of the people working in the kitchen are men."

Engraved in the stone wall where we sat was a list of all the kibbutzim of Israel, 280 in all. In 1920 Degania Bet (B) was founded. The last was founded in 1989.

The first stone courtyard is still in use. In the early years, the buildings around it were the cow and tool sheds, stables and housing for members. The communal laundry is there as well as a movie theater, library, and a social hall that is rented out for celebrations. Kibbutz life has improved. Facilities are air-conditioned.

The kibbutz museum also has a photo of strong-willed Miriam at her wedding wearing the only dress at the kibbutz. "When she had a baby," Gil said, "there was a debate, 'whose baby is it?' They thought they had erased the word 'mine' from the dictionary. But Miriam said, 'This baby is mine.' She named it and since then Degania, unlike other kibbutz in the early decades, has never had sleeping arrangements where the children are separated from parents."

Polish born Moshe Bersky joined the group a few months after it began. He was killed by Arabs when he left the kibbutz to get a doctor and medicine. Degania honors him, Gil said, "as the first victim of the national struggle." When his parents heard of his death, they sent their second son and then they came themselves.

The second kibbutz baby was born a year later and was named after Moshe Bersky. He was Moshe Dayan. He is shown in a 1920 photo, sitting in a small kindergarten class. Degania has been home for many luminaries of the socialist Zionist narrative. Joseph Trumpeldor, the one-armed Jewish soldier who had served in the Russian army, joined in 1911. Later, he led the Jewish brigade in World War I. Killed in an Arab attack on his kibbutz Tel Chai in 1920, he became a symbol of Jewish self-defense. Ideologist of the socialist Zionist movement A. D. Gordon joined Degania a few years before he died in 1922. So did "Rachel," the famous poet who died in 1931. Prime Minister Levi Eshkol had a hand in founding Degania Bet.

At the end of the photo exhibit is a wall honoring those of Degania, twenty in all, who died defending Israel. Moshe Bersky was the first. There are soldiers who fought with the British in both world wars; an air force pilot who died in the Independence War; brothers who died in the '57 and '67 wars and cousins in the Yom Kippur War.

Then there was the soldier from Degania who disappeared in a plane crash in the Sinai Desert during the Suez War. He was missing in action until several years ago when his bones were discovered in the roots of a date tree in the Sinai. Local Arabs called it the Grave of the Jew. That soldier's nephew was killed in the late '90s in a helicopter accident in Lebanon in which seventy Israelis died.

By the '70s Degania and other kibbutz across Israel saw that agriculture was not enough to stay economically viable. It became a divisive issue in the kibbutz movement: If members founded factories then they would wind up becoming employers of workers who were not members. But reality dictated ideology and Degania began a company called Toolgal, which makes and exports diamond saws for the cutting of marble, granite, and glass. It has been very successful, but now is getting competition from the Far East.

Gil said about half of the kibbutz members return to Degania to live after army service and attending college. The average age is thirty-five. An average of six babies are born a year. And the kibbutz has taken in three new members in recent years, two immigrants from Russia and one from Hungary.

In addition to those working at the kibbutz, members include a history professor at Hebrew University in Jerusalem, a judge in Tiberias, and a Knesset member, the seventh in the history of the kibbutz. Kibbutz members today are a small percentage of the Israeli population, but in the history of Israel, much of the country's early political and military leadership were drawn from them.

Kibbutz life provides an intimate community that is rare in our lives of increasing privacy, individuality, anonymity, choice, and mobility. Gil called the kibbutz a village, one among three types in Israel. The other two are Arab villages and "haredi" or ultra-Orthodox communities.

What I saw at Degania was the lore, the heroes, the harsh realities of climate, economics, and enemies and the deaths that came with forging a nation. This small community is almost a family; at the same time it is one microcosm of the nation.

And this microcosm had its roots in the Russian Pale and the ideologies spawned there. Today a new flood of Jews has come in Israel from the former Soviet Union. Gesher Theater tries to make a bridge between the Second Aliyah immigration and those today. They perform *Kfar* at their theater in Jaffa. The play was written by Joshua Sobel, a well-known Israeli playwright who grew up in the village Tel Mond. The artistic director, Yevgeny Arye, had been a successful director in Leningrad. "He has an intellectual and artistic curiosity about Jewish culture that could not be satisfied under the Soviet regime. 'I started to get interested in this culture that had completely disappeared,'"[2] He said he decided to emigrate in 1980 but waited a decade to leave.

The Gesher Company formed in the early '90s and is made up of Jewish actors from Russia who emigrated in the recent wave. When the play first opened, it was performed in Russian, then later in Hebrew as the company became fluent in the language. It has since been performed in London and New York and on the evening I saw it headsets were provided with an English translation.

The play portrays the intimacy of Jewish village life in the *yishuv*, the pre-state Jewish community in Palestine, from 1942 to the War of Independence. So the past and present Russian presence in Israeli life is tied together by means of this idealized village life.

It is a wonderful, yet nostalgic view. Most Russians who have come to Israel today are well-educated and urban. They left the *Kfar* life long ago as did most Israelis, if they ever lived it. Still, the image of "village" has a potent resonance to some encapsulated memory, passed along in families from a time when Jewish life was whole, when to be Jewish meant to belong, to have an intimate Jewish relationship to God and to the dream of the Messiah. And this force continues to animate a strain of Jewish thinking, with its vigilant eye to improve community.

Even in the religious, ideological, and geographical fracturing of Jewish life that has occurred over the last century, these strands of utopia have persisted. This is the image of Israel that was passed on to me, even though long ago we became urban and capitalistic, if we were ever anything else.

And these images get in the way of a more realistic picture of Israel and the real-life problems it faces on the ground. Since the 1967 war, a new competitive ideology has arisen in Israel regarding "the land:" the religious settler movement. And that land, the West Bank and Gaza, is still in dispute between Israel and the Palestinians.

Yet, at Degania, it occurred to me that this ideal must have been the wellspring that drew my mother to send us to high school on a farm in Vermont. What she found was an experiment in progressive education, on a farm—Putney School, whose first mission was community. Students worked the farm and learned to value physical labor, community, and the development of the individual within it. It was a kind of New England variant of kibbutz life, albeit decidedly un-Jewish. Considering our drive to be part of America's center, perhaps that too was intentional.

How critical I had become of her choice of school, this community where I felt an outsider, even though I have never questioned the good values I got from it.

Degania appealed to me. In the evening I heard the sounds of children playing by the pool and relaxing with their families. A pomegranate tree, laden with fruit, hung low in front of Gil's front door. Old people rode by in golf carts, younger ones on bicycles with baskets on the back. But Degania is not utopia. Clashes with Arabs occurred early on. A Syrian tank is at the entrance, stopped during the War of Independence, and the entrance to a bomb shelter, last used in the '67 war, was visible. Laboring in the extreme heat must be something to endure. Degania sits at the edge of the Golan Heights, once a part of Syria that one day will likely be up for negotiation. Communal life surely came as much out of necessity as ideology.

Still, this idealism is one of the strains of my Jewish narrative. And it has also been part of my Israel mythology that stood in the way of a more realistic picture of Israel and the very real problems it faces.

NOTES

1. Howard M. Sachar, *A History of Israel from the Rise of Zionism to Our Time* (New York: Alfred A. Knopf, 1996), 79.

2. Blake Eskin, "A New Wave of Actors Revives Israeli Theater," *Forward* (July 3, 1998), 11.

21

ZION AND DIASPORA

In 1939, there were 16.6 million Jews in the world.[1] Then the Jewish world was radically, surgically altered. Six million were murdered in the Holocaust. In the past half-century, many of those who were left migrated.

In 2000, there were 13.2 million Jews in the world, less than half the number of people who live in Tokyo. Population had shifted to the United States and Israel. Both became centers of Jewish life and power. Today, 5.7 million Jews live in the United States,[2] 4.9 million in Israel. Together they comprise a little over 80 percent of the world's Jews. The countries with the next largest Jewish populations are: France, 521,000; Canada, 362,000; Russia, 290,000; United Kingdom, 276,000; Argentina; 200,000; Ukraine 100,000.[3]

Before the Holocaust, 9,648,000 Jews lived in Europe, west and east: Today it is 1.6 million.

Like a lot of orphaned siblings, American Jews and Israelis share a powerful bond. That bond contains a deeply etched understanding of the Jewish story as well as questions about what it means to be a Jew today and where home is. Yet American Jews and Israel are also foreign to each other. Like a lot of powerful relationships this one has been filled with myth and unrealistic expectation.

"It's a miracle," an Israeli remarked to me of the astonishing success of Jews in America. He was referring to the fact that senators, university presidents, CEOs, Supreme Court justices, and the chairman of the Federal Reserve are Jewish.

"It is something of a holocaust, you know," another man told me. He also was referring to Jewish life in America. What he meant was assimilation, a purported intermarriage rate of 52 percent leading to, he believed, the extinction of American Jews.

His use of the word "holocaust" made me cringe. Choosing to marry outside one's faith is one thing; mass murder is quite another. Yet his comments reflected the Jewish obsession with demographics, a natural preoccupation of a small people, especially in the aftermath of genocide.

Here were two Israelis expressing dichotomous views. Each expressed some truth, be it extreme, about the paradox of American Jewry, its success and its vulnerability.

We have a similarly dichotomous view of Israel. On the one hand we see Israel's miracle: The return to Zion after two thousand years, the revival of Hebrew as a spoken language, cultivation of the land, the presence of a powerful Israeli army.

On the other hand, we see Israel as always on the edge of annihilation. We see an Israel not at ease in the world, despite its military prowess and superiority in the region. It is an Israel still fighting for legitimacy in the Middle East. These views express some truths about Israel and the United States but hardly the whole or most realistic picture.

Israel was founded largely by secular Jews but they came out of a religious culture and they put out a biblical call: It was for an ingathering of Jews from all over the world, an end of Jews living in exile. This was to be no ordinary emigration. It had religious significance, aliyah or ascending. Zionists believed it would lead to "the negation of the diaspora."

Jews came to Israel from around the world, though relatively few from the United States, only 77,282 since 1948.[4] American Jews do not need a refuge. And most have not felt the need to answer this religious calling; they could live freely as Jews and practice Judaism here. In fact five hundred thousand Israelis have left Israel, many after war.[5] Most live in the United States in New York or Los Angeles.

Where one lives as a Jew is perhaps as old a question as the Jewish people themselves. It includes matters of what is desirable and what has been possible, both existentially and politically.

In Jewish thinking, Zion is the center. Jews are in exile in the diaspora because of *galut* or sin. They will return when the Messiah comes. These concepts have deep roots in Jewish thinking about what is home and what isn't, about where you belong and where you are an outsider, the meaning of exile and return. They are not only about Jewish political existence, writes Arnold Eisen in his meditation of Jewish homelessness and homecoming,[6] but the deepest questions of human existence—the human longing for the innocence of the Garden of Eden, for childhood, and for a sense of wholeness in life.

"Paradise, it seems, has never preoccupied the Jewish imagination nearly as much as exile," Eisen writes.[7] He raises fundamental questions: Can you be Jewish and normal, or is that only when the Messiah comes? Is that when one achieves a sense of belonging? Is the state of exile part of the creative tension of being a Jew or of human existence for that matter? "Not-yet-home remains the condition of Israel and the human species."[8]

"Home in Genesis is a place remembered and revisited but never really known," writes Eisen.[9] In Deuteronomy, exile is the most powerful reality known to the Israelites, he continues. Jewish time and space were created by establishing a sacred order—a way to live one's life in a world that was not Jewish. Jewish time and space became portable.

"The rabbis could not turn the world right side up. They could not depose Roman rulers, establish jurisdiction in Jewish courts, or restore the Temple to its glory. All they could do was protect the purity of the Israelites —eating, drinking, having sex, and marrying, according to rabbis comprehensive regulations."[10]

Following Torah and Jewish law was "nothing less than putting the shards of God's cosmos back together again," he wrote.[11]

"Deuteronomy insists that law and justice are the only paths to homecoming."[12] Morality is social as well as personal and inextricably linked to politics, to *mitzvot*, laws or commandments.

Under conditions of persecution, Jewish time and space contracted. The crypto Jews of Spain practiced Judaism surreptitiously. Later, with the advent of citizenship in western Europe, Jewish law gave way to that of the nation state. The space of Jewishness contracted further. Secular Jews, other than in Israel, made Jewish space smaller and less visible.

With modernity, hope was placed in politics on the ground. Zionism was about Jews taking matters into their own hands. It took hold in the secular context of the late nineteenth-century political dilemmas (of nationalism and the struggle for citizenship) in which Jews found themselves.[13] The Zionists hoped to make Jews a normal people by ending exile and returning to "the land."

I found these stark themes of Holocaust and miracle, exile and return, laid out before me at the Diaspora Museum, Beit Hatfetfuzot, in Tel Aviv. The message of the section called Remembrance is, we shall not forget. The museum intends to inform and imprint the ideas that Jews are "a people apart" who will always be turned against in the end. Acts against Jews are on display in this Scroll of Agony for each of the fifty-two weeks of the year, from the destruction of the Temple in 70 C.E. to the Holocaust, including the Crusades and the many expulsions, false accusations, and pogroms.

Then there is the culture section, which celebrates the richness of two thousand years of Jewish life in the diaspora. It portrays the endurance and yeasty presence of Jewish life. I saw wonderful displays, of the flowering of Yiddish theater in Moscow and New York, artists like Marc Chagall and Ben Shahn, even the magician Houdini. There were the poets of the golden age of Spain; the lively Jewish press; and Boris Pasternak, Saul Bellow, I. B. Singer, and Nadine Gordimer among the ten Jewish Nobel Prize winners. What I felt looking at this section was a sense of the well-formed capacity of Jews to sustain their own culture and at the same time live among others and contribute creatively.

But the museum is really the Israeli story of how Jews lived in the diaspora. It is the tribal religious story of Jews who made a covenant with God in Sinai and later lived in the diaspora. That ended in the Holocaust. Then came Jewish redemption in the form of Israel. It is a neat story, but it is not exactly the whole story. It is as if the diaspora was something makeshift, temporary and bad, and yet it went on for close to two thousand years and is vibrant today even after the establishment of Israel. The American experience is minimized: Israel is the Jewish homeland. It is as if the museum is saying that the two-thousand-year diaspora is of the past. We have put it in a museum. Most of all, remember how it ended. The museum has arranged the diaspora as a way of life on the way to Israel, rather than a legitimate and ongoing part of the Jewish experience, past and present.

What I didn't see there was the portrayal of how to be a Jew and be among others. That is the American experience and also part of the Jewish experience. It is actually the struggle of Israel as a nation: How to be itself, secure and strong, and be accepted by and accepting of others.

I went to Israel to explore Jewish life and found it rich beyond my expectations. For the first time I experienced in a fully positive way what it meant to be a Jew. Yet while I was there I also gathered a sense of why the American environment has been an exceptional place for Jews not only to survive, but to thrive.

America's separation of church and state gave Jews a chance to thrive on the relative safety of secular ground. That may be why, for American Jews, secular ground, protected in the Constitution, has become practically sacred. America is a nation based on citizenship that puts everyone, at least legally, on an equal footing. It is not based on any tribe of religion, race, or ethnicity.

The chief American struggle has been and is over slavery and race, not religion. Jews are a minority group but they are white, so whatever the history of antisemitism, they have been able, to a great extent, to blend.

America is a meritocracy and merit has been increasingly determined by education. For centuries Jews have placed a central value on learning and that value was easily transferred to secular education.

The role of outsider, living in the borders of a society, is a well-developed one for Jews. It goes back to the Middle Ages when they had to find ways to earn a living as traders because they were not able to own land. The outsider has the vantage of seeing new opportunities that lie outside the traditional ways of doing things.[14] America's capitalistic milieu has depended on an ability to see and take advantage of opportunities, try new things that had not been done before.

The scholar Simon Rawidowicz wrote a jaunty essay first published in Hebrew in 1948 called, "Israel: The Ever-Dying People."

> He who studies Jewish history will readily discover that there was hardly a generation in the Diaspora that did not consider itself the final link in Israel's chain. Each saw before it the abyss ready to

swallow it up. . . . Each generation grieved not only for itself but also for the great past that was going to disappear forever, as well as the future of unborn generations who would never see the light of day.

. . . Maimonides, the great Jewish thinker of the golden age of Spain, when he finished his famous *Guide to the Perplexed,* wrote to scholars in France, "This I have to tell you, that in our difficult times there are none left who care for the Torah and Talmud except for you and your neighbors.

. . . Maimonides did not realize . . . that new Jewish settlements were growing up on both sides of the Rhine . . . and that hundreds of scholars would study the Torah.[15]

Not only did religious Jews through the ages lament the end of Torah, piety, and faith, but with the coming of modernity secular Jews did as well. Y. L. Gordon, the leading poet of the Haskalah, burst out in this famous lamentation, writes Rawidowicz, "For who do I labor? Who will tell me the future, who will tell men that I am not the last poet of Zion, and you my last readers?"[16]

Rawidowicz continued:

Now after our great European tragedy—'tragedy' is too weak a word for this third great disaster in our history—the traditional dread of being the last naturally assumes dimension of great magnitude.

. . . We are confronted here with a phenomenon that has almost no parallel in mankind's story: A people that has been disappearing constantly for the last 2000 years, exterminated in dozens of lands all over the globe, reduced to half or third of its population by tyrants, ancient and modern, and yet it still exists. . .[17]

Rawidowicz concludes with a heavy tone of irony: "A people dying for thousands of years means a living people. . . . But if we are the last, let us be the last as our fathers and forefathers were. Let us prepare the ground for the last Jews who will come after us, and for the last Jews who will rise after them, and so on until the end of days."[18]

Rawidowicz was born in Lithuania, educated in Germany and London, and taught at Brandeis. He was controversial. He did not accept traditional Jewish thinking about center and diaspora. He believed that since the destruction of the Temple two centers to Jewish life have existed, the land or center, *and* the diaspora. Not only has creativity flourished in both, but every Jew, he believed, is rooted in both.

Not only has the Jewish diaspora failed to disappear, diasporas are hardly exclusively Jewish these days. With an increasingly mobile world made so by political struggles or globalization, African, Hispanic, Asian, Indian, and Palestinian diasporas have formed, each with a powerful connection to the homeland.

In recent years a tectonic shift has taken place in the relationship between American Jews and Israel. Each side has had to give up some sustaining myths. Israel has been faced with the reality that Jewish life in the diaspora did not end. And American Jews have been faced with the reality that something more than support of Israel is needed to sustain Jewishness in multicultural America.

"We don't need your money anymore," said Yossi Beilin, who was minister of justice under Ehud Barak. He was referring to the $280 million that was raised annually from world Jewry to support Israel. "I am insulted by it. I do not want money for poor Israel. It is right in the '50s. It was already wrong in the '60s."[19]

For many American Jews, giving to Israel was a potent way of being Jewish. Now others ways will have to be sought to sustain Jewish identity. Israel does not want to serve as that kind of repository. American Jews have had to come to grips with Israel rejecting its paternalism.

Other factors are changing the relationship. There has been a tremendous growth in the last decade of the Israeli economy in high technology. The presence of Israeli companies on the U.S. stock exchange is making for another kind of reciprocal relationship, blurring the old narrative.

And a major shift has occurred in recent years among some historians in the way the Zionist story of redemption is told. Israel is much more cognizant of Palestinian national aspirations. With the release of government records for the years in which the state was established, a cadre of Israeli historians have acknowledged more fully Israel's responsibility for the Palestinian refugee problem. A majority of Israelis have come to accept that some day, two states —one Israeli, one Palestinian—will likely occupy the land.

So the two orphans have grown up. Each has established its own fulsome family and household—one in the United States, one in the Middle East. Both have their problems. But neither, really, seems set to disappear.

They no longer need to cling to each other for survival. That blood-brother relationship that was once symbiotic has given way, for me at least, to one of mutuality. In this severing of that symbiotic tie, there is a chance to actually draw closer.

It takes a great deal of demystifying on both sides. Israel still needs American support and the political power of American Jews. American Jews need a connection—emotional, historical and religious—to Israel. But each side must have its own identity and expectations need to be more in line with current realities. After more than a half a century, perhaps it is time for the high dramas of "miracle" and "holocaust," "exile" and "return" to tone down. It is not a question of choosing one or the other but drawing from both to gain the sense of home, of belonging, that ultimately comes from within. In both, there is perhaps a chance to recover from the dark side of Jewish history.

NOTES

1. Census Bureau of Statistics of the Israeli Government.
2. The 2000 Jewish Population Survey, Council of Federations, New York.
3. The American Jewish Committee, *The American Jewish Yearbook 2000*, 489–90.
4. This figure is from the Central Bureau of Statistics in Israel and is higher than the actual immigrants as it includes "potential immigrants" as well as "immigrants."
5. World Jewish Congress, Israel Office, September 15, 1998, Profile of World Jewry.
6. Arnold M. Eisen, *Galut: Modern Jewish Reflection on Homelessness and Homecoming* (Bloomington: Indiana University Press, 1986).
7. Ibid., xi.
8. Ibid., 18.
9. Ibid., xv.
10. Ibid., 49.
11. Ibid., 52.
12. Ibid., 183.
13. Ibid., xi.
14. Shulamit Volkov, speaking at the Alma Hebrew College in Tel Aviv, July 25, 1999.
15. Simon Rawidowicz, *State of Israel, Diaspora, and Jewish Continuity: Essays on the "Ever-Dying People"* (Hanover, N.H.: University Press of New England, 1997), 54–57.
16. Ibid., 59.
17. Ibid., 60–61.
18. Ibid., 63.
19. Yossi Beilin, speaking at the Alma Hebrew College in Tel Aviv, July 25, 1999.

TISHA B'AV

The past is a vital and disruptive part of existence.

—Sigmund Freud

Lou told me that on the eve of Tisha B'Av, he wanted me to go with him to the Western Wall of the Old City in Jerusalem.

Tisha B'Av is a Jewish day of commemoration, which I had never heard of before. Again, I was in this odd position of being introduced to something new that is Jewish through my son. It is the ninth day of the Jewish month of Av and it commemorates the destruction of the First and Second Temples in Jerusalem, which, at least as tradition tells it, happened on the same day, some five hundred years apart.[1]

On that night observant Jews read the Book of Lamentations. It begins:

Alas!
Lonely sits the city
Once great with people!
She that was once great among nations
Is become like a widow;
The princess among states
Is become a thrall [enslaved].[2]

How deep is this longing for Jerusalem, this city that is part of Israel now! I was astonished at how long and literal the collective memory is of its loss. And this was not some ideal called Jerusalem or some imagined loved place but the actual political entity. No, in Israel, religious longings pour unchecked into the politics of the day.

Before Lou arrived I began to notice newspaper advertisements: "Join an old Jerusalem custom, walk around the walls of the Old City, on the eve of Tisha B'Av." An editorial in the paper argued that Holocaust Remembrance Day, now in April or May, should be moved to this day associated with these other Jewish national catastrophes. It was a day also associated with Jewish militancy. Women in Green, a group that opposes the peace efforts and supports the Jewish settlements in the West Bank, had a newspaper advertisement asking supporters to join their walk.

At dusk, Lou and I walked to the Old City. The sun was setting as we joined a long, quiet procession of people making their way to the Western Wall. Extra security was evident: Groups of soldiers were everywhere. Police and ambulances were at the ready.

Along the inner wall of the Armenian quarter, we passed a group of secular Israelis. The guide, speaking in Hebrew, was giving a detailed account of exactly what happened at that particular spot, how Israel took that wall in the 1967 war. There must have been two hundred people listening in rapt attention to the story.

Jerusalem figures prominently in Israel's political and military history. But there, on that night, recent history mingled freely with the rich, deep and contentious religious tributaries of the distant past that are remembered in liturgy and ritual.

It was a comfortably warm Jerusalem night. The Western Wall was lit with floodlights. The gold of the Temple Mount gleamed. Across from the wall were six huge lighted candles, commemorating the six million Jews who died in the Holocaust.

The area in front of the wall was slowly filling up with amazing communal activity. People stay till dawn reciting prayers, I was told. On the male side were old and young men, clean-shaven modern and long-bearded ultra-Orthodox. Groups were sitting on the ground on mats they had brought. Many had their young sons at their sides. One sat on a small orange plastic chair. To the left another group was chanting from their prayer books.

> *Her enemies are now the masters,*
> *Her foes are at ease,*
> *Because the LORD has afflicted her*
> *For her many transgressions;*
> *Her infants have gone into captivity*
> *Before the enemy.*[3]

Two men sat on the ground, back to back, supporting each other, chanting. A father chanted as his young son sat against him in tennis shoes and shorts, asleep, his mouth open, his hand on the prayer book. A man gestured constantly to the sky as if conducting.

On the women's side, a group of observant women stood together, one holding onto a crib on wheels with two babies in it. Modern Orthodox women were there, too—most standing, some rocking forward and back, davening (uttering silent or whispered prayer while standing). A woman held her baby in her arms. He sucked his thumb and she rocked side to side, reading prayers. Another crib, momentarily unattended contained a baby girl and her mother's purse. I was struck by how seamless this religious observance was with daily life.

Further back from the wall, a young woman, an off-duty soldier, with a long thick braid, carried a rifle. A haredi (ultra-Orthodox) man talked on his cell phone. Three religious men stood nearby, dressed elegantly in black bowler hats, long black coats, and wire-rimmed glasses.

Lou and I climbed to the arch of the synagogue across from the wall. I looked down on the hundreds, maybe thousands, of people reading from the book of Lamentations, each at his or her own pace, and the hundreds more standing, soaking up the solemn air, contemplating Jewish loss.

Standing there, watching all those around me recite the prayers at this solemn communal event, I felt in the bowels of existential Jewish thought. My mind fixed on the question Zipperstein posed early on in my exploration: What is remembered? He was referring to immigrants' recollection of the old country, but *lizkhor*, to remember, is a potent Hebrew word, with a particular Jewish resonance. What are we to remember? And how does it imprint us? What we remember of Jewish history and the meaning we give to it is central to Judaism. And central, too, to my disquiet: Can post-Holocaust Judaism offer sufficient hope?

There, surrounding me was a liturgy of lamentation. I thought about how much the Jewish mind has been shaped by the catastrophes of Jewish history. The Scroll of Remembrance at the Diaspora Museum in Tel Aviv outlines fifty-two acts of suffering for each of the fifty-two weeks of the year. They include the destruction of the Temple, Masada, the Crusades, the expulsions from France, Spain, and Portugal, pogroms, blood libels, shouldering blame for the plague, and finally the Holocaust. Liturgy and its repetition etches Jewish suffering in our minds. And memory of recent catastrophes, like the Holocaust, is kept alive in families, memoirs, and memorials. Grieving permeates Jewish culture.

The past gives powerful meaning to the present, and especially so in Judaism. Yosef Haim Yerushalmi writes: "Only in Israel and nowhere else is the injunction to remember felt as a religious imperative to an entire people."[4]

Certain historical events are so pivotal that they become the way to view and interpret all subsequent events.

When Ben Gurion brought the proposed reparations agreement with Germany before the Knesset in 1952, Menachem Begin led demonstrations opposing it. Money for Jewish blood, he called it.[5] It marked the beginning of his rise in Israeli politics and Holocaust memory as a force to be reckoned with in Israeli public life.

Demonstrators wore yellow stars with the word "Jude" on them, as Jews, including some of the demonstrators, had been made to wear in Germany. Under the word "Jude" were the words, "Remember what Amalek did to you" (Deut. 25:17).[6]

In the biblical story of Amalek, the prophet Samuel in the name of God ordered King Saul to kill all the Amalekites and "utterly destroy all that they had in retribution for their violence against the children of Israel." But Saul and his people had mercy on the Amalekite king and coveted their wealth so they "saved the best of the sheep and kept all that was good." Samuel killed the Amalekite king with his own hands and Saul was stripped of his kingdom. Saul's sin was his choice to disobey God and take halfhearted revenge out of greed.[7]

Although the demonstrators didn't carry the day, invoking the story of Amalek bolstered their side with the authority of Torah, the voice of God.

The story of Amalek, like that of the exile or the exodus, was not "a series of facts to be contemplated at a distance, but a series of situations into which one could somehow be existentially drawn."[8]

When Israel decided to put Eichmann to death in 1962, seventy-eight-year-old professor of philosophy at Hebrew University Shmuel Hugo Behrmann, who opposed it, wrote in his diary at the time. "There have always been in Judaism, from time immemorial, two strains grappling with each other in a duel. One is the isolationist. It hates the stranger, fosters the Amalek complex, and at every opportunity emphasizes 'Remember what they did to you.' And there is another Judaism, which I would characterize perhaps with the verse 'Love thy neighbor as thyself.' This is a Judaism whose prayer is 'Allow me to forget Amalek'—a Judaism of love and forgiveness."

Historian Tom Segev sees these strains as the basic division in Israeli politics: the nationalistic isolationism versus humanistic openness. In another place in his diary, Bergman wrote, "There are two peoples of Israel."[10]

Rabbi David Hartman of the Shalom Hartman Institute in Jerusalem draws a similar distinction. He poses this question, What is done with memory? Are we to be a victim people or are we to "channel memory into a larger ideal of aspiration. 'Love the stranger because you were once a stranger in the Land of Egypt.'"[11]

Hartman says he is not suggesting forgetting or denying but channeling experience into a constructive force. If not, he says, we are "locked into a past where we are unable to breathe new air and the joy of life is destroyed. "Amalek," he said, "is a state of permanent vengeance."[12]

How drawn I am to this dichotomy, how familiar it is to me. It is the dichotomy of my parents. Their parents may have forgotten the old countries from which they came, but they passed on intact these deep contours of the Jewish mind. My father had a sobered darkness, a sense in his bones of the tragedy in Jewish history. His was not a vengeance but an intractable sense of aloneness and belief that in some mysterious way the very darkness of collective memory was, paradoxically, linked to survival.

My mother epitomized the other side, with her unending energy and optimism, an insistence that hardship could be transformed into good or at least into good actions. She did, as Hartman said, let in new air. Her thinking found fertile ground in America where the climate was more optimistic and opportunity, it seemed, was endless.

I grew up in this divide. I know it as part of the construct of the Jewish mind, the dichotomous strains I bring to understand every story, every new event. I have come to believe these seemingly contradictory ways of viewing the world is one of the strengths of Judaism. It makes a diversity of response possible, depending on the historical situation. Jews, as a people, have developed a capacity to endure hard times as well as a capacity to transform hard times. Having this ability to behave in two conflicting manners enhances chances of survival. It is also what has made Jews so fractious.

Historians, however, do not ask, what is remembered? They ask, what happened? How did it happen, and why? Historians have a different mission. Theirs is not to provide solace or meaning to life, but to explain by looking at evidence, causation, and context. Sometimes they find a narrative different than the Jewish one.

Robert Wistrich writes in his study of antisemitism that the "eternal hatred" for the "eternal people" is ahistorical. "It ignores that Jews have often been welcomed in the surrounding society . . . and Jewish participation . . . since the western Enlightenment has been a remarkable success story. "Yes," he says, "there has been a backlash to Jewish integration but that is not innate Gentile antisemitism."[13]

Salo Baron, who was chair of Jewish history at Columbia University, also interpreted history differently than the Jews. Baron, who died in 1989, made the word "lachrymose" part of our daily vocabulary. He used the word to describe an entrenched view of Jewish history as unending hardship.

"Surely it is time to break with the lachrymose theory of pre-revolutionary (i.e., French) woe, and to adopt a view more in accord with historic truth," wrote Baron, whose research focused on the medieval period.[14]

When Baron testified at the trial of Nazi Adolf Eichmann in 1961 in Jerusalem, he said, "I am not a historical determinist. . . . History develops by reason of causes and changes within society, many of which are unpredictable. Accident is very important. Personality is very important. Together all these things create history."[15]

Rabbi and Jewish historian Ismar Schorsch argues that "at the heart of Baron's legacy pulsated the conviction that Jews were more than the hapless victims of persecution."[16]

And yet elsewhere Schorsch says, "the unvarnished truth is that Baron failed. The Holocaust overwhelmed his lifelong agenda to present a version of Jewish history that would do justice to all the evidence."[17]

So here is the dilemma. I am in search of a usable past. But how, in my generation, is it possible to feel that Jews, despite their successes, are more than hapless victims? For me, the Holocaust only etched the Jewish story of unending travail deeper.

For all of my life, the Holocaust has seemed beyond explanation. Yet I do not believe it happened because of demonic forces or because of a wrathful God. Humans are to blame for the Holocaust and, in time, historians will explain fully the complex of human forces that created it. Perhaps we are still too close to the tragedy.

Standing at the Western Wall on Tisha B'Av eve, I observed religious Jews praying:

> *The Lord vented all his fury,*
> *Poured out his blazing wrath;*
> *He kindled a fire in Zion*
> *Which consumed its foundations.*[18]

And I saw secular Jews reconstruct the battle of forty years ago. I felt the presence of those two worlds. The religious one—this lamentation for Jerusalem in Scripture—is based on the belief that God is guiding Jewish history, and the secular one looks to military might.

These scenes made me reach for my Americanness, which gives me a wall of protection—legal and psychological—between religious and secular life. That wall holds back the full weight of tragedy in Jewish history. It may mean a sacrifice or diminishment of religious zeal, but one well worth it for safety's sake. I felt glad for my American perspective, however young, fresh, shallow, and, yes, hopeful it may be. Grateful that it stanches the free flow of the past.

Baron writes that history, including Jewish history, is a complex human creation, on the ground, set in time and forged in interaction among peoples, cultures, and nations.

So how, in my generation, to draw hope from either the Jewish story or even the recent Jewish past as told by historians? I wanted to no longer be engulfed by Holocaust history or the fifty-two weeks of agony in the Scroll of Remembrance. I wanted to no longer be subsumed by my father's dark side. I wanted a usable past, a patch of hope to stand on.

NOTES

1. Yosef Haim Yerushalmi, *Zakhor: Jewish History and Jewish Memory* (Seattle and London: University of Washington Press, 1982), 44. In the Bible, contradictory days are given for the destruction of the First Temple in the fifth century

B.C.E. and the Second Temple in 70 B.C.E., but tradition made them the same for the sake of historical symmetry.

2. *Hebrew English Tanakh* (Philadelphia, Pa.: The Jewish Publication Society, 1999), 1749.

3. Ibid.

4. Yerushalmi, *Zakhor*, 9.

5. Tom Segev, *The Seventh Million: The Israelis and the Holocaust,* (New York: Hill and Wang, 1993), 214.

6. Ibid., 216.

7. Ibid., 207.

8. Yerushalmi, *Zakhor*, 44.

9. Segev, *The Seventh Million,* 362–63.

10. Ibid., 363.

11. Rabbi David Hartman, "The Politics of Resentment," speech at the conference "Memory, History and Myth," at the Shalom Hartman Institute, June 29, 1999.

12. Ibid.

13. Robert S. Wistrich, *Antisemitism: The Longest Hatred* (New York: Pantheon, 1991), xii.

14. Ismar Schorsch, *From Text to Context: The Turn to History in Modern Judaism* (Hanover and London: Brandeis University Press/University Press of New England, 1994), 376.

15. Ibid., 376.

16. Ibid., 377.

17. Ibid., 376–77.

18. *Tanakh,* 1761.

23

LAST DAYS IN ISRAEL

The Jerusalem air was no longer so captivating. It was late in the summer, the heat extreme, and it filled me with languor. By afternoon, like many Jerusalemites, I was driven indoors. In fact, I had become a shade-seeking creature, spotting cool and darkness wherever I went. I felt myself gearing down. There were moments when I wanted to shut out hot, struggling, foreign Israel.

When I arrived I felt as though every pore in my body opened to absorb this entirely new place. It was as if what was already formed in me had been put aside, releasing a tremendous energy. But gradually the formed part of me began to reassert itself. Part of my slowing down, I felt, was this need to integrate all that I had learned, chew it over like a cud.

All three others in my family, my husband and two sons, had joined me in the last two weeks. David arrived a week before the others, then Lou and Max.

I was eager to show David my apartment, neighborhood, and all the places I had discovered. We went to the theater and had Shabbat with friends. I often wondered how perplexing my project must have been to him. He is a man of strongly held views. Our sons and I had all moved in this new direction toward Israel, Judaism, and Jewish life. On his own, I don't think it would have been a path he would have chosen. I give him a lot of credit for being willing not only to wade in with us but to allow the experiences to embrace him as well. Even before coming to Israel, he often traipsed along with me to museums or lectures about Jewish life and would exclaim with me at how interesting it all was and how much he had learned.

When my sons arrived, they made a beeline for the bakery at the shuk that makes chocolate rugela and bought a bagful. I had never even noticed the shop. It was just as well; the rugela was not only chocolate, it was coated with butter when taken out of the oven. I saw right away that the Israel my sons had gotten to know was different than the one I experienced. They saw a faster, hipper Israel, filled with sounds of contemporary music and images of fashionable dress. They were more attuned to the young, sometimes macho culture that emanates from the potent presence of the military in Israeli life. And they were drawn more to the Old City, the Western Wall, and hard-line politics. Yet they spent a day together walking in the Palestinian neighborhood of Silwan, something that would no longer be possible with new Intifada. I saw this interest as very American or rather the America my husband and I gave them and were quite practiced at ourselves. Here were our sons reaching out to see the other side, a way of life different from their own.

In a way, their arrival took the wind out of my sails. I couldn't walk as fast as they and I felt silenced by their far more fluent Hebrew. They rattled on with the landlady, on the phone, and with shopkeepers. They got around with ease. Still, what an experience it was to be in Israel with them. They had been a big part of the impetus for my investigation into Jewishness.

One day my sons and I stood in front of Shalom Falafel on Bezalel, eating sandwiches from their favorite storefront stand. Traffic rushed by; construction workers pulled their trucks onto the sidewalk and shouted out their orders in rapid-fire Hebrew. As Lou said, it may not have been exactly what Theodor Herzl had in mind, but there we were, together in Jerusalem in the Jewish state. Each of us had gotten there following a different path. We had all struggled with Hebrew and now we were sharing something much more than a delicious falafel sandwich with each other. Individually and as a family, we had grown in our Jewishness.

At my last Hebrew class the teacher read a story. We were to explain it back to her in Hebrew. I strained to understand as I always did in that class. Then I sat back. I could feel myself letting go of this intense labor, no longer poised to write down every new word. I felt sad to be going. The class would not end for another month and the others would continue.

That beautiful evening sun came through the window of the classroom. It was oddly cool—perhaps a hint of fall was in the air. I felt a touch of regret that I did not get as fluent in Hebrew as I had wanted. Despite my work, the Israeli pace was daunting. Still, I loved learning Hebrew and I had the sense I would continue to study.

My next to the last day in Israel was a Friday. David had gone home the week before and Max that morning. Lou and I were left. We were a little at loose ends, not sure what the day would bring. So we rambled, he with his camera, me with my notebook.

We took the bus to Herzl Cemetery. It seemed fitting on the last day: Go back to the beginning, visit the grave of the founder. To our surprise the cemetery was closed. We were both disappointed. Then we saw people inside the gate. So we walked down the road along the fence of the cemetery and saw some religious boys coming out. They were picking their way over barbed wire that had been trampled down at this unobtrusive place. So we crawled in, as they had crawled out.

As we walked to Theodor Herzl's grave, an American tour group came through. "Remember, he had the vision for Jews to have their own homeland," the guide told them. The kids, high school age, were wearing an array of T-shirts—IDF "Israeli Defense Force," Maccabee beer, as well as Led Zeppelin and the Dave Matthews band. They looked exhausted.

A circle surrounded the large austere grave. To the side was a half-dome shading bleachers where tour groups sat to hear a capsule of Zionist history. Olive and pine trees surround the area. "National Site of the State of Israel and the Jewish People," it said at the grave, an interesting statement encapsulating for me that I am both part of this history and not part of it.

Standing there, I felt caught again in the force of Zionism, what an amazing feat it was and what a strange path it has had. Herzl's articulation of it was meteoric. In 1895, when he was thirty-five, he published *The Jewish State*. The First Zionist Congress was held in Basel, Switzerland, three years later. He died seven years after that. Zionism was born out of the battle for human and national rights. In Europe, the two struggles were assumed to proceed together with some congruence. But as the intersection of Herzl with the Dreyfus trial so graphically illustrated, the story of

Jews in Europe did not follow that path. Those who were different may have been granted citizenship but were viewed suspiciously when it came to being trusted and included in the nationalist fold. That was true in France and elsewhere in Europe, as Jews moved into the larger societies.

What an incredible twist it was for Jews that with modernity—increased opportunity, success, and visibility—antisemitism rose. It was an anti-progress, anti-Enlightenment idea to be sure, that when things began to go well, it could actually mean more danger. But such a consequence was familiar to the dark Jewish mind, which has a facile grasp of tragic contradiction. The question became, where was the land to grow this Jewish nationalism and, later, was life possible for Jews in Europe?

We walked along the graves of Israeli leaders and Zionist heroes and heroines: Chaim Herzog, Golda Meir, Levi Eshkol. At the simple grave of Yitzhak Rabin stones were in baskets and candles were all around. In the military section was the grave of Ze'ev Jabotinsky, the revisionist leader and those of paratroopers like the heroine Hannah Senesch, who was dropped into Germany in a rescue effort in World War II. Even the geography here points to the power and the triumph of the Zionist idea. Yad Vashem, the Israeli memorial and museum for the Holocaust, is down the hill, intentionally below this cemetery.

We walked to the part of the cemetery for Jewish soldiers from the city of Jerusalem. The graves, raised out of the ground, are many. Their dead are from all of the wars and they died young—fourteen, seventeen, twenty-five years old. Some had small boxes with candles in them on the side, potted evergreens or cactus or glass vases with flowers.

I walked along a path where I saw, at a lower level, a woman tending the grave of her son. Lovingly, she pulled weeds. Then she got water from a nearby spigot with her can and poured it on the plants. She was a large woman with dyed reddish-blonde hair and her fingernails were painted red. She picked away stray dead leaves. She filled jars with water and put in the white and pink carnations she brought. She flicked away leaves or twigs on the stony edge, cleaned as one would tidy up a kitchen table, readying it for her son to come for dinner. He was eighteen. He died in 1993 in Gaza.

A few graves down, a white-haired man was doing the same tidying. When he was done he sat down on the grave's edge and lit a cigarette. The woman leaned her arms on the grave's edge, as if she and the man were sitting across the table from each other for a conversation. But neither acknowledged each other's presence, so deep were they in thought.

She got up and found her broom, swept the stone ground around the grave, as though it was time to do the floors. She was in a reverie of work. They were the gestures of loving, grieving parents.

The graves go on and on. Some of the engraving is in Russian, perhaps the grave of a young man who had been a new arrival in Israel. I saw a poem left by a girlfriend. I felt the poignancy of loss for those visiting these graves, how their lives will always be shaped by these deaths. And I felt the ruthlessness of Zionism. The story of the Jewish state is not only the idealistic self-actualizing socialist one passed on to me by my mother. This state's arc of nationalism was late compared to other nations and it established itself in a hostile surround. And it is still on a collision course with another national story, the Palestinian one. Yet if the Jews who came here and made their stand had not had that single focus, that uncompromising stance, even the hubris and intoxication with power, there would be no Jewish state. It would not have come to be.

At the end of the day Lou and I went to the shuk. It was frenzied before Shabbat, people caught up in this riot of food. Off Agrippas Street boys were peddling baby chicks and Arab women selling figs and grape leaves. Young men carrying huge trays of steaming pita on their heads made their way through the crowds of people. "Pitot, pitot, pitot," yelled the sellers, like auctioneers.

I was caught up again in the exotic bustle of this market. Crates of eggs, thirty in each, were piled high, as were mounds of fruits, stacks of green onions, radishes, and celery. Soldiers stood by the entrance near a large ice cream freezer. Shoppers made their way around babies in carriages to the piles of tomatoes, buckets of flowers, vats of lush olives. You could also buy underwear, tablecloths, glassware, and shampoo.

"Shabbat Shalom! Shabbat Shalom!" someone yelled. It was almost time.

I wasn't interested in buying anything, only watching. How different than when I first came. Then, the market was visually intoxicating and intense with all its sensations and evocations of color, taste, and texture. I had thought I might buy some of everything in sight, even a large chunk of a giant coned-shaped mountain of paprika-looking spice. Now I was leaving. I felt saturated with place and food, an inner peace and security. It was an odd day too, cloudy and with an unusually a cool breeze, like September at home when summer is over.

My son and I walked home from shuk, past the now familiar alleyways through the neighborhood of Nachlaot. The people no longer seemed quaint as I had felt when I arrived. I could now imagine myself, as an old woman, being one of them.

At sunset, Lou went to the Western Wall as Shabbat was coming in. Later, I walked to meet him for dinner at the restaurant at the Cinemateque. On my way I passed the Great Synagogue. I knew to listen to the horn of Shabbat, this orchestration of community I had come to feel part of. The services were letting out.

Walking along the streets, I saw people through windows getting settled into their homes for Shabbat, flowers on the table. What I felt was what a complex society Israel is. Before I came, all I saw was the Israel I needed to fortify my sense of being a Jew. But this place has its own intricacy and mystery, its own dark side, blind spots, and growing pains; its own excitement, accomplishment, and many problems to solve. It is a place to delve into, try to understand, support, and enjoy but let be. I was at the margin and with minimal language. Much was truly foreign.

No, Israel was no longer the quaint place I had needed it to be. It has its musicians and criminals, tribalism and hi-tech companies, women's rights, multiculturalism, and new immigrants. It faces difficult problems— a shortage of water, a fragile ecology, increasing inequality among its citizens, and coming to peace with Palestinians. Some of its citizens support fundamentalism and others are part of leading the global economy. Many issues Israel struggles with—how to be part of and advance in modern society, and at the same time keep alive a sense of community, heritage, and identity—are the same ones America faces.

Modernity is not simply a matter of education and income, skills and acquisitions, mobility and choice. It is also about how we think about ourselves in the world, the history we allow in. My journey to Israel has been a process of updating and allowing myself to engage with Jewish life and its past. If I had let it lie fallow, it would have been lost to me as part of my history. And that would have been a loss indeed. I marvel at this people I was born into and the richness it brings my life.

Is there a more dramatic place than the terrace of the restaurant Cacao at the Cinemateque? I was out with my grown son on a beautiful night. We sat at a small table in the cool air. Before us was the outer wall of the Old City and the Silwan Valley below. Couples and friends talked quietly, drinking wine.

From there we walked to the courtyard of Beit Shmuel for a Rami Kleinstein concert. Rami and the piano. Shaved head, big smile, ears sticking out. Perhaps he compares himself to Billy Joel because at one point he

breaks into English with, "Sing us a song, Mr. Piano Man, we are all in the
mood for a melody. And you've got us feeling alright." What a Jerusalem
night. He sat at his raised platform, lit by spotlights flickering in the trees.
A couple hundred people sat all around; it had the intimacy of a nightclub,
only better. The people sitting in the row behind us knew all the words and
sang them out.

So we rambled through Herzl cemetery, the shuk, dinner, and concert.
We drank up Israel together, Lou and I. We spent Shabbat together. The
next day I left for the States.

In New York, I left El Al and went to Continental to get my flight home.
At the gate next to mine a celebration was underway. Sand was on the
ground, tables were covered with blue and white stripe cloths, and Israeli
flags and blue and white balloons floated about. I was momentarily puzzled
to see these suggestions of Israel again. This was a celebration of the inau-
gural flight to Tel Aviv. What sounded like a salsa band played, then klezmer,
and the food included fried rice and chicken. There is a leveling here; the
specificity of all ethnic groups are made kind of generic. The effect is a kind
of flattening. Employees came to share in the food and the prospect of new
business. In this instance, and many others, American ethnicity involves
commercialization. How simple it makes the matter of differences. Yet this
journey of mine had not been simple at all.

My husband and son greeted me at the airport. Then I was home—
the quiet streets, green trees, and dappled sun in the dark rooms of my
house. This place I live is warm and rich with my dishes, clay pots, and
people I love.

I was different now. The old dichotomies—Israel and us, religious and
not—once so important, had dissolved. I now had an appreciation of
Jewish history far beyond the Holocaust. Israel had a place in my Jewish
identity but it was by no means all. Israel will always have the age-old purposes it has served in the minds of Jews, but it is a foreign country, a different culture. Our relationship cannot be parasitic or surrogate. I felt
closer to Israel, with a more realistic view, and at the same time farther
apart. I have an appreciation of their enormous job in achieving peace and
multiculturalism.

Visiting Israel transformed me, yet outwardly I was the same. I did not
take up Orthodoxy, or find lost relatives or the perfect synagogue. But what
did happen was that Jewishness in me found room to breathe and to grow.
The fractured pieces came together; I felt whole. The passionate center

that is Judaism can now nurture me. It is important for me to preserve it and carry it on.

And now, there was another place I felt I had to go. It is one thing to explore issues of immigration, modernity, the diaspora, and the Holocaust from the Jewish perspective. But I would never get out from under the shadow of the Holocaust without experiencing the other side, without going to the place of the perpetrator. And so I set out for Berlin.

Part Three

G E R M A N Y

ENCOUNTERING GERMANY

I never expected to actually go to Germany voluntarily. Germans and Germany were closed off in a blank, silent space.

Still, I paid attention to its goings-on. Perhaps it was more like I had Germany perpetually on trial. Germany was to be watched—from a safe distance. And I was grateful for my distance. My greatest hope was that Germany would not stray, as it did twice in the last century, with catastrophic result.

Watching turned into a more intense vigil after unification in 1989. My fear was that Germany would fold back into its old skin, reconnect with its past, in a way it was not able to when it was divided. A reunited Germany gave me a queasy feeling.

I started following news more carefully: The strength of the German economy, Germany as the leader of a new integrated Europe. And most intriguingly, occasional glimmers of Jewish life: The death of Estrongo

Nachama in January 2000, the famous cantor of Berlin who survived Auschwitz because of his beautiful singing voice. Originally from Salonika, Greece, he wound up in Berlin after the War and stayed. His son Andreas Nechama became the elected head of the Berlin Jewish community, one emblem of its diversity.

But most astonishing to me was that Germany was repopulating with Jews. I had thought of it as poisoned barren ground. Why would any Jew live in Germany? My impulse was to condemn those who moved there. But I had to wonder, had the new post–Cold War climate changed so dramatically that Jews would find a home in this inhospitable place?

Still, I stayed away—distance and revulsion. Like many American Jews, a part of me still wondered whether it was OK to buy a Volkswagen. It was a kind of principle, or protest, to be repelled by anything German. I was frozen in the past.

Growing up, we had closed the door on German Jews as well. Looking back, it was classic "blame the victim." The air was filled with unhistorical questions: Why did they not see what was coming? Were they blinded by their unrequited love affair with Germany? And that most shrill condemnation: Why had they not resisted?

We felt lucky to be having our own more successful love affair with America. We were smug—before September 11, 2001—with our protected rights, and notions of pluralism. We were always telling ourselves that our experience was different, trying to reassure ourselves that what happened in Germany would never happen here. And we were so carefully schooled in keeping the vigil over our democracy and any outbreaks of antisemitism.

But what I felt toward German Jews was more complicated. Our success followed in their footsteps. We emulated them in our Reform Temple and we were bound up with them in this business of assimilation, of how a Jew goes about living in a wider culture.

I was afraid to look at the life they had. Our own assimilation, growing up, was laced with guilt and a sense of danger. The Holocaust was inexplicable. The only explanation had a theological cast. The assimilation of the German Jews was like the biblical exile from Israel—because of sin. Only now the sin that they committed was assimilating, straying from traditional Judaism. And it brought this grotesque punishment: obliteration. The Israeli Zionist view we heard growing up went even further: All diasporan Jews risked danger, not only those who had lived in Germany. The only safe place was Israel, so the conventional wisdom went.

Yet, ironically, it was in Israel that I was first jolted out of this view of Germany so stuck in the strong currents of my childhood. American Jews may still feel a prick of conscience about buying a German product, but in Israel, the bus or cab you ride in may be a Mercedes. Daimler Chrysler has a factory there. On my first trip to Israel in 1986, I remember being jarred by the many Germans students I saw everywhere. I wondered what on earth they were doing there. I have found out since that numerous inter-cultural understanding programs exist between Germany and Israel.

As early as the 1950s, Israel took a pragmatic approach and developed a relationship with Germany. Ben Gurion, speaking somehow for all Jewish people, hammered out a reparations agreement with Konrad Adenauer in 1953. The two countries established diplomatic relations in 1965. "It is doubtful whether bridges were ever built so quickly over so deep an abyss," writes Israeli historian Tom Segev.[1]

A total of $820 million was paid to Israel in German goods over twelve years. It helped to build Israel's infrastructure: the railways, the Haifa port, the electrical system, heavy equipment for agriculture and construction.

A predominant strain of Israeli society is European. The early immigrants were from the Russian Pale and Poland. Before the war, fifty thousand German Jews—called by the derogatory term "Yekkes"—made it to Palestine. By 1948, another hundred thousand Holocaust survivors came on illegal ships. More than a million Jews have gone to Israel from the former Soviet Union since the fall of communism.

"Israel is not in Europe, but it is of Europe," said history professor Dan Diner, who holds posts at University of Beersheva and Leipzig University. He added starkly, "Europe is a large Jewish cemetery." Now, he says, the third generation wants to know more about their European heritage. "In their ears are the sounds of their grandparents."[2]

Israelis see images of a Germany that show a heterogeneous society. Some Israelis are interested in getting closer to the younger generation of Germans. And they admire German products and want to pursue economic links, he said.

Diner says that Israelis deal with Germans with two attitudes. One is like a black and white documentary film; that is the history. The other is in color and it is the Germany of the present—soccer, cars, industrial and other capabilities. The two attitudes are parallel but utterly separate. The existence of the color does not diminish the potency of the black and white. Germany's history with Jews remains a vivid part of Israeli self-awareness.

Today, Israel, isolated in the Middle East, wants a relationship with Europe, and that means Germany, the leader of Europe. Israel needs it for markets for its growing technology industry. It is not the once heralded "German-Jewish symbiosis" but the perpetrator is now a partner.[3]

As I got further into my investigation of Jewish identity, I knew Germany was exactly the place for me to go. I had to stand on German soil as a Jew and see and feel what it was like. Jews there had grappled first with the major question still before us: How to be a Jew and be part of a larger society. I realized that the lives they led were hidden from me behind a screen of shame, blame, and fear. Yet in many respects we, American Jews, with our astonishing accomplishments in every facet of society, are their legacy.

When I announced I was going, friends asked me in disbelief: You are going there? Why would you go there? Is this a vacation, some kind of tourist destination? And they would shudder as if Germany would be the last place they would go. It seems to be one of the few remaining group condemnations—perhaps like "whitey"—that have not been politically corrected.

For all my education, I lived—was stuck—in certain simplistic polarities: Holocaust and Israel, darkness and light, destruction and salvation. Of course I had experienced none of this history directly. Yet perhaps what happened over there in the Holocaust mattered so much precisely because it was so alien to my Jewish experience in America, one of comfort and predictability.

So I set out to Berlin—at one time the heart of darkness. It had been that concentration of totalitarian, fascistic power, where right and wrong did not fade into grays. I was excited and scared. For the first couple of days, I felt as though my body resisted being there. I felt lifeless in this deeply alien land. How to breathe here, as a Jew?

If for most of my life, I had held Germany perpetually on trial, going there felt as though finally I had been called to a parole hearing, years after an unspeakable crime against beloved family members. What I saw was that life had gone on. The rehabilitation process, so we are told, has been carried out; the prisoner, the perpetrator had done all that he was expected to do. Immediately, what was apparent was the blatant normalcy—women in hip clothes, fancy shops, busy streets, and all the impressive rebuilding. Looking into the faces of Germans, I felt strangely at home. They were the faces of thousands of Americans of German descent—political leaders, business men, mothers, and farmers, what we think of as quintessentially American. So, too, on the streets of Berlin is the undeniable sense of a

Germany thriving, of German power, its strategic place in Europe, and of German industrial and technological competence.

How deflating, that life had not only dared to go on, but was going on rather well. Not that I didn't know this; I read the papers. I realized what a primitive level I was operating on, stuck, despite facts, in my own misperceptions, unaccountably at the same place, mired in the Holocaust.

Even that word "normal" gave me a twinge. Here, as I looked out on the streets I saw how we, Jews and Germans, victims and perpetrators, despite our being in such vastly different universes over this more than half a century, have been shackled together. We are forever playing leading roles in each other's histories, however tucked below the surface they may be.

For one, we have the same deep longing. We both keep asking the same question: Are we normal yet? I think of Israel in the swirls of yet another confrontation with Palestinians, a conflict that resonates so deep into the Jewish past. It is a pariah in the Middle East as Jews were once in Europe. No, for Jews, at least, it is not normal yet. And I think of Germany's increasing impatience recently with being reminded of its Nazi past. Are they normal yet? And I think of the high level of security surrounding Jewish institutions in Germany. Are Jews really threatened in Germany, or are Jews and Germans just that nervous around each other? Is the echo of the past still deafening?

NOTES

1. Tom Segev, *The Seventh Million: The Israelis and the Holocaust* (New York: Hill and Wang, 1993), 384.

2. Dan Diner, speaking at the conference, "Germany: from Perpetrator to Partner," King David Hotel, Jerusalem, June 21–22, 1999.

3. The title of a conference at the King David Hotel in Jerusalem, June 1999.

JEWISH IN GERMANY

Several rows in front of me, in a Berlin synagogue on Yom Kippur eve, a mother sat between her two daughters. During the long periods of standing, the girls, bored, leaned into their mother. The older one, with a long mane of striking red curly hair, looked about twelve. The mother put an arm around each and whispered to them. In this conservative synagogue, the women sat on one side, men on the other. Occasionally, the father came over and whispered to the mother, as if, stuck on the other side with the men, he was left out of this family togetherness.

How reminiscent this felt to me, this sweet intermingling of boredom and intimacy. How familiar were those scrubbed, well-turned-out children. I too had leaned into my mother at Yom Kippur services. But what I remember most was the prayer for the dead, when we stood for the six million.

And here I was in Rykestrasse synagogue in Berlin, the city from which the plan to murder the six million emanated. The family a few rows in front of me were from Russia, part of a wave of newcomers to Germany in the past decade. The synagogue was beautiful; four huge candelabras lit the altar, which was surrounded by an ornate arc of vivid blue, gold, and earth tone. I too found the service dull. But I was transfixed by something else: Simply breathing deeply there as a Jew, on German soil, in that place of private Jewish space. The old Gestapo headquarters was not far away.

This large red brick synagogue was set back from the street behind a building and large brick courtyard. It was not among the more than two hundred synagogues burned in Germany on Kristallnacht in 1938, spared because it was built too close to other houses where Nazi officers lived. During the war it was used for a horse stables and to store munitions. And during the Cold War, it was the only surviving synagogue in use for the tiny Jewish community of two hundred in East Berlin.

This is what it was like in Berlin. History bleeds through. I seemed to be unable to let events of the past, near or more distant, fall into history.

The synagogue was in Prenzlauer Berg, a working class neighborhood that was also home to the poets and artists under the German Democratic Republic. Since unification Prenzlauer Berg has been rapidly gentrifying. The narrow streets of rundown apartment buildings are side by side with those that have been redone and now have trendy shops and cafes at street level.

Today, this vibrant corner of Prenzlauer Berg is a bustle of activity in the astonishing rebirth of Jewish life. A newly constructed sukkah (temporary outdoor structure for Sukkot) was in the courtyard. Yeshiva students dashed about. They were part of the new *Beit Midrash*, the only yeshiva in Germany, which opened recently with fifteen students in the building across the courtyard. The students came from nine cities in Germany but were originally from Russia or other parts of the former Soviet Union. It is part of the Ronald S. Lauder Foundation's effort to revive Jewish learning in twelve countries in central and eastern Europe.

Before the war 170,000 Jews lived in Berlin, 500,000 in all of Germany. In 1946, 7,000 Jews emerged in Berlin, 12,000 in Germany. Lately, the number of Jews has surged. "The Jewish population is triple what it was ten years ago, making Germany the fastest growing Jewish community in the world other than Israel," estimated Joel Levy of the Lauder Foundation. Now 85,000 are registered with the official Jewish community. The actual number is between 100,000 and 130,000, 60 to 70 percent from the former Soviet Union.

Up the street from the synagogue was a charming circular corner of outdoor cafes: Pasternak, Kost.Bar, and Gordon's. Gefilte fish is on the menus as well as other Jewish and Russian foods. People relax outside in the October afternoon sun.

But history is never far away: Across the way was an old water tower. Under the Nazis, the basement was used as a place of torture. It was being converted to apartments.

Germans Jews were once an accomplished prosperous group, in the vanguard of early twentieth century science, medicine, business, and arts. I recalled an exhibit of photos of prominent German Jews I had seen at the Leo Baeck Institute in New York. They included Albert Einstein, James Franck, and Otto Stern in physics; Otto Heinrich Warburg and Otto Meyerhoff in physiology and medicine; Otto Wallach and Fritz Haber in chemistry; Max Liebermann, who put Berlin on the map in the art world. Thinking about that exhibit then on the street in Prenzlauer Berg, I had to wonder whether Germans have ever felt they lost something when they did away with their Jews.

It was in Germany that the break was made with traditional Orthodox Judaism and the Reform and Conservative streams were spawned. Those who fled before the Holocaust, some 250,000, scattered around the world. The legacy of German Jewry goes on in Israel, the United States, Canada, Argentina, and elsewhere.

Today, Berlin Jews present a diverse picture. A small number are elderly and only a few of these are German. Others came to Berlin from the DP (displaced persons) camps in Poland after the war, like Leo Kutner, seventy-nine, who survived the Lodz ghetto and Bergen-Belsen and then ran a jewelry store in Berlin. His son, he told me proudly, is a pilot for Lufthansa.

But the young are the majority, the new immigrants from the east, the highly educated offspring of the several million Jews who survived the war because Germany was defeated. Like the Chamilov family from the Caucasus, who emigrated a year ago and hope their two sons, nineteen and twenty-one, will enter German universities. Why Germany? Economic prospects are good and, unlike Israel, it is European, perceived to be safer and not so far from home. Also, it is difficult to emigrate to the United States.

And now that Berlin is a cosmopolitan capital at the center of the new Europe, an increasing number of young educated Jews may be drawn there. Like Richard Tarasofsky, thirty-eight, an environmental lawyer from Canada who wound up in Bonn for a job and then settled in Berlin; or a thirty-seven-year-old doctoral candidate in environmental policy, whose parents are German Jews who moved back to Berlin from the United

States when she was ten. Others too, feel this pull to Germany, despite the history. The father of Michael May, the executive director of the centralized Berlin Jewish community, fled to Palestine before the war and returned to Germany in the 1950s.

People drifted in throughout the Yom Kippur service and by the end the large first floor was full. Most wore secular dress but there were men with tzitzit (fringe), others with only talit and observant women with their heads covered. Some had prayer books in Russian and Hebrew, like the teenage girls down the pew from me. And others, like the two middle-aged Russian women on the other side of me, were simply listening to the service, which was in Hebrew and German. Near the end of the service I felt a warm comfort in this place with these people.

Yet the evening also had an uneasy quality to it. Coming in through the outside gate, the security check was meticulous. The German police not only scanned each person with a radar device, but private Israeli security searched bags and purses. It's routine for German police to patrol in front of all Jewish institutions. The Jewish community hired the private Israeli security firm.

Five days earlier, on German Unity Day, a Molotov cocktail was thrown into a synagogue in Düsseldorf and a swastika was scrawled at Buchenwald. A new nationalism is surging in Germany since unification. The strain that showed itself on Unity Day—hatred of foreigners and anyone different—is disconcerting. Many say it is a fringe phenomenon coming from a lost generation, mainly in the east, that glorifies Nazis. German officials showed great concern for the Jewish attacks: Chancellor Gerhard Schroeder visited the Düsseldorf synagogue; members of the Reichstag attended Shabbat service in Berlin to show their support.

And in Israel, the new conflagration with Palestinians broke out. Israel, which is to be the refuge for Jews, is now contributing to the wave of antisemitic incidents across Europe, hundreds in France. Some of these incidents are a result of sympathy with Palestinians. "We have our problems (in Germany), said Jewish Cultural Center head Irene Runge, without a trace of irony, "but nothing like what is going on in Israel."

Sitting there in the full synagogue, I wondered, would this burgeoning Jewish community and a nationalism that does not like foreigners someday collide? Or were times now different, Germany different?

What I sensed most in Berlin were the broken pieces, the shards of Jewish life: what was there before, what is now, what is dead, what is elsewhere. Berlin represents most accurately what I have felt as a Jew—this absence of wholeness.

Sachsenhausen concentration camp, just twelve miles outside the city, is a reminder of the anonymous victims of genocide.

Weissensee cemetery is where prominent Jewish Berliners—Jews with names—who lived before the Holocaust are buried: Rudolf Mosse, founder of the Mosse publishing house, and Hermann Tietz, founder of successful department store chains. Tietz bought KaDeWe, which was then "aryanized" by the Nazis. Now it is considered to be the largest department store in Europe. Natalie Baeck is also buried there, wife of Leo Baeck, the rabbi who led the Berlin Jewish community under the Nazis.

In Berlin, memory itself is a political issue. Who should remember, how to remember, where to remember, how long to remember hangs in the air: The controversial memorial to the six million Jewish victims of the Holocaust to be built near the Brandenburg Gate, at the center of the city, is just being constructed.

I think of the way Jews, once of Europe, are now scattered, some not knowing who they are. Sarah Aynor, who I met in Jerusalem, taught Hebrew in DP camps after the war to children preparing to go to Palestine. "Over the years, I have gotten many phone calls from people." she told me. "They say, I don't know who I am. I don't know where I am from. I don't know my parents' names. Maybe I have a brother." The calls were from people with breaks, disruptions, blank spaces in their identities.

Real Jewish life here, in the schools and synagogues, is surrounded by heavy security. And free speech, unlike in America, has limitations; Nazi paraphernalia, slogans, and symbols are against the law.

In 1986, Peter Sichrovsky, an Austrian Jew, wrote about the few Jews who wound up somehow on the scorched earth of Germany or Austria. He said they lived as though their suitcases were packed. Their biggest struggle was whether they, unlike those before the Holocaust, would be able to read the signs and know when to leave.

In the flurry following the synagogue attack on Unity Day, Paul Spiegel, the elected head of the Jewish community of Germany, said to the *International Herald Tribune*, "After such repeated attacks on synagogues one is justifiably entitled to ask whether it was right to rebuild Jewish communities in Germany."[1]

Yet Russians have poured in. Newly arrived immigrant Irene Chamilov said, yes, she worries about incidents like the attack on the synagogue in Düsseldorf, yet she feels America and Israel won't let anything happen to Jews in Germany.

Deidre Berger of the American Jewish Committee in Berlin says anti-semitic incidents have an echo in Germany they do not have elsewhere. Incidents are increasing, she said, but government officials are also paying attention. Yet she sees the incidents of violence against Jews a symptom of a larger problem: "Many Germans are not comfortable with people of other races and religions."

About nine million people living in Germany are considered non-German; three million of them are Turks, some third-generation. Attacks have been reported on Turks, Africans, ethnic Germans (Germans who lived for generations in Russia or Ukraine and are now recent immigrants), homeless, anyone who is or looks non-German. "It is a tenet of the right wing philosophy, the arrogance to make a judgment of others," Berger said.

Several months before the synagogue attack, in a terrorist bomb attack in Düsseldorf, ten recent immigrants from the former Soviet Union were wounded leaving a language class, seven of them Jews.

"Germans want the Jewish landmarks, they like the kitsch like klezmer, but they do not want Jews," Irene Runge, who heads the Jewish Cultural Center, told me in an interview.

And it has always been so. Jews in the early part of the century may have felt German, but Germans didn't feel one with Jews. Jews I talked to in Berlin were careful to point out that there never was a German-Jewish symbiosis. Michael May spoke of the "wrongly called symbiosis that co-defined a German Jewish culture. (Jews were seen as) a pollution of German culture," he told me.

The German Jewish symbiosis was an illusion, Berger said to me. "Germans did not accept it. German is based on German Christian blood."

"In Germany, it is them and us, it is not 'e pluribus unum,'" said the German doctoral student who lived for a time in the United States.

The term German Jew may have been a Jewish invention; for Germans it may have been only Jew. There isn't, now or before, anything like American style multiculturalism—African American, Irish American, Jewish American. In fact, it is rather new for us, this loosening of the cultural bonds to allow for these dual identities.

The situation in Germany before the Holocaust, from the 1870s to 1933, was perhaps more accurately a time of unparalleled opportunity for

Jews coupled with unparalleled antisemitism. The anti-Jewishness coming out of the Arab world today toward Israel and especially since September 11, 2001, has some resonance for me to that earlier time.

I was reminded of another exhibit at the Leo Baeck Institute in New York of Jews who had fought in the German military. It included those who fought to liberate Germany from Napoleon to those who served in World War I. What pathos this exhibit had, this display of Jewish loyalty and sacrifice to Germany, as if German Jews in America were still trying to prove themselves to an alien world.[2]

But loyalty went only one way. In 1916, rumors circulated that Jews were shirking military service. So the German army carried out a census. When it proved that Jews were serving their share, the army refused to release the results. Jews experienced a profound sense of betrayal.[3]

Jews were heady with emancipation but they were not accepted, as time went on, for many reasons and in many quarters. The situation was particularly hard to grasp as it defied the belief in reason and progress, so prevalent at the time.

The granting of citizenship to Jews did not overcome antisemitism then. So, too, the development of democracy in Germany now does not necessarily overcome an intolerance of those who are different.

Yet many Germans are horrified by the attacks. Jewish community director Michael May said he receives letters after such incidents, a recent handwritten one from a wine merchant expressing shame about what happened and offering to help in any way he could. He calls it a "mend the world" impulse. Runge too, said she had many phone calls that day, including one from a mother of a twelve-year-old girl also offering help.

"There is a kind of philosemitism in Germany," said Richard Tarasofsky in an interview. He is a Berlin lawyer who had family from Ukraine killed in the Holocaust. Klezmer may be heard several nights a week at the Hackescher Hof. And one can even learn the Jewish dances. Yet the infatuation with things Jewish has a ghostlike quality; the musicians, and likely most of those attending, are German. Berlin Jews I spoke with are uncomfortable with the German interest in klezmer: They find it odd to have their culture represented by Germans.

Tarasofsky said Germans do not have a normal view of Jews. For example, Germans tell him how upset they are seeing Israelis beat up Palestinians. "They like to see Jews as moral victims. In today's world, their sympathies are with the Palestinians," he said. Nor do Jews feel normal in

Germany. Tarasofsky said Jews would be mortified if some financial scandal were exposed involving someone from their community.

Jews are unknown to most Germans. Before Hitler, Jews were less than 1 percent of the German population. Now, even with the influx from the east, they comprise only one-tenth of 1 percent. I watched Germans looking at images of children at Purim, Shabbat, and wedding celebrations at a photo exhibit of Jewish life today at the New Synagogue. They looked as though they were seeing some strange aboriginal tribe.

But it seems Jews have put down some roots. "The days when Jews sat atop packed bags are over," said Charlotte Knobloch, chair of the Israelite Cultural Community in Munich. "And those bags will not be brought back out . . . Jews cannot allow themselves to be forced into a corner by antisemitic hooligans."[4]

British historian Bernard Wasserstein has made the dire prediction that within a few generations Jews will disappear as a significant part of life on the European continent. It will not be because of antisemitism but because of assimilation made possible by living in an open society.

Yet for those living in Germany, like Tarsofsky and Runge, the search is intense to find a Jewish life in Germany, in Europe, and in themselves. Grassroots groups like the Jewish Cultural Center and those with Hebrew names like Gesher and Mushulash have sprung up outside of the official Jewish community to explore questions of Jewish identity.

Gesher, which means bridge, explores the question of what it means to be Jewish now, in Germany and in Europe. Gesher is made up of people who ended up in Germany; their parents were out of the DP camps from Poland and Russia, or they are from Argentina, Hungary, Canada, or Scotland and wound up in Berlin. They held a conference called, "Towards a European Jewish Identity," which explored questions of comfort and collective identity.

Tarasofsky is involved with Mushulash (which means triangle in Hebrew), which sponsored an exhibition of Jewish artists that attracted wide attention. The group, he says, is a "vehicle for expression of a living Jewish culture. We want to remember the past but not get stuck in it," Tarasofsky told me. Mushulash has started a magazine called *Golem*, which deals with European Jewish identity from Lisbon to Minsk.

Not only are Russians arriving, young people will be increasingly attracted to Germany's thriving cities as the country prospers and takes on more leadership in Europe. Germany itself is looking to attract workers from around the globe skilled in high-tech jobs. And the second generation of Russians Jews will grow up firmly planted in German society. I wondered whether the tensions in German society would increase as it attracts a more diverse population. And how life will be for Jews, making a home in a country that historically has had little tolerance for diversity.

NOTES

1. Roger Cohen, "Germany's Subdued Fete: Synagogue Attack Mars Unification Anniversary," *International Herald Tribune,* Frankfort, October 4, 2000, 1–2.

2. Ismar Schorsch, *From Text to Context: The Turn to History in Modern Judaism* (Hanover and London: Brandeis University Press/University Press of New England, 1994), 371.

3. "Berlin Metropolis: Jews and the New Culture, 1890–1918," catalog, The Jewish Museum, New York, November 1999–April 2000, 12.

4. "Constitutional Office Cites Far-Right Threat after Series of Anti-Semitic Incidents," *Frankfurter Allemeine,* English edition, October 9, 2000, 1–2.

26

GERMANS TELL THEIR STORY

If I lived in the Jewish polarities of Holocaust and Israel, destruction and salvation, I also lived in that other narrative, that other way the world was organized: east and west. Berlin is the place—Checkpoint Charlie to be exact—where the twentieth century's gigantic ideologies of communism and capitalism, totalitarianism and democracy, faced off with each other.

The Checkpoint Charlie Museum celebrates everybody's freedom. A bust of Brezhnev out front has this cheeky inscription, "To honor the people who were persecuted by him." On display is the nonviolent revolution in Prague, Lech Walesa's Solidarity in Poland, and the overthrow of Ceausescu in Romania. There are photos of Gandhi's nonviolent resistance, the civil rights movement in the United States, a monk's self-immolation in Vietnam. There is a painting of Brezhnev and German Democratic Republic (GDR) head Eric Honnecker in a romantic kiss called: "The Fraternal Kiss: God Help Me to Survive This Deadly Love."

The museum is also filled with cars, gliders, and other contraptions East Germans used to flee to freedom, even though, ironically, when communism fell, East Germany, unlike the Czech Republic or Poland, had no revolution. It folded into the west when West German Chancellor Helmut Kohl bought it from Gorbachev for forty-one billion marks.

Way back, the east-west divide rippled into our lives too, as we were marched to the school basement for air raid drills and terror over the Cuban missile crisis. Today, we are told it is a fault line, mending. One Europe, and Germany is at the center. The Serbs bringing down Slobodan Milosovic surely will be another freedom revolution exhibited here.

Could it really be that all that is left of the communist behemoth are the burly Russians selling kitsch on the street nearby: German military hats and Russian fur ones, handcuffs and medals, tiny models of the Trabant, the car made in East Germany? You can even bargain for a piece of the wall, although a Berlin friend told me that enough pieces have been sold to go around the world twice. It is astonishing that all that ideology has become just another souvenir market.

Nearby is the new Berlin, Potsdamer Platz, once the barren wasteland where the wall made a gash through the middle of the city. It gleams now a monument to capitalism with the new headquarters buildings of Daimler Chrysler and Sony Europe.

What to make of Germany united, settled into its old boundaries and its old capital? I think again of an imagined parole hearing. Am I some kind of witness or judge to assess these sweeping matters: the strength of German democracy, how it has dealt with its past, its ability to lead Europe, the health of its nationalism, its tolerance for difference? Was I there to make this judgment: is Germany safe? I hardly felt up to such a daunting task. Yet I wanted to know the new Germany. I was drawn to places where Germans put together their past and presented it to the world.

The Reichstag was once a symbol of German defeat, made so in part by that famous photo of a Russian soldier hoisting a Soviet flag atop it in April 1945. Now hordes of people, German and foreign, were lined up in the cold rain to get a view of Berlin's citadel of democracy. The magnificent renovated dome has a photo display of its history. How better for Germans to reassure the world that they have made a moral recovery, that Germany is safe and they are normal, than to tout the strength of its democracy.

Here was a startling revelation: the Nazi period lasted a mere twelve years, from 1933 to 1945, tucked neatly into two hundred years of German history.

The display showed Hitler coming to power in January 1933. The Reichstag fire on February 27 and 28 that year was blamed on the communists. The rights of Jews were dissolved and the concentration camps established. Then suddenly, it was twelve years—and 50 million victims— later. "Germany is largely destroyed. Soviets claim victory." A mere twelve years toward developing democracy.

I was stunned. That was the same twelve years that exploded over us, defined us, changed us so that we will never be the same. Even the episodes of Jewish persecution in the centuries before the Holocaust—the expulsion from Spain, the pogroms in Russia, the Dreyfus affair—seem to have taken on new, more potent meaning because of those twelve years. In much the same way, since September 11, 2001, the anti-American and anti-Jewish attitudes of the Arab world stand out to us in a new bold relief.

For me German equaled Nazi: Nothing came before or after. Nazi blotted out all else. All that existed of German history was what led to it and what flowed from it. Potsdam was where world leaders divided up Europe. Nuremberg was synonymous with the trials, Munich with appeasement, and Wannsee, not a lakeside villa outside of Berlin, but where the Final Solution was put into motion in 1942.

Walking down the streets I had to concede there was much more to German history; the Hohenzollerns and their fabulous homes in Potsdam, the main boulevard of Friedrichstrasse named for Frederick the Great, the beautiful baroque buildings.

The Reichstag exhibit seemed to make short shrift indeed of Germany's damage. Germany has had a long catastrophic history governing itself and finding its place in Europe. But many now applaud its development of democracy. "A stable democratic order has been established; a different political culture has taken root. The very mentality of its citizens has been changed. . . . The nationalistic sense of German superiority has been overcome," wrote Princeton historian Fritz Stern.[1]

"The Federal Republic remains a solid workaday democracy," says Harvard historian Charles Maier.[2]

Even historian Daniel J. Goldhagen, a sharp critic of Germany's historic antisemitism, lauds the development of democracy over the past fifty years and the teaching of new beliefs and values. Germany has transformed itself culturally and politically and antisemitism has declined, he said.[3]

The German Bundestag has an exhibit called "Questions of German Democracy" in the Deutscher Dom on Gendarmenmarkt Square that showed the development of democratic government in Germany. Here the same twelve years were portrayed again as unfortunate indeed but a step along the road to Germany's struggle for democracy.

The exhibit showed how Hitler came to power legally. "The most criminal regime in history ruled Germany," it said. Yet it eliminated unemployment and made "breakthroughs" in foreign policy. It also was repressive and resistance was weak. Jews were demonized but annihilation followed no plan. The German cities of Cologne and Dresden were left in ruins.

The exhibit was worthwhile and educational but Nazism it seemed, happened to them, too, not by them. First on a list of victims of World War II in the exhibit are the 5.2 million Germans, along with five (not the commonly accepted six) million Jews, 20.6 million Soviets, 4.5 million Poles. They, this exhibit seemed to say, were victims of Nazism too, bystanders to their own perpetration. As they tell their story, they too were liberated from the Nazis. Is this an attempt to be part of the late-twentieth-century attitude that says, if you go deep enough inside every perpetrator, you find a victim?

Since the wall came down, says writer Jane Kramer, Germany has negotiated for a new past, the past of Helmut Kohl. This is the Germany that Hitler seized in 1933 and occupied for twelve dark years, the Germany that was liberated in 1945 as if it were Holland or a concentration camp."[4]

Germany, divided and held hostage to the cold war, was in a hiatus from its own history, Kramer contends. The Nazi past was subsumed by the Cold War: Each side could blame the other. The west saw the war as a terrible place where fathers and sons went to a place called the Russian front and fought communism. "The East Germans thought the war was a capitalist adventure and the East Germans were the liberators."

The east-west divide has collapsed. Unification not only knit the two sides together, it folded them into a common past. "Germans want their past to have happened to them. They want to have suffered from themselves, the way everybody else suffered from them," writes Kramer.[5]

How blurred the lines can become between victims and perpetrators. In the exhibit, the causes of the war were shown to be the Depression and unemployment, the punitive reparations of the Treaty of Versailles, the threat of communism. This is the story I learned in the '60s. But I saw no explanation of how they got from these difficulties to genocide. For that you must look at only a small portion of Raul Hilberg's work. It details how every crevice of German life was drawn into the machinery of death; flag manufacturers also turned out bales of yellow stars. Hilberg banishes the passive voice. He locates individual responsibility. Someone, many someones, did this. Goldhagen estimates a hundred thousand but perhaps as high as five hundred thousand people were involved in the machinery of death. The perpetrators were people, ordinary Germans who lived, breathed, acted, and were responsible.

Even the Topography of Terror, a photo exhibit of the workings of the Gestapo, on its old grounds, to my eye presented a G-rated version of the Holocaust, "Holocaust lite." Sure, people were shown being shot but they have coats on, their heads have not been shaved. There were no masses of starving naked people with bare heads, no piles of skeletons. You do not see the horror, the full consequences of German action in these portrayals. Indeed, if you want to learn the details of what happened in the Holocaust, look to the Holocaust Museum in Washington, Yad Vashem in Jerusalem, or even TV's History Channel.

I had always assumed that at the very least some parity existed between victim and perpetrator—that we each had an equally difficult, if entirely different, time coming to grips with the overwhelming experience of what happened. For the Germans, I had thought, the experience was something along the line of what Rabbi Leo Baeck answered when he was asked at the end of the war—will you ever forgive the Germans? "I forgive the Germans?" he said, "It is for the Germans to forgive themselves."[6]

Now I don't think there was ever such parity. Each has had to grapple with vastly different stories. The inclination of the perpetrators is perhaps to flee the damage they have done, assuage their own considerable wounds, and go on. Perhaps they do not even see it as their job to remember and memorialize, except as others wish them to. Perhaps it is human nature to be far less willing to own the history of the damage we do. Hurt, damage, and loss imprint victims far more indelibly. Victims cannot escape remembering.

Yet I found places in Berlin, sometimes quite by accident, where Germans publicly recognize what happened, take responsibility, and remember. And I was deeply moved by them. I realized I had come to Berlin, in part, to stand in front of such places as a way of resolving my own feelings about the Holocaust. As one comes out of the subway at the Wittenbergplatz in bustling West Berlin there is a simple wooden sign listing the names of twelve concentration and extermination camps. I rushed up to a German woman and asked her to translate the words below the sign for me exactly. "Let us not forget the terror." She looked at me a little puzzled as I thanked her profusely, for the words, as much as the translation.

The German Museum of Technology in Berlin, a testament to German invention and mastery of the physical universe, has publicly taken responsibility too. Amid the tool and die, sewing machine, computers, and clocks are nineteen trains from 1918—"the end of the monarchy"—to the high-speed train of 1982. The year 1943 is a wood slatted transport car with this explanation: "The darkest hour in the history of the German railways is the collaboration of the Reichsbahn in the systematic murder of European Jews in the Second World War."

The Reichsbahn carried a total of three million people to the camps. "All documents between the railroad and the police in relation to this topic were carefully destroyed before the end of the war," the display said. I stood there a long time engulfed in the poignancy of this simple acknowledgement. The trains were a key element of the extermination; they got people out of cities to the crematoria. Raul Hilberg wrote a paper called "The Role of the German Railroads in the Destruction of the Jews" as part of his general thesis showing how all the German bureaucracies were drawn into the machinery of death. How survivors are filled with images of trains; Aharon Appelfeld writes about them and Yehuda Poliker sings about the Treblinka Station. Trains from all angles move in and out of Claude Lanzmann's film *Shoah*, punctuating conversations with Polish farmers around Auschwitz, Sobibor, and Treblinka about what they saw. "The train encircles the film, emerging as if from a tunnel, again and again, to mark the end of the Jewish people in Europe."[7]

Primo Levi wrote, "Almost always, at the beginning of the memory sequence, stands the train, which marked the departure toward the unknown, not only for chronological reasons but also for the gratuitous cruelty with which those (otherwise innocuous) convoys of ordinary freight cars were employed for an extraordinary purpose."[8]

And there was this apology.

Germany is now impatient with what some have said feels like being held hostage to the Nazi past. In the late '80s a controversy developed among German historians; could the Holocaust be compared with other atrocities such as Stalinist terror? If the Nazi genocide is but one specimen, "then Germany can still aspire to reclaim a national acceptance that no one denies to perpetrators of other massacres such as Soviet Russia."[9]

Others do not agree and hold the Nazi experience singular. "How understandable the wish of so many Germans to be liberated of the burden of the past, to "relativize" Nazi crimes, to seek a retrospective moral equality," writes Princeton professor Fritz Stern. "How understandable, and probably how unattainable."[10]

That controversy is likely to be debated for some time.

NOTES

1. Fritz Stern, *Einstein's German World* (Princeton, N.J.: Princeton University Press, 1999), 297.

2. Charles Maier, *The Unmasterable Past: History, Holocaust and German National Identity* (Cambridge, Mass.: Harvard University Press, 1988,), 2.

3. Daniel Jonah Goldhagen, speaking at Kent State University, April 21, 1998.

4. Jane Kramer, *The Politics of Memory: Looking for Germany in the New Germany* (New York: Random House, 1996), 257.

5. Ibid., 108.

6. Leonard Baker, *Days of Sorrow and Pain: Leo Baeck and the Berlin Jews* (New York: Macmillan, 1978), 324.

7. Raul Hilberg, *The Politics of Memory: The Journey of a Holocaust Historian* (Chicago: Ivan R. Dee, 1996), 40.

8. Primo Levi, *The Drowned and the Saved* (New York: Summit Books, 1988), 107–8.

9. Maier, *The Unmasterable Past*, 1.

10. Stern, *Einstein's German World*, 269.

GERMAN JEWISH CONTRIBUTION

The ornate blue and gold onion dome of the New Synagogue on Oranienburger Strasse stands high above surrounding buildings. It is in Mitte, an old Jewish neighborhood that has a new importance since unification when the center of the city moved east. Renovation of the synagogue began in 1988 under the GDR and was completed in 1995. The building houses an exhibit of Berlin Jewish life before the Holocaust. It is not a functioning synagogue because the main sanctuary was not rebuilt after bombs destroyed it.

But when this grand synagogue was originally built, it reflected the stature of Berlin Jews. Since gaining citizenship in the early part of the nineteenth century, German Jews rose rapidly. Completed in 1866 with a 3,200-seat sanctuary, the building expressed the mindset of German Jews at the time, their "confidence in the durability of emancipation and their pride in their religious distinctiveness."[1]

But even at the time, there were Germans who criticized the new edifice. Its grandeur was seen negatively, an expression of the rising power of German Jews. Synagogues constructed at the end of the century, as antisemitism rose, were far more modest. Its style too was seen as alien. The architecture, like the Jews themselves, did not blend in. The style was not German. It was Moorish, reflecting the admiration the Jews of Germany had for the Jews of Spain before the expulsion.

In Germany, Judaism broke with Orthodoxy. A long period of intellectual ferment preceded it. For a century, Europe had been transformed by the Enlightenment's ideas of reason and progress and the deep religious and cultural changes brought about by the separation of church and state. Jews had their own response to this ferment. The German *haskalah* was the Jewish version of the Enlightenment. It produced the intellectual figure of Moses Mendelssohn. And it brought about a break with the closed world of Ashkenazic Judaism, with its separate education and exclusive reliance on rabbinic authority and Talmudic law.

Jews were in search of a usable past.[2] The inspiration they found was Spain. What the German Jews saw in the life of twelfth-century Spanish Jews was a cultural openness, philosophic thinking, and an appreciation of the aesthetic. "The romance with Spain offers yet another perspective on the degree to which German Jewry distanced itself from its East European origins."[3]

So, too, it was the Sephardic Jews of Amsterdam, London, and Bordeaux who led the campaign for citizenship. They were also more privileged, prosperous, and assimilated.[4]

The synagogue escaped Kristallnacht because the head of the district police, Wilhelm Krutzfeld, did something extraordinary—he drew his pistol on the arsonists and called the fire brigade. "Nearly everywhere the fire brigade was not allowed to intervene," the exhibit says. Most of Berlin's synagogues fell. Krutzfeld was called to the chief of police next day and was not punished. He retired soon after.

The synagogue was used again for worship but was soon confiscated by the Wehrmacht for a leather and textile warehouse. In November 1943 it was severely damaged by a bomb and in 1958 the ruins of the main synagogue were cleared.

Rubble and falling-down buildings are nearby, side by side with renovation. There is a sense of an alive Jewish community in the area of Oranienburger Strasse—a high school, a gallery for artists from the former Soviet Union, a Jewish book store, the Jewish Cultural Center around the corner, the popular Oren Café, which is Israeli.

Again, I felt I was bumping up against layers of history that would not fold into the past. It was not only this sense of obliteration that traces back to Germany, but fundamental questions about Jewish identity that were wrestled with here. Questions of assimilation and extinction, separateness and integration, religion and secularity are also relevant today.

Across the street from the synagogue at Tucholskystrasse 9 is a newly renovated building with a white façade and Star of David above the door. It is the current offices, under heavy security, of the Central Council of Jews in Germany, the official central Jewish body. But it was once the home of what historian and dean of the Jewish Theological Seminary of America Ismar Schorsch has called, "the most important legacy of German Jewry," Wissenschaft des Judentums or the College for the Science of Judaism.

The movement to bring a historical consciousness to Judaism was begun by Leopold Zunz in early part of the nineteenth century. It was a response to the rapid transformation Jews and Judaism were undergoing at the time. Jews left the ghettos and entered schools and occupations of mainstream secular society. Well-equipped with the strong Jewish value of learning, they were able to enter German universities far beyond their proportion in the population.

The question that occupied Zunz was how would Judaism, which had been closed to the outside world, adapt and stay in the lives of those moving rapidly toward secularity. What Zunz envisioned was Judaism as "a vibrant religious culture responding creatively to the dilemmas posed by each new age."[5]

Zunz had several purposes. One was to wrest the study of Jewish history away from Christian scholars. He wanted Jewish scholars to tell the Jewish story. His innovation was to apply the modern research techniques of university scholarship to the study of Jewish history. What Zunz put forth was a new way of thinking about Judaism. He put Jewish text in a historic context.[6] It was the modern notion of using the past as a way of understanding the present. "One way of understanding Wissenschaft Des Judentums is as a collective act of translation, a sustained effort to cast the history, literature and institutions of Judaism in western categories."[7]

The movement laid the intellectual groundwork for Conservative and Reform Judaism with the synagogue as the centerpiece. Within a generation rabbis were university (rather than yeshiva) trained.

The college, established in 1872, moved to the building at Tucholskystrasse 9 in 1907 and became a seminary for rabbis and teachers. Rabbi

Leo Baeck and philosopher Martin Buber taught there; Solomon Schechter, one of the founders of Conservative Judaism and writer and teacher Abraham Joshua Heschel were students. Ransacked on Kristallnacht and closed for good in July 1942, it was the last place in Germany that Jews could attend college.

The lives of German Jews have been painted with the broad, sometimes disdainful brushstroke of assimilation. To peer into their lives there was to find a far more complex picture. The effort of Zunz and others was to rescue Judaism and those in flight from it. The Jewish rush into modern life dealt a serious blow to piety, ritual, and community, that is, to what bound Jews to God and to each other. These scholars took on the ambitious task of recasting Judaism for the modern world. "They created a historical consciousness that could serve as a base for a voluntaristic and secular Jewish community."[8] The Jewish story was to be the new glue to bind people together. History itself was to be the vehicle for continuity.

The German Jews' struggle is even more relevant today as modern life has proceeded to globalization and raised questions about how this identity is to be fostered and passed on, or kept alive at all.

Yet this new academic discipline founded in Germany never gained university acceptance there. It did reach full fruition and acceptance in the United States. In 1930, Salo W. Baron became the chair of Jewish history at Columbia University, the first at a secular university in the western world.[9]

A confluence of forces in the 1960s brought about a rapid growth of Jewish studies—the flowering of black and women's studies, the growth in religion departments, as well as a generation of scholars, most of whom were Jewish, with an avid interest in the subject. Jewish studies courses are offered now at more than five hundred colleges and universities in the United States. My son Max's exposure to Jewish history in college anchored him as a Jew—classes not only about the Holocaust, but also American Jewish life and the history of Israel.

The German Jews studied the history of Judaism for one reason: To bridge the quake made by the encounter with modernity. I have studied it for a different one—to make sense of the staggering and overwhelming events of the past in order to open up this rich cultural and spiritual legacy.

Standing there, I thought of the historians I have engaged with: Salo Baron on Russian Jews, Peter Gay on Germany, Paula Hyman on French Jewry, Robert Wistrich on antisemitism, Jacob Katz on Jewish emancipation, Raul Hilberg and Yehuda Bauer on the Holocaust, Arnold Eisen on Jewish homelessness and homecoming, Tom Segev on Israel, and many more. I saw this army of new Jewish historians as a kind of Marshall Plan. Perhaps it was never intended to be so but I saw them as a massive effort to rebuild Jewish identity from out of the vast and uncomfortable blank space left by the Holocaust. Through them, I have tried to understand what happened and how it happened, what the causes and context were. History is a way to wrap words around experiences and to give voice and dignity to those who died.

NOTES

1. Ismar Schorsch, *From Text to Context: The Turn to History in Modern Judaism* (Hanover and London: Brandeis University Press/University Press of New England, 1994), 79.

2. Ibid., 246.

3. Ibid., 71.

4. Ibid., 75.

5. Ibid., 247.

6. Ibid., 152.

7. Ibid., 154.

8. Ibid., 198.

9. Yosef Haim Yerushalmi, *Zakhor: Jewish History and Jewish Memory* (Seattle and London: University of Washington Press, 1982), 81.

THE JEWISH MUSEUM

Museums tell stories and often they are narratives the wider culture wants told. The Holocaust Museum in Washington tells an American story—What happened when human rights were not safeguarded. Yad Vashem in Jerusalem tells another story—the bitterly instructive Israeli tale of what happened to Jews in the diaspora without the power of a state to defend them.

The Jewish Museum in Berlin is a German Jewish story: It accomplishes a seemingly impossible architectural task—capturing the void left by the German elimination of Jewish life from its midst. The museum investigates the intertwining of two peoples and how one was first marked, then disentangled, extricated, severed, and exterminated.

The Berlin museum is not to be about the Holocaust. It is about the one thousand years of Jewish life in Germany. Still, the Holocaust hovers in Daniel Libeskind's architectural form and fills the air with what happened here like an eerie, almost sacred mist.

Aharon Appelfeld once said, "The tragedy of the Holocaust is epitomized by, among other things, our inability to grasp its enormity."[1] This building comes as close as anything I have experienced. It evokes the loss, the emptiness, and the fractures left behind.

Libeskind, a renowned reconstructivist architect, is an American whose design was selected recently for the September 11, 2001, memorial in New York. Born in 1946, he is a child of Polish Holocaust survivors. He calls the museum's seven spaces voids. "How to give voice to an absent Jewish culture without attempting to speak for it? How to bridge an open wound without mending it?" he said of his architectural task.[2]

The building is experientially disorienting. The floor is at a slant, giving a sense you are losing your bearings. The walls are at odd angles; the windows are jagged lines making for slits of light.

The intellectual, rational processes that normally mediate experience are bypassed. The experience of standing in this oblique space tampers with your sense of balance and equilibrium. I felt slightly sickened by the disorientation. I was not to see but feel how the life of German Jews came to an end. Libeskind is a sophisticated architect, taking us out of the spatial dimensions we are accustomed to, reminding us sharply that this happened in the heart of European civilization.

The building, with its odd shape and jagged slits on the outside, does not blend with its surroundings: It stands as a kind of island in the Kreuzberg neighborhood, modern and difficult to discern. It is not defiant as much as simply different, as Jews were in Germany, despite how hard they tried to fit in.

Libeskind told one writer who interviewed him that certain angles were determined by stretching a Star of David. Other angles and the lengths of windows were based on connecting the street addresses of Jews and non-Jews in pre-Holocaust Berlin. It is interesting to know these things, but not essential to one's appreciation of the building.

When you enter, you first pass through, once again, that vigilant security. Then, three paths open up before you. One leads up a staircase three flights, to where the exhibition spaces are on the upper floors. On the way up, I stopped at a window, strangely in the shape of a cross, barely at eye level. The stairway climbs on to the dead end, going, it seemed, nowhere, capturing a "no exit," trapped sensation. The light comes through the slits in the ceiling. Here I felt, oddly, in safety of a museum, the legacy of vulnerability passed on to me.

Another path leads to the Holocaust void. It is a narrow high space with the raw concrete walls converging at strange angles. Once inside, the door closes. Through some holes in the wall, I heard sound from the outside street. But I had the sense I was completely removed from it. The sound is near, but I was no longer part of it. I caught a glimmer of the extrication, what Holocaust writer Daniel J. Goldhagen called "socially dead." I felt a need to beat back a rising terror in this void.

The third path goes to the Garden of Exile and Emigration. It is paved in Belgian cobblestone pitched at a slight angle, again making for a sense of being thrown off center. The symbolism is simple and literal. The garden has forty-nine columns, in seven rows of seven, each twenty-three feet high. Willow oaks, whose leaves resemble olive trees in Israel, are planted in the top of each and in time the branches will thicken and form a canopy. Forty-eight of the columns represent the year Israel was founded, and the soil contained in them is from Berlin. The central column holds soil from Israel and stands for Berlin.

So there it was—the paradigm of my generation, the binding of the Holocaust and Israel, destruction and redemption, I thought standing in that garden. I felt a note of quiet triumph among those pillars, especially the forty-ninth with the soil of Israel coming back to Germany, standing tall.

Leaving, I glanced at the book where visitors signed their names. They were from all over—Japan, Italy, Germany, Turkey, Norway, Korea, and Australia. My eye caught one in Hebrew, a woman from Tel Aviv. Something about seeing that name written in Hebrew letters filled my eyes with tears. "Never ever will I forget my trip through—thank you Libeskind for your creation," it said.

All of this loss and the survival too. I also wrote my name and message of thanks in Hebrew, proud I could make the letters and immensely glad I could slip into what Israel had fortified me with, a skin, a bulwark of Jewish survival. Signing my name in Hebrew gave me a sense of healing and wholeness. For all of Israel's difficulties, it is a life source. It is why we cling to it as to life itself.

I thought of all of the new knowledge and experience I had gained during my investigation. What I did not anticipate was that there would be loss as well, that this journey would also involve giving something up. But that was exactly what happened. A certain mindset I had lived with all my life lifted. The Holocaust's heritage was no longer my burden.

I am done, I thought, after signing my name, done with this search. I had reached the end. This museum was transforming. It connected me to some loss or void that had lived inside. For so long I had been shackled to these dead. I will never forget them, but I am among the living. I needed to let go of the Holocaust and its binding, overly defining connection to Jewish persecution.

I saw, suddenly, that my imagined parole hearing was not to consider anything about Germany and its big questions—whether it was time to be released from its Nazi past, whether it was safe in its old boundaries and old capital, and in its new nationalism. I was not a judge, a witness, or even a victim. I was there for me, for my own release. What a startling revelation; I was the one to be set free. I was here to breathe freely as a Jew on German soil.

I caught a glimpse of what was fast becoming the outer edge of my generation. I thought of the daughters, one with the long mane of red hair, at Rykestrasse synagogue on Yom Kippur leaning into their mother. Jewish life is not vanishing here. I thought of my own sons' questions on the beach at Netanya. What are the particulars, they wanted to know. Where is our Judaism, not the tense one in a cramped crouched vigil, but the one that lives and breathes? That is the new generation. They are all reaching for a Jewish existence that is about something more than what I was shackled to. They will have their own struggles, to be sure—new threats are already before them—but they will be different from mine. They will not carry the burdens of the Holocaust in the way my generation did.

I came to Germany and entered the dark space of the past. I saw the new Germany and its new Jewish community. I puzzled over how Germany has put together its story. And I connected to an important Jewish heritage hidden from me by the Holocaust. But mostly I saw the layers of history that would not fall into the past. It was time to let them.

NOTES

1. Aharon Appelfeld, "Buried Homeland," *The New Yorker,* November 23, 1998, 56.

2. James E. Young, *At Memory's Edge: After-Images of the Holocaust in Contemporary Art and Architecture* (New Haven, Ct.: Yale University Press, 2000), 164.

Part Four

HOME

ANTISEMITISM

Contrary to liberal expectations, antisemitism has proved
to be the most durable ideology of the twentieth century.

—Ruth R. Wisse, professor of English and Yiddish Literature at Harvard

A number of years ago, I would have this perplexing conversation with a journalist friend. When a Jewish cemetery would be desecrated or swastika graffiti painted on a synagogue, she would be dismissive. She saw such acts as ticks in America's rollicking, background noise. It was part of living in a multicultural society and, perhaps more importantly, part of the price we pay for our hallowed freedom of speech. Not to worry, she would say, the vandals would be dealt with through the justice system.

But I could never be dismissive. I would dwell on such events. Were they really just disagreeable background noise? Or did it mean we were in the foothills of a new and potentially overwhelming assault on Jews? I seemed to be always in wait for cataclysm, for antisemitism to become out of control and for a holocaust to rise again.

I didn't seem to have the proper mechanism to evaluate the threat. The question went directly to the dark recesses of my Jewish mind. Was I over-reacting or did I have a finely tuned early warning system? I simply could not tell when a swastika was just a swastika and when it had the power to ignite and do damage. She, on the other hand, was grounded in Christian America. Was she a better or worse judge than me?

More recently, that is, since the second Intifada, I have come to realize that I have the same difficulty evaluating Israel's actions toward Palestinians. First, I don't live in that hostile neighborhood, so it is hard for me to say if Israel is overly aggressive or simply acting like a state. And there is the more personal Jewish question: How to disentangle Israeli aggressiveness from Jewish vulnerability? On the one hand, Israel is among the strongest mil-itarily and economically in the Middle East. "On the other hand," wrote Israeli writer David Grossman, "Israel is also a surprisingly fragile country, profoundly almost tragically unsure of itself, of its own ability to survive, of the possibility of a future for itself in this region. These two characteristics are on prominent display right now—Israel is today a clenched fist, but also a hand whose fingers are spread wide in despair."[1]

But I am getting ahead of myself. Before this second Intifada, in the days of hope for peace, I spent four days at a conference on antisemitism at Hebrew University in Jerusalem.[2] I had been keen to get this global pic-ture from the experts. I thought it would help me discern more accurately what was dangerous antisemitism and what was not. On the last day Hebrew University's Yehuda Bauer, a slight, soft-spoken man, considered an elder statesman among Holocaust scholars, called the conference, with a touch of humor, an exercise in "constructive masochism, three days of lis-tening to what they don't like about Jews." There was plenty for the para-noid mind, in fact, after some thirty-eight papers more than enough for those not paranoid to feel paranoid about. Sitting there took fortitude. Scholars presented papers on antisemitism in Poland after the war, East Germany under the GDR, postwar France, present-day Hungary. I heard about antisemitism in the Catholic Church, among Protestants, on the Internet, at the United Nations, and the continued proliferation of the Russian forgery called *Protocols of the Elders of Zion*—especially in the Arab world—that one-hundred-year-old antisemitic diatribe.

I was struck again by this mysterious Jewish paradox: power and vul-nerability. What kind of a people is it anyway, that first has this amazing force of scholars. In the United States alone Jews now hold 20.7 percent of positions at American universities. And this same people find it necessary to devote this considerable brainpower to the study of those who plot its extinction. What a stunning reversal of that cabal of international conspiracy Jews have so frequently been accused of.

At the time I attended the antisemitism conference I found it ironic that it was held in Israel. Israel has fought five wars, has since become embroiled in a second Intifada, and does not yet have its boundaries firmly drawn, but antisemitism, as I had thought of it, was a diaspora worry. It was part of the burden of living in a diverse culture with deep roots in European Christendom where a Louis Farrakhan can rant about that "gutter religion" Judaism.

Zionists told us that two thousand years of Jewish powerlessness and vulnerability in the diaspora ended with the Holocaust. The advent of the Jewish state with its ability to defend itself was to make it normal like all others. But how normal is Israel? The Intifada rages and Cairo intellectuals—as well as New Jersey poet laureate Amiri Baraka (formerly Leroi Jones)—claimed Israel knew of the September 11, 2001, World Trade Center bombing in advance and told 4,000 Israeli workers to stay home.[3] The negative image of Jews in Arab textbooks was a subject at this conference. Israel and the diaspora have come much closer together. Israel may have disowned the diasporan history of persecution, but some altered form of that narrative has intruded itself into the new surround.

Some say that Israel is now a pariah state, as Jews were once the pariahs of Europe. Since 1967, despite its military triumph and power, Israel has lived with a sense of isolation and insecurity, with an "ideology of survival."[4] History did not so much begin anew with Israel as continue, in certain respects, in the same vein. Israel is seen by many in the Arab Muslim world as the cultural, political and religious foreigner in the Middle East in much the same way as Jews were seen in Christian Europe.

In one sense this think tank is yet another piece of the massive defense or security apparatus Jews have erected. The American Jewish Committee could be seen this way, as could the World Jewish Congress, the Simon Wiesenthal Center, and the Anti-Defamation League. So could the Israeli Defense Force and perhaps even the new separation fence between Israelis and Palestinians. Each group battles for Jewish survival, the fence by being there, the IDF with weapons, the others with words in the forums of public opinion and politics. It is a fine line where exactly defense melds into offense.

For many in the United States and elsewhere, vigilance is the primary posture of how to be a Jew. As I have said, that silent guarded posture is well formed in me. Unlike my journalist friend, I can always react, even overreact to Jewish vulnerability. That warning system is part of my mental construct.

Some months after my travels to Israel and Germany, as I was grappling with writing a measured piece about antisemitism, Anita Gordon, or Nicki as we called her, was shot to death in her living room.

Nicki was my sister's sister-in-law. She and I were bridesmaids in my sister's wedding, wearing white scoop-necked dresses with pink rosebuds. Nicki gave the shower. She had pasted funny childhood pictures of the bride and groom on the place cards. I, in my teens, was in awe of how she did things even then.

At sixty-three, she was murdered by Richard Baumhammers, thirty-four, who had been her next-door neighbor for thirty years. He was the same age as one of Nicki's daughters. In fact, Baumhammers' parents, prominent Pittsburgh dentists, had attended the wedding of one of the Gordon daughters. These families lived in a well-to-do section of Mt. Lebanon, a Pittsburgh suburb known for its good schools, safety, and quality of life.

Gunning down Nicki in her living room was the beginning of an hour-plus rampage in which Baumhammers, an unemployed lawyer, shot five people—a Jew, an Indian, two Asians, an African American—and critically wounded a sixth.[5] It was a multicultural spectrum of hate.

In life, Nicki was the glue that held many relationships together even as they frayed over the years. At the time of her death, she was planning a ninetieth birthday for her mother-in-law. Instead, Nicki opened the door to her neighbor and likely asked him how she could help. He shot her six or seven times in the face, throat, neck, and hands, which she must have tried to put in front of her as a shield. Then he set the carpet on fire with a Molotov cocktail. In the rampage that followed, Baumhammers shot out the windows of Nicki's synagogue and painted a red swastika and the word "Jews" on the façade. And he sprayed six bullets at another synagogue in nearby town. The summer before the rampage, Baumhammers had walked into Ace Sporting Goods in a town outside of Pittsburgh and bought the gun used in the shootings, a .357 Magnum revolver.

While the four-day Hebrew University exercise on antisemitism was cerebral, in the end, it analyzed some of the same forces that later left

Nicki dead in a pool of her own blood on her living floor. Antisemitism can live in crevices, be ignited after long periods of latency, be spread by the Internet, and thrive in freedom as well as be state sponsored. In other words, it can appear before us in ways the mentality formed by the Holocaust, heavy-duty as it may be, does not prepare us for.

The longevity of the dislike of Jews is staggering. "If the Jews want to become citizens of Alexandria, why don't they worship the gods of Alexandria?" said the Greek polemicist Apion following the anti-Jewish riots in 38 C.E. in Alexandria, the first pogrom.[6] What a ring of familiarity that has. How we still struggle to accept those who are different.

As Christianity blossomed, it added a deadly charge: Not only did you (Jews) kill the Son of God, you do not accept him as the savior. Ideas of reason and progress flourished in the Enlightenment but the views of one of its leading voices, Voltaire, were tinged with the medieval hatred of Jews. The French Revolution ushered in citizenship. But Jews were given a stringent standard: You may become citizens but only if you become French. Give up ideas of homeland, of chosen people, that is, stop being Jews. So began the era of Jewish assimilation. Later came obliteration. In Germany the Nazis espoused racial inferiority to exterminate the Jews.[7]

"German antisemitism," wrote historian Peter Gay, "was a way of confronting—or rather not confronting—the pressures of contemporary life which were remaking Germany. . . . Specialization, mechanization . . . the speeding up of existence, the burgeoning threats posed by godless morality, socialist revolution and cultural nihilism; Antisemitism was in short an irrational protest against the modern world."[8]

Societies, it seems, have a need for safety valves, for scapegoats perhaps especially as they become increasingly complex, fast-paced, and unequal, as they are today. Historian Bernard Lewis argues that some of these same tensions and upheavals exist now in the Islamic world, making a fertile ground for extremism and hate.[9]

All these years as scapegoat have marked Jewish sensibility. My parents taught me that the world is against us. Don't trust. We dwell alone. This sense that we are "a people apart" runs deeper than antisemitism; it is part of Judaism itself. This was what I resisted so in my father. As a young person, I could not accept this long view of history that carried such a bitter verdict.

Historian Robert Wistrich cautioned his colleagues at the Hebrew University antisemitism conference about the enduring capacity of the old hatred to mutate and reemerge to serve new religious, psychological, or political purposes. "It is one of the fundamental expressions of human baseness and depravity," in which he included racism and ethnic hatred. "History teaches us to be cautious about antisemitism. How many times has it been declared dead?"

I got the idea that antisemitism is like cancer cells; one form is rooted out only to have it mutate and reappear. Or like a ground bass, always there, even though at times its rumble may be faint.

Progress has been made. In the West at least, antisemitism is no longer state sponsored as it was in Nazi Germany and for periods of time in the Soviet Union. In the United States Jews are no longer barred from employment or housing. The Catholic and Protestant churches have made considerable progress coming to terms with their contributions to antisemitism, to the "teaching of contempt." Martin Luther, the German church reformer, who wrote *About the Jews and Their Lies,* was virulently antisemitic. The charge that the Jews killed Christ stood until the 1960s when the Catholic Church finally revised it.

Pope John Paul II made admissions that not long ago might have been unimaginable: In 1990 he declared antisemitism a sin and in 2000 he apologized to Jews. Then he went to the Western Wall in Jerusalem and put his own small piece of paper there expressing his brotherhood with Jews and his anguish of Jewish suffering.

The Anti-Defamation League surveys report that in 1999, 12 percent of the U.S. population held antisemitic attitudes compared to 29 percent in 1964.

Several years ago, such progress led some to declare antisemitism dead, especially when compared to the threat of assimilation. Others were more cautious. Arthur Hertzberg wrote, "All the older forms of antisemitism have been undermined: it would be foolish to say it is dead, but it seems to be dying out and to have force only when it is redefined."[10]

Redefined, indeed. While much has improved, new virulent forms have appeared. One is Holocaust denial. The UN, which created Israel, has also been a platform. Canadian professor Irwin Kotler, at the Hebrew University conference, called the treatment of Israel at the UN a "thirty-year de-legitimization," making for the emergence of Israel as "the collective Jew among nations."

The 2001 UN conference against racism saw a resurgence of the "Zionism is Racism" campaign. Hate has found new formats such as on the Internet. Some Arab governments, such as Saudi Arabia, foster hatred of Jews. So do the government-controlled media there and radical clerics.[11]

But the second Intifada has opened the floodgates. Many consider Israel the aggressor in the conflict with Palestinians, deserving of international condemnation, divestment, and isolation. Following Israeli incursions into the West Bank, synagogue and cemetery desecration have dotted numerous European countries, especially in France. Some academics have called for a moratorium on grants by European educational institutions to Israeli scholars and researchers. And Palestinian groups have called for a divestment-in-Israel campaign on North American college campuses.

If just a few years ago antisemitism was at a low rumble, today, to my ear at least, it is a roar. And if the low rumble had come from neo-Nazis and other right wing extremists—such as Richard Baumhammers—the roar is coming from a new alignment. It is the left in Europe and elsewhere that has Israel in its sights.[12] A cacophony of voices today condemns Israel: human rights and peace groups, antiglobalists, anticolonialists and anti-imperialists, and of course many who are anti-American.

All of these developments put me squarely into my dilemma: how to disentangle legitimate negative reactions to Israeli policy from antisemitic hate. My sensibility about Jewish danger, formed in the wake of the Holocaust, is deeply imprinted, fixed, and intractable. And so I have a hard time discerning—am I overreacting, do I have a finely attuned early warning system, or am I right on target? Unlike my Christian journalist friend I find it very difficult to be sure.

A year almost to the day after Nicki and the others were murdered, Baumhammers' trial got underway. When I walked into the courtroom, I had this powerful sense of Nicki's presence, of her utter helplessness as she was gunned down. The judge, prosecutor, defense attorneys, court reporter, and defendant Baumhammers took their places. It was a small comfort that this public machinery of justice would try to make things right, as much as could be at this point.

I sat with Nicki's sister and two of her daughters. Nearby were a cluster of relatives of the Chinese victim, an Indian man, and the mother of the twenty-two-year-old African American man. The defense argued that Richard Baumhammers was legally insane. His lawyer told the jury that he had been hospitalized twice for mental illness since 1993 and had been prescribed various antipsychotic medications. The prosecutor said that Baumhammers was a racist and white supremacist who targeted racial, ethnic, and religious minorities. A computer forensics specialist testified that Baumhammers frequently visited Internet sites of white supremacist, neo-Nazi, and other hate groups. Baumhammers was the self-appointed chairman of the Free Market Party, whose objectives included ending Third World immigration and affirmative action. The defense was unsuccessful in convincing the jury that Baumhammers was legally insane. They found him guilty and he was sentenced to die.

His antisemitism did not fit any of my previously held fixed understandings. It was elusive, an undetected, lethal, fragment fomenting in this placid safe suburb. His hate grew unchecked in the crevices of our free and open society. Mental health professionals did not find him a danger to society. And despite his history of mental illness, he easily managed to buy a gun.

His hate was not caught in our society's normal mechanisms of surveillance and control. It was a microcosm of the way the nineteen hijackers were able to carry out their plans here, undetected, taking advantage of our trust. Baumhammers was certainly beyond the reach of Jewish or other defense organizations. Yes, he was dealt with by the justice system, but five people are still dead and one paralyzed because of his hate.

What Baumhammers' trial did to me was break apart the mentality of cataclysm, amplified by the Holocaust that I had inherited and that seemed to come into play for me with each antisemitic incident. Such a mentality is calcified. It does not always help us understand today's circumstances. History never repeats itself in exactly the same way. If we are watching for it to, the new forms that antisemitism has taken will elude us. That mentality did not help me understand how, in a nation which condemns antisemitism and ethnic hate, a thirty-year neighbor could leave Nicki in a pool of blood on her living room floor. And the lens of the Holocaust will not bring clarity to a world in which a powerful Jewish state is an actor. Israel, like any state, will be judged and criticized. But, with our history, how easily that criticism resonates to the virulent antisemitism that lies in history. Just as for many Jews a swastika is never an inert object, so too criticism of the Jewish state doesn't stay confined to just that. Yet those with whom Israel is in conflict, as well as many others, care not a whit about the dark insecure Jewish past. They are only interested in holding to the fire today the actions of the Jewish state.

For sure, hearing Sharon compared to Hitler and terms like apartheid state, human rights violator, and colonialist applied to Israel has a harsh dissonant ring to my ears. Such terms are lacking in nuance and context. They blur distinctions and use historical analogy carelessly. They also shatter some Jewish mythology about Israel.

Still, my dilemma remains: How to discern legitimate criticism of Israel's current policies from critiques that are anti-Zionist, antisemitic or a delegitimizing of the state of Israel? How to disentangle them? They seem balled together and weighed down by history in much the same mysterious way that Israeli power and Jewish vulnerability are.

I do know that the old vigilance, that mentality of cataclysm, is no longer sufficient. It is not up-to-date enough or finely calibrated enough to help me grasp the complexity and variety of forces at work today. I feel the need to develop some new lens, new ways of discerning the nuances of the anti-Israel, anti-Jewish nexus we live in today. This new lens would be mindful of the presence and wisdom of the Jewish past, but open and ready to engage with the today's new challenges, whether they be conflicts in Israel, a murder in Pittsburgh, academic deliberations in Jerusalem, or conversations with a journalist friend.

NOTES

1. David Grossman, *Death as a Way of Life* (New York: Farrar, Straus and Giroux, 2003), 164.

2. "The Dynamics of Antisemitism in the Second Half of the 20th Century," conference organized by the Vidal Sassoon International Center for the Study of Antisemitism, an academic think tank.

3. Matthew Purdy, "New Jersey Laureate Refuses to Resign over Poem," *The New York Times*, September 28, 2002, B1.

4. David Biale, *Power and Powerlessness in Jewish History* (New York: Schocken Books, 1986), chapter on Israel.

5. The others were Anil Thakir, thirty-one, at an Indian grocery; Je-Lin Sun, thirty-four, and Thao Pham, twenty-seven, at a Chinese restaurant; Gary Lee, twenty-two, at a karate school. Sandit Patel, twenty-five, was critically wounded.

6. Jasper Griffin, "Their Jewish Problem," a review of Peter Schafer's *Judeophobia: Attitudes Toward Jews in the Ancient World*, in *The New York Review of Books*, December 18, 1997, 57–59.

7. Leonard Glick, *Ashkenazic Jews in European History*, tapes of summer program in Yiddish culture, National Yiddish Book Center, Amherst Mass., 1995.

8. Peter Gay, *Freud, Jews, and Other Germans: Masters and Victims in Modern Culture* (New York: Oxford University Press, 1978), 20–21.

9 Bernard Lewis, "The Roots of Muslim Rage," *The Atlantic* 266, no. 3 (September 1990), 47–60.

10. Arthur Hertzberg, "Is Antisemitism Dying Out?" New York Review of Books (June 24, 1993), 57.

11. Gabriel Schoenfeld, "Israel and the Anti-Semites," *Commentary* 113, no. 6 (June 2002), 13–20.

12. Ibid.

30

RITUAL

The four of us, David and I, and Lou and Max, spent a weekend together in a cottage in a pine forest overlooking the bay in Cape Cod. On Friday evening Lou set up four stubby candles—purple, pink, white, yellow—on the corners of a small glass table on the patio. The shells that Max collected that day at the bay were drying in the center of the table, making a breathtaking tableaux in the orange liquid light of the setting sun that was coming through the stark black trees. Lou put on his crocheted kipa, which he got in Israel. He lit the candles, "Baruch ata adonoy . . ."

In those flickered flames, blown gently by the wind, was the creation once again of Shabbat. For those brief moments, Jewish time and space were alive and well. When we finished saying the prayer, Lou hugged each of us and each of us, each other. "Shabbat Shalom." (Good Sabbath.) He had erected the scaffolding of this ancient ritual through which we could express our love.

I felt such pleasure partaking in this ritual with my family. There I stood, in a generational line next to my mother. That line reached back into history, across all of the pain and sorrow to the richness of Jewish life and its remarkable survival.

It was not that long ago that I felt uncomfortable with such display of religiosity, even in the privacy of family. Like the day I was walking on Ben Yehuda Street in Israel, the busy pedestrian mall in the heart of Jerusalem, and I saw a man selling tefillin from a cart. Men walked by, stopped, picked them up, handled the leather straps and tried them on. I watched, stopped in my tracks. It was the middle of a busy commercial district, bagels at one end, McDonalds at the other. And here were these religious objects being sold like so much cabbage at an open market. It had the effect of thawing some long frozen and erroneous idea of mine, that the religious objects of Judaism were scarce, private, and to be shrouded in the family.

What a discrete, cramped Jewish world I had grown up in. We had few Jewish objects and the ones we had could only be found at special places: Chanukah candles at the temple, a menorah at the temple gift shop or perhaps at a religious shop that carried Judaica.

Today it is not only in the Jewish state that the objects of Judaism are public, available and commercial. At my local Bed Bath and Beyond was a display of mass-produced, affordable Passover items. They included the Haggadah and a cookbook called *Matza 101*. There was a seder plate with spaces for all the symbolic foods, and even a wine cup for Elijah. All of this was alongside the heart candies for Valentine's Day and the bunnies and eggs for Easter, in kind of a parity, as Chanukah had developed long ago with Christmas.

However disposable and commercial these items may have been, they expressed a Judaism turned outward, Judaism in the marketplace, an accessible, confident Judaism.

Jewish religious objects had begun to come into my life. When Lou came home from his first year in Israel, he brought us a gift: two mezuzot, the small decorative objects, containing a piece of Torah scroll, placed at the right side of the entryway to a Jewish home. He stammered a bit when he presented them to us. He wasn't sure how we would like them or if we would feel comfortable displaying them.

At one time I would not have been comfortable being marked as a Jew. It was too frightening as a historical memory. "Marking" Jews by making them wear yellow stars was what the Nazi regime did prior to the Final

Solution. I wanted to blend in. Now it seemed exactly right to put the mezuzot up on the front and back doors. It was a Jewish home, why not mark it? They were beautiful; two shades of blue stained glass in an ornate silver case. David liked the idea too and put them up right away. Here was this moment of rebirth of a Jewish ritual. And I could embrace it without any of my old discomforts.

After Lou's arrival home, I dug out an artifact that had come into my possession after my father died more than thirty years ago. It was my grandfather's tefillin, still in its embroidered Russian bag. It was a remnant of our fractured legacy, a small relic of where we had come from and who we once were. I gave it to Lou.

For a long time I had thought of this book as about Jewishness, not Judaism. But in time I saw that this hair-splitting was a hair that would not be split. This reach into history was a reach into Judaism itself. It was about the story of a people and their search for meaning through a covenant with God.

I had been working on this book more than two years when I bought myself a Tanakh, the Jewish Bible. The Hebrew Publication Society version is a beautiful edition, large, bound in blue leather with gold leaf pages. It has Hebrew on one side of the page and the English translation on the other.

I had read more than one hundred books and now finally I had gotten to *the* book of the Jewish people. I realized I could not continue without opening up to its religious center. I had come across quotes from Exodus and Deuteronomy and I wanted to see them for myself in the original and even try to read them in Hebrew. After being at Tisha B'Av in Jerusalem, I wanted to read the Book of Lamentations. Suddenly I felt it was *this* Jewish story that I must read. It was part of what defined who I am.

I was surprised what a big step it was for me to buy and engage with Torah. I was surprised too by the extent of my alienation. I saw that owning and drawing from this book did not have to be a fundamentalist endeavor.

"Jews kept Torah, but Torah has kept the Jews," the sages say. Torah, the first five books of what Christians call the Old Testament, is the Jewish story. Several generations ago, my line of Jews put Torah aside as revealed text. They stepped out of that protective Jewish membrane and began to advance in and absorb the larger culture. Still they held onto the importance of the story of the Jewish people, as a central part of who they were, with a passionate attachment.

Torah lays out the covenant between God and the Jewish people, explained Rabbi Roger Klein at Temple Tifereth Israel in Cleveland. It gives laws and commandments. It lays out a moral universe and gives shape to time. And it conveys a message of hope, a refusal to succumb to despair. Klein, a Reform rabbi, gave a series of lectures on Torah, midrash, Talmud, and other Jewish texts. I sat in a roomful of people, who, like me, wanted to know, what is the *Gemara* anyway?

To answer that, you must start with Torah and move on to midrash. Midrash is a process of interpreting the Bible for later generations. "The answers of one generation are not always sufficient for the next," Klein said. Those who engage in midrash apply the Bible's teachings to current situations as well as clear up confusions in the text. Through midrash, which means study or investigate in Hebrew, the authority of the Bible is maintained. "Midrash never ceases," Klein said. "It still goes on. Judaism itself is a product of midrash." Klein said.

Then there is the Talmud. Displayed on an entire wall at the permanent exhibit at the Jewish Museum in New York is an enlarged page of Talmud. This particular page pertained to Yom Kippur and the rules for pregnant women, young children, and the infirm in regard to fasting. The original passage from the Bible is in the middle. Then in squares and rectangles around this passage are the commentaries from scholars and rabbis across the ages, each adding their own new interpretations. A page of Talmud, which looks like a large puzzle, represents a conversation of Jewish thinkers across the generations, as if all were sitting around a table considering this particular question. It has served as a powerful way for Jews to maintain the sense of their covenant with God, especially once Jewish communities were scattered.

The Talmud was completed in 500 C.E., Klein said. Before that, going back to 1000 B.C.E. was the oral Torah, the Mishnah. It defined aspects of a Jewish life, such as marriage laws or how to use tefillin, which were not spelled out in the Torah. The Mishnah itself was incomplete and so was followed by commentaries. These two together are known as the Gemara, the Aramaic word for study. The Mishnah and Gemara together form the Talmud.

Later came the Codes, the *Mishneh Torah* written by Moses Maimonides between 1170 and 1180 and *Shulchan Aruch* by Joseph Caro, who left Spain for Tsfat at the time of the expulsion. And, predictably, more commentaries followed these Codes.

All of this forms Jewish law or *halakha*. When the Reform movement came along, it said that halakhic law was not the word of God but rather the response of Jews to conditions of exile, that such high walls regulating Jewish life were necessary for survival, Klein said.

This was the Orthodox tradition that we had left behind. It was what we thought of as backward, closed, and ignorant. How we feared that somehow this heritage would not allow us entry into the larger society or would somehow diminish our rationality.

Yet here was this astonishing history, what it has meant to be the People of the Book. It was these books, these commentaries that held the Jews together over many centuries. Jews were not defined by land, by place, by skin color but by the power of ideas, by the meaning given to life. To that question, how is a Jew imprinted? This is the first way: Torah and its streams of offspring, believed to be from God. It was this amazing body of literature and ritual that spun a web around Jewish existence, ensuring its survival by making it come alive in each new generation. What respect I felt for it. The divisions among Jews no longer held any importance to me. I wanted access to the whole heritage.

31

CONCLUSION

Tradition is not reproduced. It is thrown and it is caught.
It lives a long time in the air.

—Leon Wieseltier in Kaddish

For three years, I lived in a self-imposed cocoon, insulated physically, intellectually, and emotionally from most things not related to Jewish life. In the last months, I thought a great deal about why I had undertaken this investigation. I recalled that day when I sat in the kitchen listening to my sons speaking Hebrew. How powerfully it had evoked the kitchen of my childhood, listening to my parents speaking Yiddish. I was an outsider, the English-only speaker, a role not unfamiliar to me as a Jew. Ironically, that position isolated and alienated me from both my Jewish heritage and a Jewish future. I sought to create a new Jewish story for myself that strengthened the scaffolding to the generations on either side.

In the kitchen that day I caught a glimpse of my generation that took Judaism deep inside. The impetus had come from two powerful forces— the contracting Jewish space made by assimilation and the sense of obliteration left by the Holocaust.

One night on the phone, in one of those rare moments with offspring, Max began talking about what he thought David and I had given him: An ability to empathize, an ability to see the world as bigger than himself and as not only about him, an ability to tackle problems out in the world, an ability to work hard.

I saw the first three as part of what Judaism had given to me. Yet he described these values in universal secular terms. I was of a generation that was practiced in making Judaism crypto. I was no longer comfortable with that. I wanted to describe Jewish values as Jewish even if they were also values shared by others.

It was no longer paramount to blend. But what a long road it had been, through my father's fears and into the dark side of Jewish history, until finally I gained this capacity to feel comfort and ease making Jewishness legible in my life.

When I look back, it takes my breath away to recall my own enormous optimism as I came of age. How hard I had fallen for John F. Kennedy and the belief that we could stop a war and remake the world. Only fifteen years had passed since World War II and the Holocaust. Perhaps in order for each generation to make its mark, it must for a time have amnesia to history.

I had lived a defensive, fear-based Judaism, purged of much of its visible, identifiable, and nurturing content. Many of my generation expressed our Judaism through the fight for equal rights. It was a Judaism that reached out to others, "tikkun olam," repair the world. They are the values of the liberal secular Jew that have suffused into this fluid modern society and flow from other groups as well. It is a wonderful inheritance. We spent much of our lives working to make the world safe for Jews, but reaped little of the nurture and pleasure of being Jews. When I began, I was after a Judaism that could nurture. I wanted to partake in this sense of belonging. Tikkum olam is not only about what we do for others, but healing ourselves so that we have some inner sense of well-being.

In New York City, off of Fifth Avenue, between Sixteenth and Seventeenth Streets, is the new Center for Jewish History. It was under construction when I visited. Scaffolding was still in front of the three-story building, which was the old Helen Keller School. An atrium connected it to another building, making a single structure. I peered in through the windows one late afternoon.

The new organization now houses the archives and offices of the YIVO Institute for Jewish Research, the Leo Baeck Institute, the American Jewish Historical Society, and the American Sephardi Federation. Thus, this new organization has brought the past of American Jews—the eastern European, German, American, and Sephardic threads—into a single repository of Jewish history.

"Yes, YIVO is in business upstairs," a guard told me.

Upstairs the atrium reading room is lit by skylight; the tables have green shaded reading lights. The YIVO archives are stored all around and the Leo Baeck reference collection, the single largest archive of the life of German Jewry, was soon to be housed here.

So here it is, my history, I thought, taking in this new facility being constructed just as I was constructing my own Jewish identity.

Lou once said to me, "Three thousand years—what an amazing story of survival." I saw his awe and deep appreciation of what I had taken for granted. He made me wonder if I had been neglectful and careless with this heritage. I had thought, like my father, that Jewishness was fixed and immutable, like antisemitism itself seemed to be, and would be passed on, if only by osmosis.

But I have learned that Jewish life in this open society will no longer be sustained by the tremendous force of tradition, communal life, and religiosity that came from Europe in my grandparents' generation. "The self-segregating, all embracing world of European Jews before the Holocaust is for many a distant fading memory. Today it is an emotional, complex of feelings, beliefs, associations and occasional voluntary actions."[1]

Today, if you want to be Jewish you have to *do* something to make it happen. You have to sort out what you wish to take from this complex heritage and find a way to live it in this varied society. That was not possible for me until I had faced squarely some of the discomforts that emanated from the difficult history.

There are many ways to live the Jewish imprint—religiously, ethnically, and culturally. Another way is to study Jewish history. That was the insight of Leopold Zunz in Germany as the institutions of Judaism lost their force under the pressures of assimilation. Yet after the overwhelming events of the Holocaust, history itself is an extremely difficult force to reckon with. How easy it is to be either stuck in it as a perpetual victim or to disconnect from it altogether.

There is still this question, how Judaism and Jewish culture will thrive in the modern world. Vilna, erased in the Holocaust, was one model, a vibrant Jewish community of Yiddish culture existing alongside communities. Sephardic Jews, most of whom are now in Israel, are another. They did not experience the upheaval in Jewish identity caused by modernity. Consequently, today they have greater ease in combining their Jewishness with modern life.

And we have another model in American culture. It is what African Americans of this generation have given—the gift of multiculturalism.

Jewish life will continue to have this wide spectrum from ultra-Orthodoxy to secularity that resulted from the splintering of Jewish life. But no matter where you are along that spectrum, the sense of identity that comes from situating yourself in the center of your own history is a most potent way to know yourself and belong. David Biale writes, "many Jews will choose to remain Jews, to identify with the powerful narrative that is Jewish history. This identification will no doubt take many forms, revealing a type of pluralism that has its justification in Jewish history itself."[2]

But deriving a sense of Jewishness from a consciousness of Jewish history is not the same as nostalgia for Yiddish, the old neighborhood, the old country, or a corned beef sandwich. Nor is it the same as Jewish memory, those potent elements of the ancient Jewish story such as the exile and the exodus that are part of Judaism. Nor is it Jewish genealogy. Most of us will not live our lives in some kind of village, shtetl, or even kibbutz, much as we may have some vestigial longing. The old sense of community we came from does not have the force it once did. For many today a sense of Jewishness is internal and not centered in particular institutions. We live in a far larger, more complicated world made up of many communities. The sense of religious and ethnic identity must be put together within.

I stand now in what is for me a nascent Jewish American culture. The ties have been loosened from both Israel and the Holocaust. I am more solidly planted in this pool of Jewish culture with its own richness that feeds and fortifies a deep internal Jewish identity.

The word Israel means "he who wrestles with God."[3] Amos Oz calls it the anarchic gene in Jewish civilization, this open-ended dialogue across generations of interpretation and counter-interpretation with no central authority to decide, that goes all the way back to Abraham.[4] Now I too am in the ring, wrestling with this legacy.

NOTES

1. J. J. Goldberg, *Jewish Power: Inside the American Jewish Establishment,* (Reading, Mass.: Addison Wesley, 1996), 73.

2. David Biale, "Jewish Identity in the 90s," *Tikkun* (November 1, 1991), 61.

3. Arnold Eisen, *Galut: Modern Jewish Reflection on Homelessness and Home-coming* (Bloomington: Indiana University Press, 1986), 182.

4. Amos Oz, "Where Will Israel Be 50 Years from Now," lecture at the Cleveland College of Jewish Studies, May 10, 1998.

RESOURCES

BOOKS AND ARTICLES

Alhadeff, Gini. *The Sun at Midday: Tales of a Mediterranean Family.* New York: Pantheon Books, 1997.

Amichai, Yehuda. *Open Closed Open.* New York: Harcourt, 2000.

Amichai, Yehuda. *The Selected Poetry of Yehuda Amichai.* Berkeley: University of California Press, 1996.

Appelfeld, Aharon. "Buried Homeland." *The New Yorker* (November 23, 1998), 48–61.

Appelfeld, Aharon. "The Kafka Connection." *The New Yorker* (July 23, 2001), 38.

Appelfeld, Aharon. *The Age of Wonders.* Boston: David R. Godine, 1981.

Appelfeld, Aharon. *The Conversion.* New York: Schocken Books, 1998.

Appiah, Anthony K., "The Multiculturalist Misunderstanding." *The New York Review of Books* (October 9, 1997), 30–35.

Arendt, Hannah. *Eichmann in Jerusalem: A Report on the Banality of Evil.* New York: Viking Press, 1963.

Arnold, Michael. "Bringing Secular Israelis Back to their Jewish Roots." *Forward*, July 31, 1998.

"Audit of Anti-Semitic Incidents." New York: Anti-Defamation League, 1997.

Baker, Leonard. *Days of Sorrow and Pain: Leo Baeck and the Berlin Jews.* New York: Macmillan, 1978).

Baron, Salo W. *The Russian Jew under Tsars and Soviets.* New York: Macmillan, 1964–1976.

Bauer, Yehuda. *Rethinking the Holocaust.* New Haven: Yale University Press, 2001.

Bekar, Avi, ed. *Jewish Communities of the World*, Institute of the World Jewish Congress, 1998–99 edition. Minneapolis: Lerner Publications, 1998.

Ben-David, Calev. "An Artful Life: Israel Prize Winner Bezalel Narkiss . . ." *The Jerusalem Post* (May 14, 1999).

Berger, Joseph. *Displaced Persons: Growing up American After the Holocaust.* New York: Scribner, 2001.

Biale, David. "Jewish Identity in the 90s." *Tikkun* (November 1, 1991), 60–62.

Biale, David. *Power and Powerlessness in Jewish History.* New York: Schocken Books, 1986.

Biale, David, Michael Galchinsky, and Susannah Heschel eds., *Insider/ Outsider: American Jews and Multiculturalism*. Berkeley: University of California Press, 1998.

Bilski, Emily D., ed. *Berlin Metropolis: Jews and the New Culture 1890–1918*. Berkeley: University of California Press, 1999.

Burns, Michael. *Dreyfus: A Family Affair 1789–1945*. New York: HarperCollins 1991.

Chanes, Jerome R., ed. *Antisemitism in America Today: Outspoken Experts Explode the Myths*. Seacaucus, N.J.: Carol Publishing Group, 1995.

Cohen, Steven M. *American Modernity and Jewish Identity*. New York: Tavistock Press, 1983.

Cohen, Steven M., and Arnold M. Eisen. *The Jew Within: Self, Family and Community in America*. Bloomington: Indiana University Press, 2000.

Cowan, Paul. *An Orphan in History: Retrieving a Jewish Legacy*. New York: Doubleday, 1982.

Davis, David Brion. "Jews and Blacks in America." *The New York Review of Books* (December 2, 1999), 57–61.

Dawidowicz, Lucy. *From That Place and Time: A Memoir 1938–1947*. New York: W.W. Norton, 1989.

De Lange, Nicholas, ed. *The History of the Jewish People*. New York: Harcourt Brace, 1997.

De Silva, Cara, ed. *In Memory's Kitchen: A Legacy from the Women of Terezin*. Northvale N.J.: Jason Aronson, 1996.

Ehrenburg, Ilya, and Vasily Grossman, eds. *The Black Book*. Jerusalem: Yad Vashem, 1980.

Eisen, Arnold M. *The Chosen People in America: A Study in Jewish Religious Ideology*. Bloomington: Indiana University Press, 1983.

Eisen, Arnold M. *Galut: Modern Jewish Reflection on Homelessness and Homecoming*. Bloomington: Indiana University Press, 1986.

Elon, Amos. *Israelis: Founders and Sons*. New York: Holt, Rinehart and Winston, 1971.

Eskin, Blake. "A New Wave of Actors Revives Israeli Theater." *Forward* (July 3, 1998), 11.

Ezrahi, Yaron. *Rubber Bullets: Power and Conscience in Modern Israel*. New York: Farrar, Straus and Giroux, 1997.

Finkielkraut, Alain. *The Imaginary Jew*. Lincoln and London: University of Nebraska Press, 1994.

Fleischner, Eva, ed. "After Auschwitz: Beginning of a New Era? Reflections on the Holocaust." Papers given at the International Symposium on the Holocaust, Cathedral of St. John the Divine, New York, June 1974.

Foreman, Seth. *Blacks in the Jewish Mind: A Crisis of Liberalism*. New York and London: New York University Press, 1998.

Friedman, Lawrence J. *Identity's Architect: A Biography of Erik Erikson*. New York: Scribner, 1999.

Fromer, Rebecca Camhi. *The House by the Sea: A Portrait of the Holocaust in Greece.* San Francisco: Mercury House, 1998.

Gaon, Hahom Dr. Solomon, and Dr. M. Mitchell Serels, eds. *Del Fuego: Sephardim and the Holocaust.* New York: Sepher-Hermon Press, 1995.

Gartner, Lloyd P. "Jewish Migrants en Route from Europe to North America," in *The Jews of North America.* Ed. Morris Richin. Detroit: Wayne State University Press, 1987, 25–43.

Gay, Peter. *Freud, Jews and Other Germans: Masters and Victims in Modern Culture.* New York: Oxford University Press, 1978.

Gerber, Jane S. *The Jews of Spain: A History of the Sephardic Experience.* New York: Free Press, 1992.

Gilbert, Martin. *The Atlas of Jewish History.* New York: William Morrow, 1969, 1992.

Gitlitz, David M. *Secrecy and Deceit: The Religion of the Crypto-Jews.* Philadelphia: Jewish Publication Society, 1996.

Glazer, Nathan. *We Are All Multiculturalists Now.* Cambridge, Mass.: Harvard University Press, 1998.

Glick, Leonard B. *Ashkenazic Jews in European History.* Four lectures on tape from the National Yiddish Book Center, Amherst, Mass., 1995.

Goldberg, J. J. "Interfaith Marriage: The Real Story." *The New York Times,* August 4, 1997, op-ed page.

Goldberg, J. J. *Jewish Power: Inside the American Jewish Establishment.* Reading, Mass.: Addison Wesley, 1996.

Goldhagen, Daniel Jonah. *Hitler's Willing Executioners: Ordinary Germans and the Holocaust.* New York: Alfred A. Knopf, 1996.

Greenberg, Irving. *The Jewish Way: Living the Holidays.* New York: Summit Books, 1988.

Griffin, Jasper. "Their Jewish Problem." *The New York Review of Books* (December 18, 1997), 57–59.

Gross, Jan T. *Neighbors: The Destruction of the Jewish Community in Jedwabne Poland.* Princeton, N.J.: Princeton University Press, 2001.

Grossman, David. "Fifty is a Dangerous Age." *The New Yorker* (April 20, 1998), 55–58.

Grossman, David. *Death as a Way of Life.* New York: Farrar, Straus and Giroux, 2003.

Grossman, David. *The Yellow Wind.* New York: Farrar, Straus, and Giroux, 1988.

Grossman, Vasily. *Life and Fate.* New York: Harper and Row, 1986.

Hafner, Katie. *The House at the Bridge: A Story of Modern Germany.* New York: Scribner, 1995.

Hall, Stuart. "Cultural Identity and Diaspora." In *Identity: Community, Culture, Difference.* Ed. Johnathan Rutherford. London: Lawrence and Wishart, 1990.

Hall, Stuart, and Paul DuGay, eds. *Questions of Cultural Identity.* London: Sage Publications, 1996.

Hartman, David. "The Bearable Rightness of Arguing." *Moment* (August 1998), 38–39.

Heppner, Ernest, G. *Shanghai Refuge: A Memoir of the World War II Jewish Ghetto.* Lincoln: University of Nebraska Press, 1994.

Herberg, Will. *Protestant, Catholic, Jew: An Essay in American Religious Sociology.* New York: Doubleday, 1956.

Hertzberg, Arthur. "Is Anti-Semitism Dying Out?" *The New York Review of Books* (June 24, 1993), 51–57.

Herzl, Theodor. *The Jewish State: An Attempt at a Modern Solution of the Jewish Question.* New York: Dover Publications, 1988.

Heschel, Susannah, ed. *On Being a Jewish Feminist: A Reader.* New York: Schocken Books, 1983 and 1995.

"Highlights of the CJF 1990 National Jewish Population Survey," Council of Jewish Federations, New York, and the Mandell Berman Institute-North American Jewish Data Bank, the Graduate School and University Center, City University of New York, 1995.

Hilberg, Raul. *The Destruction of the European Jews.* Student edition. New York: Holmes and Meier, 1985.

Hilberg, Raul. *The Politics of Memory: The Journey of a Holocaust Historian.* Chicago: Ivan R. Dee, 1996.

Hirschberg, Peter. "Beyond the Rage." *The Jerusalem Report* (September 14, 1998), 14–17.

Hoffmann, Eva. *Shtetl: The Life and Death of a Small Town and the World of Polish Jews.* Boston, New York: Houghton Mifflin, 1997.

Hyman, Paula." Jewish Studies in the Jewish Community," *Association of Jewish Studies Newsletter* (Fall 1996), 8.

Hyman, Paula, E. *Gender and Assimilation in Modern Jewish History: The Roles and Representation of Women.* Seattle: University of Washington Press, 1995.

Hyman, Paula E. *The Jews of Modern France.* Berkeley: University of California Press, 1998.

Kamenetz, Rodger. *The Jew in the Lotus.* San Francisco: HarperSanFrancisco, 1994.

Kaplan, Robert P. *The Arabists: The Romance of an American Elite.* New York: Free Press, 1993.

Karpin, Michael, and Ina Friedman. *Murder in the Name of God: The Plot to Kill Yitzhak Rabin.* New York: Metropolitan Books, 1998.

Kassow, Samuel. *Vilna: The Jerusalem of Lithuania.* Four lectures on tape from the winter seminar on Yiddish culture, National Yiddish Book Center, Amherst, Mass., 1996.

Katz, Jacob. *Out of the Ghetto: The Social Background of Jewish Emancipation 1770–1870.* New York: Schocken Books, 1978.

Kleebatt, Norman L., ed. *too Jewish?: Challenging Traditional Identities.* Piscataway, N.J: Rutgers Univesity Press, 1996.

Kovaly, Heda Margolius. *Under a Cruel Star: A Life in Prague 1941–1968.* New York: Penguin Books, 1986.

Kramer, Jane. *The Politics of Memory: Looking for Germany in the New Germany.* New York: Random House, 1996.

Kristeva, Julia. *Nations Without Nationalism.* New York: Columbia University Press, 1993.

Lansky, Aaron. "Back on the High Wire Again." *Pakn Treger* (summer 1997), 46–49.

Lanzmann, Claude. *Shoah: An Oral History of the Holocaust: The Complete Text of the Film.* New York: Pantheon, 1985.

Levi, Primo. *The Drowned and the Saved.* New York: Summit Books, 1988.

Levi, Primo. *If Not Now, When?* New York: Summit Books, 1985.

Levi, Primo. *Survival in Auschwitz.* New York: Simon and Schuster, 1958.

Lewis, Bernard. "The Roots of Muslim Rage." *The Atlantic* 266, no. 3 (September 1990), 47–60.

Lewis, Bernard. *Semites & Anti-Semites: An Inquiry into Conflict and Prejudice.* New York: W.W. Norton, 1986.

Lewy, Guenter. *The Catholic Church and Nazi Germany.* New York: McGraw-Hill, 1964.

Mahfouz, Naguib. *Palace Walk.* New York: Doubleday, 1990, published in Arabic in 1956.

Maier, Charles S. *The Unmasterable Past: History, Holocaust and German National Identity.* Cambridge and London: Harvard University Press, 1988.

Mayer, Egon. *Children of Intermarriage: A Study in Patterns of Identification and Family Life.* New York: American Jewish Committee, Institute of Human Relations, 1983.

Melman, Yossi. *The New Israelis: An Intimate View of a Changing People.* Syracuse, N.Y.: Carol Publishing, 1992.

Memmi, Albert. *The Liberation of the Jew.* New York: Orion Press, 1966.

Michaels, Anne. *Fugitive Pieces.* New York: Vintage International 1996.

Morris, Benny. *Righteous Victims: A History of the Zionist-Arab Conflict 1881–2001.* New York: Vintage, 2001.

Oz, Amos. *In the Land of Israel.* New York: Vintage, 1983.

Oz, Amos. *Under This Blazing Light.* Cambridge, U.K: Cambridge University Press, 1979.

Ozick, Cynthia. "The Impossibility of Being Kafka." *The New Yorker* (January 11, 1999), 80–87.

Ozick, Cynthia. *Metaphor and Memory.* New York: Alfred A. Knopf, 1989.

Pawel, Ernst. *The Labyrinth of Exile: A Life of Theodor Herzl.* New York,: Farrar, Straus and Giroux, 1989.

Peretz, Martin. "Zionism at 100: The God That Did Not Fail, a Symposium." *The New Republic* (September 8 & 15, 1997), 1–24.

Purdy, Matthew. "New Jersey Laureate Refuses to Resign over Poem." *The New York Times,* September 28, 2002, B1.

Rawidowicz, Simon. *State of Israel, Diaspora, and Jewish Continuity: Essays on the "Ever-Dying People."* Hanover, N.H.: University Press of New England, 1997.

Remnick, David. "The Afterlife." *The New Yorker* (August 11, 1997), 50–63.

"To Renew and Sanctify: A Call to Action, The Report of the North American Commission on Jewish Identity and Continuity." Council of Jewish Federation, New York, November 1995.

Robinson, George. *Essential Judaism.* New York: Pocket Books, 1999.

Roden, Claudia. *The Book of Jewish Food: An Odyssey from Samarkand to New York.* New York: Alfred A. Knopf, 1996.

Roskies, David G. *The Jewish Search for a Usable Past.* Bloomington: Indiana University Press, 1999.

Rubenstein, Joshua. *Tangled Loyalties: The Life and Times of Ilya Ehrenburg.* Tuscaloosa: University of Alabama Press, 1996.

Sachar, Howard M. *A History of Israel from the Rise of Zionism to Our Time.* New York: Alfred A. Knopf, 1996.

Said, Edward, W. *Orientalism.* New York: Pantheon, 1978.

Sartre, Jean-Paul. *Anti-Semite and Jew: An Exploration of the Etiology of Hate.* New York: Schocken Books, 1948 and 1976.

Schorsch, Ismar. *From Text to Context: The Turn to History in Modern Judaism.* Hanover and London: Brandeis University Press/University Press of New England, 1994.

Segev, Tom. *Elvis in Jerusalem: Post-Zionism and the Americanization of Israel.* New York: Metropolitan Books, 2002.

Segev, Tom. *One Palestine Complete: Jews and Arabs under the British Mandate.* New York: Metropolitan Books, 2000.

Segev, Tom. *The Seventh Million: The Israelis and the Holocaust.* New York: Hill and Wang, 1993.

Schoenfeld, Gabriel. "Israel and the Anti-Semites." *Commentary* 113, No. 6 (June 2002), 13–20.

Shehadeh, Raja. *Strangers in the House: Coming of Age in Occupied Palestine.* South Royalton Vt.: Steerforth Press, 2002.

Sholem Aleichem. *Teyve the Dairyman and the Railroad Stories.* New York: Schocken Books, 1987.

Sichrovsky, Peter. *Strangers in their Own Land: Young Jews in Germany and Austria Today.* New York: Basic Books, 1986.

Silberman, Charles E. *A Certain People: American Jews and Their Lives Today.* New York: Summit Books, 1985.

Slyomovics, Susan. *The Object of Memory: Arab and Jew Narrate the Palestinian Village.* Philadelphia: University of Pennsylvania Press, 1998.

Smith, Huston. *The Illustrated World's Religions: A Guide to Our Wisdom Traditions.* San Francisco: HarperSanFrancisco, 1991.

Spector, Michael. "Traffickers' New Cargo: Naïve Slavic Women." *The New York Times,* January 1, 1998, 1, 6.

Spitzer, Leo. *Hotel Bolivia: The Culture of Memory in a Refuge from Nazism.* New York: Hill and Wang, 1999.

Stern, Fritz. *Einstein's German World.* Princeton, N.J.: Princeton University Press, 1999.

Tanakh, Hebrew English. Philadelphia: Jewish Publication Society, 1999 (*5759).

Trunk, Isaiah. *Judenrat: The Jewish Councils in Eastern Europe under Nazi Occupation.* New York: MacMillan, 1978.

Vital, David. *A People Apart: The Jews in Europe 1789–1939.* New York: Oxford University Press, 1999.

Walzer, Michael. *On Toleration.* New Haven, Ct.: Yale University Press, 1997.

Wasserstein, Bernard. *Vanishing Diaspora: The Jews in Europe since 1945.* Cambridge, Mass.: Harvard University Press, 1996.

Waters, Mary C. *Ethnic Options: Choosing Identities in America.* Berkeley: University of California Press, 1990.

Wertheimer, Jack, Charles S. Liebman, and Steven M. Cohen. "How to Save American Jews." *Commentary* (January 1996), 47–51.

Wiesel, Elie. *The Night Trilogy.* New York: Noonday Press, 1972.

Wieseltier, Leon. *Kaddish.* New York: Alfred A. Knopf, 1998.

Wisse, Ruth R. "By Their Own Hands: How the Jews of Russia Outwitted Themselves to Death." *The New Republic* (February 3, 1997), 33–42.

Wisse, Ruth R. *If I Am Not for Myself . . . the Liberal Betrayal of the Jews.* New York: Free Press, 1992.

Wistrich, Robert S. *Antisemitism: The Longest Hatred.* New York: Pantheon, 1991.

Wolitz, Seth, L. "The Americanization of Tevye or Boarding the Jewish Mayflower." *American Quarterly* 40 (December 4, 1988), 514–36.

Yehoshua, A. B. *Between Right and Right.* New York: Doubleday, 1981.

Yerushalmi, Yosef Haim. *Zakhor: Jewish History and Jewish Memory.* Seattle and London: University of Washington Press, 1982.

Yezierska, Anzia G. *Bread Givers: A Struggle Between a Father of the Old World and a Daughter of the New.* New York: G. Braziller, 1975.

Young, James, E. *At Memory's Edge: After-Images of the Holocaust in Contemporary Art and Architecture.* New Haven, Ct.: Yale University Press, 2000.

Zweig, Stefan. *World of Yesterday: An Autobiography.* New York: Viking Press, 1943.

FILMS

After the End of the World. Ivan Nichev. Bulgaria, 1999.

As If Nothing Happened. Ayelet Bargur. Israel, 1999.

Because of That War: Yehuda Poliker and Ya'akov Gilad. Directed by Orna Ben-Dor Niv. Israel, 1988.

Children of Chabannes. Lisa Gossels. France, 1999.

The Trial of Adolph Eichmann. Narrated by David Brinkley. 1998.

Endurance. (The story of Haile Gabrselasse, the Ethiopian long distance runner who won the 1996 Olympics event in Atlanta). Leslie Woodhead. 1998.

Europa, Europa. Agniestza Holland. 1991.

From Swastika to Jim Crow. Lori Cheatle, Martin D. Toub. United States, 1999.

Hotel Terminus: The Life and Times of Klaus Barbie. Documentary by Marcel Ophuls. 1988.

Into the Arms of Strangers: Stories of the Kindertransport. Produced by Deborah Oppenheimer, directed by Mark Jonathan Harris. 2000.

Kadosh. Amos Gitai. Israel, 2000.

Kippur. Amos Gitai. Israel, 2000.

Le Chambon: The Hill of a Thousand Children. France, 1994.

Left Luggage. Jeroen Krabbe. Holland, 1998.

Nadia. Amnon Rubenstein. Israel, 1987.

One Day in September. (The murder of Israeli athletes at the Munich Olympics in 1972). Kevin MacDonald. 2000.

Sallah. Written and directed by Ephraim Keshon. 1964

17–23: Forty Things You Have to Go Through. Dan and Noit Geva. Israel, 1999.

Shoah. Claude Lanzmann. 1985.

A Sign From Heaven. Ariella Azoulay. Israel, 1999.

The Song of the Siren. Directed by Eytan Fox. Israel, 1994.

The Sorrow and the Pity. Documentary by Marcel Ophuls. 1970.

The Summer of Aviya. (Story of Gila Almagor). Directed by Eli Cohen. Israel, 1988.

Sunshine. Itzvan Szabo. Hungary, 2000.

Tkuma. Documentary of Israeli history. Israel, 1998.

The Truce. Francesco Rossi (based on Primo Levi's *The Awakening*).

Voyages. Emmanuel Finkiel. France, 1999.

Weapons of the Spirit. Pierre Sauvage. France, 1989.